The Economics of
HIV and AIDS

The Economics of HIV and AIDS

The Case of South and South East Asia

Edited by
David E. Bloom
Peter Godwin

DELHI
OXFORD UNIVERSITY PRESS
CALCUTTA   CHENNAI   MUMBAI

Oxford University Press, Great Clarendon Street, Oxford OX2 6DP

Oxford New York
Athens Auckland Bangkok Calcutta
Cape Town Chennai Dar es Salaam Delhi
Florence Hong Kong Istanbul Karachi
Kuala Lumpur Madrid Melbourne Mexico City
Mumbai Nairobi Paris Singapore
Taipei Tokyo Toronto
and associates in
Berlin Ibadan

© United Nations Development Programme (UNDP) 1997

This work is published for and on behalf of UNDP
under the administration of UNOPS

First published 1997
Second impression 1998

ISBN 0 19 564150 7

Typeset by S.J.I. Services, New Delhi 110 024
Printed at Pauls Press, New Delhi 110 020
and published by Manzar Khan, Oxford University Press
YMCA Library Building, Jai Singh Road, New Delhi 110 001

Contents

Acknowledgements

In completing this book, the editors owe an enormous debt of gratitude to the United Nations Development Programme (Regional Bureau for Asia and the Pacific) for primary sponsorship of the research reported herein. They are also indebted to the Asian Development Bank (especially Myo Thant) for support of the project, including the organization of two conferences in Manila, at which the research was presented and deeply enriched by the generous suggestions of researchers and policymakers from throughout Asia, and of participants from several bilateral and multilateral organizations. The editors also wish to thank the Harvard Institute for International Development for administrative support and the Oxford University Press for its commitment to rapid production and dissemination of this volume. Special thanks also go to Alice Dowsett, Sarah Newberry, and Staci Warden for superb editorial assistance, to Ponnuswami Thayaparan, Beverly-Ann Agard, S. Gurumurthy, and Noni Singh for extremely efficient management of the project, and to Ajay Mahal for his valuable comments and tireless support on all aspects of the project. Useful comments were also provided by several anonymous reviewers.

Introduction

David E. Bloom and Peter Godwin

AIDS is an unusual disease in that it is easily avoidable, yet incurable once developed and invariably fatal. AIDS is also unusual because those infected with HIV (the human immunodeficiency virus, which causes AIDS) typically show no symptoms of infection for eight or more years after infection, when AIDS and its related illnesses start to appear. In its early stages, AIDS is thus an invisible disease.

An important aspect of this invisibility is the considerable epidemiological uncertainty surrounding the disease: in many countries where the reach of health information systems is still limited, the spread of HIV is difficult to establish. The burden of AIDS and its associated increases in mortality are still in the future, and estimates and projections can offer only an imperfect indication of the likely impacts on morbidity and mortality. These are poor data for hard-pressed officials to rely upon, which explains in part the slowness with which many policy makers have reacted to the epidemic. Addressing an invisible problem takes great wisdom, foresight, and determination, especially in the face of the many visible health problems—such as malaria, tuberculosis, hepatitis, cholera, typhoid, and diarrhoea—that openly ravage many populations. Responses to the AIDS epidemic are also complicated by the technical difficulty of establishing priorities for allocating resources to various health and other social problems, and by uncertainty about the appropriateness of particular policies and programmes for HIV prevention and AIDS care.

According to World Health Organization (WHO) estimates, 19.5 million people world-wide had contracted HIV through the end of 1995, with 4.5 million cases of full-blown AIDS (WHO 1995). WHO projects a cumulative global total of 30 to 40 million cases of HIV infection by the year 2000, at which time some 2 million people will be dying of AIDS each year, which will represent roughly 4 per cent of all deaths world-wide.

Among the most striking developments in the global HIV/AIDS epidemic is the rapidity with which the epidemic's centre of gravity is moving towards Asia. Although Asia currently accounts for less than 17 per cent of those infected with HIV, well below its 55 per cent share of world population, the continent has already overtaken Africa as the dominant location for new infections. WHO projects that Asia will account for more than half of the world's new HIV infections before the end of the decade.

As these statistics suggest, Asia is just as susceptible to the rapid spread of HIV as other regions. Asia will not be spared because of its culture; its values; or any of its ayurvedic, traditional Chinese, or homeopathic cures. On the contrary, Asia is extremely vulnerable to the epidemic. Many factors contribute to this vulnerability: the integration of Asian economies with each other and with the world economy; Asia's changing social customs; its pockets of widespread injecting drug use; its medical practices; its systems of commercial blood supply; its large domestic and international migrant populations; and its population's age distribution, which has a large proportion in the sexually active years.

The HIV/AIDS epidemic is a dark cloud on Asia's horizon. The large number of projected cases, the relatively high cost of caring for those with AIDS and HIV, and the fact that the disease is concentrated among individuals in their prime productive years all suggest that the epidemic has the potential to affect Asia's remarkable trajectory of rapid and sustained economic growth. The epidemic's effect may also extend beyond economic growth to a wider set of human development indicators, such as life expectancy, poverty, household security, family composition, and educational attainment. Establishing the scope and scale of these effects is the primary purpose of this book.

The first generation of economic research on the impact of AIDS focused on the epidemic's influence on the pace of national economic growth. This research found that the epidemic is likely to have a substantial macroeconomic impact in developing counties. Both elaborate macrosimulation models and standard cost-of-illness (COI) calculations suggested that the AIDS epidemic could cost as much as one-third of one percentage point of the growth rate of per capita income in developing countries through the year 2010. However, these models require many assumptions that are difficult to verify.

At the core of this book is the second chapter in this volume, by David Bloom and Ajay Mahal, which re-examines the impact of the HIV/AIDS epidemic on economic growth in a relatively assumption-free framework. This study finds a resounding lack of evidence to support the view that AIDS impedes economic growth. Bloom and Mahal analyse economic growth across a sample of fifty-one industrial and developing countries for which national AIDS prevalence data are available. They estimate the parameters of a standard empirical growth model that permits them to isolate the effect of AIDS on the growth of gross domestic product (GDP) per capita, controlling for other influences on economic growth, such as initial levels of income and human capital, openness of the economy, government spending, and so on. While the authors do not deny that AIDS is a costly disease on a per case basis, they find no evidence that it is also costly at the level of the national economy. Their analyses of the impact of the Black Death on wages in Western Europe during the fourteenth century and that of the 1918–19 influenza epidemic on agricultural output per capita in India further support this basic finding. Based on these results, Bloom and Mahal argue that economic research on AIDS should be reoriented to focus more on individuals, families, and households directly affected by HIV/AIDS; on women, children, the poor, and other vulnerable groups; on particular industrial and occupational sectors; on the economic roots of the epidemic; and on the economic evaluation of alternative policies and programmes for AIDS care and HIV prevention. The remainder of this volume is largely devoted to these 'second generation' issues.

This volume has three fundamental premises. The first is the observation that HIV and AIDS are more than just health problems; they are also problems with deep social and economic roots and potentially far-reaching and severe economic consequences. The second is an abiding faith in the power of appropriate and rigorous analysis. Such analysis can yield deep practical insights into the nature and implications of the epidemic, insights that can help guide the development of policies to address the care of people living with AIDS and the prevention and control of HIV. The third is the belief that lessons learned from studying one country's experience with the AIDS epidemic are valuable not just to that country, but to other countries as well.

The chapters that follow were prepared in connection with a joint project of the United Nations Development Programme (UNDP, Regional HIV Project for Asia and the Pacific, based in New Delhi) and the Asian Development Bank. This volume includes the studies commissioned by the UNDP. A separate volume is planned for publication of those studies commissioned by the Asian Development Bank.

The country studies in this volume focus on Thailand, India, and Sri Lanka. In the first study, Sumalee Pitayanon, Sukhontha Kongsin, and Wattana S. Janjareon measure and analyse the economic impact of adult AIDS deaths on rural households in Chiangmai province, Thailand; investigate the link between AIDS mortality and poverty in rural areas; and analyse the coping ability of households of different economic status. Alaka Basu, Devendra Gupta, and Geetanjali Krishna use data from New Delhi, India to investigate how socio-economic status affects the risk of contracting HIV and the nature and extent of the impact of fatal illness on household welfare. In the last paper, Bloom, Mahal, and their co-authors undertake a comprehensive study of the impact of HIV/AIDS in Sri Lanka. They calculate the cost of AIDS using both cost-of-illness and willingness-to-pay methods and investigate the social and economic roots and consequences of HIV/AIDS among specific groups (free trade zone labourers, commercial sex workers, prison inmates, and overseas workers) and within specific segments of the economy (tourism and health care).

The Impact on Households

Both the Thai and Indian studies found that the negative impact of AIDS on household income was sizeable despite the methods people devised to cope with the burden. In addition, the AIDS epidemic had a negative impact on household welfare beyond the direct loss of household income. Both studies showed that the consequences of the death of a productive member of the household were higher than just loss of income. For example, they found negative impacts on the elderly, because traditionally household members of prime working age care for older members of the household; children, who might have to be withdrawn from school to help with care giving or to earn an income; and the family as a whole, because of social discrimination against the person living with AIDS and that individual's family.

The Thai study also compared the cost of an AIDS-related death with that of a death from other causes. It found that the economic impacts of an AIDS-related death were more severe, because AIDS is more likely to infect a population that is already disadvantaged and less able to cope. In this survey, households in which the main income earner died of AIDS had an average income level that was only 66 per cent of the income of households in which the main income earner died from other causes. And because AIDS affects people at a younger age, the foregone income of the deceased was 30 per cent more than in households that experienced a death from other causes.

Both studies investigated the demographic impacts of the disease, and both concluded that the households that suffered the most were the poorest and least educated. These studies lend support to the claim the HIV/AIDS will have a disproportionately strong effect on those parts of society least able to cope with the epidemic. The studies show that the household impact on the poor will be greater, because poorer households have limited resources on which to draw.

The Prevalence of HIV/AIDS among Specific Demographic Groups

The impact of HIV and AIDS on a specific demographic group depends on that group's awareness about the disease and the way it is transmitted, and the susceptibility or vulnerability of that group to high-risk situations. The Indian and Sri Lankan studies investigated these issues.

Both studies found a strong positive correlation between education and income levels and knowledge about HIV and how it is transmitted. The Sri Lankan study, for example, found that 96 per cent of the households surveyed had both heard of AIDS and were generally well informed about its methods of transmission. This awareness, however, was highly correlated with both income and education levels.

The link between income levels and the prevalence of situations that increase the risk of HIV infection is not well established empirically, however. For example, the Indian study found that, while richer people could better afford to engage in risky sexual behaviour, they were also more inclined to use condoms. The Sri Lankan study investigated whether poverty levels were correlated with entering risky professions, such as prostitution, and found that there is a disproportionately large representation of individuals from economically disadvantaged households in the sex industry. The same study found that male prostitutes, street walkers, and prison inmates were at highest risk because of the high levels of casual sex and the low levels of condom use in these situations.

In short, the evidence from these studies suggests, at least anecdotally, that poor households will be disproportionately affected by the HIV/AIDS epidemic because they will be less likely to be sufficiently informed of the risks associated with the disease, and because they are more likely to engage in activities that put them at high risk of contracting HIV. Furthermore, poor households will be disproportionately affected by a premature adult death in the household, because these households have limited coping mechanisms.

Coping Mechanisms

The Sri Lankan, Thai, and Indian studies all show that irrespective of wealth, individual households bear the brunt of the cost of illness and death from HIV/AIDS. In these and most other developing countries, government health care systems and social safety nets do not reach enough people and most are not covered by private health or other types of insurance.

To accommodate the large financial burden imposed when a productive member of a household becomes sick and dies, households use a number of coping mechanisms. They draw upon their household savings, sell households assets, reduce their consumption, reallocate labour among the remaining household members, seek transfers from extended family members, or apply for loans. Both the Thai and Indian studies investigated the link between both the type of coping mechanisms employed and the ability to cope as a function of household's socio-economic status. Both studies concluded that poorer households were less able to cope with the effects of HIV and AIDS mortality.

Policy Implications

To date, HIV and AIDS policies have focused primarily on controlling the spread of the disease. Although preventing the spread of HIV is undeniably important, the current high levels and growth rate of the epidemic make it crucial that policy makers devise social protection mechanisms that directly address the impact of the epidemic on households. Policy makers need to address the costs that are unique to HIV/AIDS because it so often afflicts productive people during their prime working age. These policies must focus on addressing the need to adapt and extend the health care system (whether public, private, or NGO) to deal with the increased morbidity and mortality associated with the epidemic, and reversing the reduced functioning of families and communities, the lost economic production, and the increased social burden on those other than the AIDS sufferers (such as caring for orphaned children). In addition, policy makers will have to target those demographic, geographic, and sectoral groups that are most vulnerable to contracting HIV. Considerably more work is needed, however, for a better understanding of which groups these will be. The studies reported here for India and Sri Lanka focus primarily on urban households. Yet rural areas (particularly tribal or otherwise marginalized or distressed communities) contribute disproportionately to migrant labour, and the extent to which they are particularly vulnerable because of this is an area that urgently needs further study.

The Thai and Indian studies both reveal the inadequacy of current social protection mechanisms and offer specific policy proposals. Among those mentioned are proposals to improve the access of the poor to free or subsidized health care and basic social services, to improve credit markets and expand existing formal sources of credit, to enhance insurance schemes, to protect human rights by safeguarding the confidentiality of health records (thereby permitting HIV-positive people to continue working as long as they can), and to initiate government-sponsored campaigns against discrimination.

Finally, the studies only reported *single* adult deaths in households. Because the epidemic is relatively new in Asia, the propensity for HIV-related deaths to *cluster* in households, as spouses infect each other, has been little observed so far. This highlights both the fact that it is the minimum effect of the epidemic that is reported here, and the urgent need to consider gender differentials in further work. This latter may well be the most important of the next generation of socio-economic research and analysis on the epidemic.

1

The AIDS Epidemic and Economic Policy Analysis

David E. Bloom and Ajay S. Mahal

Economists have a vital role to play in helping public health officials and policy makers understand the AIDS epidemic and design efficient policies to limit its impact. AIDS is first and foremost a public health problem, but it is a problem with deep economic roots and potentially devastating economic consequences. The main purpose of this article is to document this assertion.

The Costs of AIDS

To understand the economic consequences of AIDS, a useful starting-point is to examine the costs associated with this disease. These costs fall into four main categories. The first includes the personal medical care costs associated with AIDS, that is, the costs of detecting, treating and caring for people with AIDS. In the second category are the nonpersonal costs, such as the costs of blood screening, the costs of information, education and communication, and the costs of basic research on AIDS. In the third category is the cost of lost output and lost income because of AIDS morbidity and mortality. The fourth consists of the psychological costs associated with the epidemic, such as the pain and suffering caused by AIDS, and the cost imposed upon people who must behave differently to avoid contracting or transmitting HIV.

The first two categories of AIDS costs jointly make up the direct costs of the epidemic, so named because they involve a direct diversion of scarce resources from other uses. The third category is referred to as the indirect cost of the epidemic. It is not an out-of-pocket cost like medical expenditures on AIDS patients. Rather, it is what economists term an opportunity cost, because it reflects the value of lost opportunities to work and produce the goods and services whose consumption yields satisfaction. Indirect costs are just as important a component of the total cost of the epidemic as direct medical costs. The epidemic's psychological costs are rarely discussed or quantified.

The first generation of economic research on the AIDS epidemic has involved measuring the direct costs of HIV and AIDS and the income forgone because of AIDS morbidity and mortality in many countries throughout the world. Every study of this issue of which we are aware concludes that AIDS is an unusually costly illness on a per case basis, for two main reasons. Firstly, many of the opportunistic infections with which AIDS is definitionally associated, such as tuberculosis, pneumonia and cryptococcal meningitis, are costly to treat relative to the cost of treating other common illnesses; and secondly, AIDS disproportionately afflicts individuals in their prime productive years, thereby causing a considerable loss of income to them and their families.

Economists have estimated, for example, that the lifetime personal medical care costs associated with AIDS in India are more than double India's per capita income, assuming that people with AIDS receive medical care that conforms fully to local protocols for the treatment of AIDS and the opportunistic infections with which AIDS is associated. The income lost because of AIDS morbidity and mortality is estimated to be far greater: more than ten times India's income per capita, in discounted terms (Bloom and Glied 1993). This estimate of the loss of private income should not be confused with social output losses, especially in a labour surplus setting, although the two concepts can be linked. Overall, these estimates of medical care costs and lost income indicate that each case of AIDS is quite costly in India, just as it is elsewhere in the world.

Economic Determinants of HIV Transmission

The contribution of economics to understanding the AIDS epidemic is not limited to quantifying its impact in monetary terms. Economics also provides a powerful way of examining the pattern of the epidemic's spread. The central idea is that HIV is not spread randomly, as tends to be the case with the bacteria that cause tuberculosis or the virus that causes the common cold. Rather, HIV is most often transmitted as a consequence of purposeful behaviour that often has a strong economic foundation. For example, some of the sex that contributes to the spread of HIV is sold on the street and through brothels (Centre for International Research 1993; Nataraj 1991). As another example, a close connection seems to exist between labour migration and HIV transmission (See Bloom and Mahal 1993; Gharpure et al. 1992; Solon and Barrozo 1993). This connection seems to arise because the behaviour of migrants is not easily subject to monitoring by their families and communities, because migrants often have considerable amounts of cash to spend, and because they may be lonely because of being separated from their families. In addition, because migrants are often poorly educated and not closely connected to stable communities, making them aware of the behaviours that put them at high risk for contracting or transmitting the virus that causes AIDS can be challenging. All these factors increase the likelihood of migrants engaging in commercial sex, an activity that puts them at high risk for contracting HIV, and ultimately places their spouses and unborn children at risk.

Considering India again, the country has a huge migrant population, both internal and international. Rural-urban migration is significant, especially in Maharashtra, Tamil Nadu and West Bengal. So too is the floating population of migrant workers (Stiglitz 1988). India also experiences substantial cross-border population movements with Bangladesh, Nepal, and to some extent Myanmar, as well as strong migration flows to and from the Middle East and a growing influx of foreign tourists, businesspeople, and others. Add to this a continuing process of economic reform, which is likely to promote the movement of people into, out of, and within India, and the situation is one of continuing and increasing vulnerability to the spread of HIV, especially among the general population.

We conclude from this reasoning and these examples that economists have a key role to play in understanding the nature of the HIV and AIDS epidemic and in assessing its impact. Economics is a crucial ingredient in any explanation of why HIV spreads so rapidly among lorry drivers, fishermen, sailors, construction workers, overseas contract workers, the military, commercial sex workers, injecting drug users, and commercial blood donors. That so many countries throughout the world share this pattern of spread is no coincidence.

Does Government have a Role to Play?

Government intervention in the area of HIV/AIDS encompasses a myriad of activities aimed both at controlling the spread of HIV and coping with the immediate shock of the epidemic and its wide-ranging echo effects. Interventions may be justified on the grounds that they promote efficiency (that is, increase the size of the economic pie) or promote equity (achieve a more desirable distribution of the pie).

Intervention can promote efficiency if one individual's behaviour imposes costs upon others for which no compensation is paid, a market failure that economists refer to as a negative externality. As an example, an externality may arise if a person with AIDS and tuberculosis coughs or sneezes in public, and thereby subjects other nearby individuals to the risk of tuberculosis infection. Costs that are not easily deterred are being imposed without offsetting compensation. As another example, consider women who are powerless to negotiate the use of condoms with their sex partners, a situation that arises in many commercial sex establishments as well as in many marital relationships. To the extent that these women, along with their unborn children, are exposed to the risk of HIV infection, costs that are not easily deterred are again imposed without compensation, a classic market failure for which government intervention is a natural remedy.

Intervention may also promote efficiency if private individuals are poorly informed about the risks and costs of HIV transmission. Indeed, under certain conditions the government can improve well-being either by providing information about HIV and AIDS or by adopting tax, subsidy or regulatory policies that induce people to act as if they had this information.

An equity justification for intervention could arise if the costs of the epidemic fall disproportionately upon the poor (Bloom and Glied 1993; Stiglitz 1988). If the government deems the ensuing distribution of economic well-being, under which the poor are further immiserized, to be socially undesirable, government intervention aimed either at preventing HIV transmission or redistributing resources is well justified.

Contribution of Economic Reasoning to Policy Making

Even though making a case for some government intervention in the area of HIV and AIDS in Asia's developing countries is not difficult, the complexity of the mechanisms that lead to HIV infection and that determine their social and economic impacts make effective policy making an especially challenging task. We offer three examples to illustrate this point.

The first example relates to HIV transmission via the sharing of needles among injecting drug users. To reduce the rate of HIV transmission, some policy makers have suggested reducing the number of drug users by cracking down on the supply of opium. From an economist's perspective, however, destroying opium fields might actually promote HIV transmission, a result exactly opposite to the one desired. This could happen if a reduced supply of opium leads to an increase in its price, which in turn leads habitual opium smokers to cut back on their opium consumption by switching to injection, a far more efficacious mode of opium use (Strang et al. 1992: 473–83).

Throughout North America and Western Europe, policy makers are increasingly responding to the problem of HIV transmission through the sharing of nonsterile injection equipment by establishing needle exchange programmes (Lurie and Reingold 1993). Under these programmes, injecting drug users can receive new injection equipment at no charge in exchange for used injection equipment. Needle exchange programmes are controversial because they try to improve the conditions under which illegal drug use takes place, which critics claim promotes greater drug use. Nonetheless, preliminary evidence for the United States suggests that the rate of new HIV infection among injecting drug users who participate in such programmes is lower than the corresponding rate among nonparticipants (De Jarlais et al. 1994: 271, 1–7).

As a second example, consider a policy of isolating or imprisoning seropositive commercial sex workers, as India did for a brief period several years ago in a highly publicized case in which 854 commercial sex workers, 457 of whom were HIV-positive, were moved from Bombay to Madras and confined (Nataraj 1991). On the surface, this policy might seem to be a sensible way to curb HIV transmission, because it prevents seropositive sex workers from selling sex. However, it fails to address the demand side of the market for sex, that is, the fact that certain individuals, be they foreign businessmen or native sailors, fishermen or migrant workers, will continue to demand and be willing to pay for sex. Under the economic conditions that currently prevail throughout most of the world, that demand will be satisfied by a new group of women who will supply sex commercially, not because they are social deviants, but because they lack better economic opportunities. Although these women may be seronegative when they enter the sex industry, without information about HIV and without the power to negotiate the use of condoms, they too will become infected and then infect others.

A third example concerns HIV testing. Some policy makers believe that mandatory testing is a useful approach to HIV prevention. Their rationale is that people will respond altruistically to the knowledge that they are HIV-infected by curbing behaviour that puts others at high risk of infection, especially if they receive appropriate counselling. Altruism is, however, not the rule in economic behaviour. Selfishness is much more common, and in this context might actually cause HIV testing to promote further transmission as people who learn that they are seropositive recognize that they no longer face a key discentive to high-risk behaviour: the risk of HIV infection. Although research findings vary, a number of reputable studies have found evidence that positive HIV test results trigger increases in high-risk behaviour, thereby supporting the view that testing may promote HIV transmission (Bloom and Glied 1992: 339–65; Philipson and Posner 1993).

These three examples are not meant to suggest that economic reasoning provides a complete explanation of individual decisions about drug consumption, the supply of and the demand for sex, or other high-risk behaviour. They do, however, illustrate one of the hallmarks of economists' approach to policy making: the need to understand the mechanism that is generating undesirable outcomes as a prelude to effective policy design and implementation.

In the first example, the economics of drug injection suggests that a policy of destroying opium fields might increase drug injection more than it decreases drug use, the net effect being a higher rate of HIV transmission. This reasoning does not, of course, imply that the government should promote opium production as a way of driving prices down and encourage smoking in place of injection. While such a policy might, in principle, curtail the spread of HIV, it would probably do so quite slowly, because heavy drug injectors rarely revert to smoking. More important, it might simultaneously increase the number of drug users, which is clearly not a desirable outcome. However, this bit of economic reasoning does help explain the calls for decriminalizing the sale, possession and use of drugs that one increasingly hears in North America and Western Europe. It also highlights the fact that many practical policies for HIV prevention may conflict with other social goals and policies. For example, needle exchange programmes may increase the number of drug users, early sex education and free contraceptives may encourage promiscuity, condom distribution in the prison system may condone illicit homosexual activity, and policies mandating the use of condoms in brothels may undermine the illegality of prostitution.

In the second example, a policy of imprisoning seropositive commercial sex workers is little more than a temporary solution, what might best be termed a band-aid solution, to the problem of HIV transmission. It ignores both the demand side of the market for sex and the readily available supply of additional sex workers.

In the third example, as already noted, mandatory testing may actually promote HIV transmission. This observation highlights the fact that the HIV epidemic can, in principle, be controlled without identifying a single HIV-infected person. As long as the population behaves carefully, a goal that is presumably promoted by the provision of information, those who are infected will not transmit the virus and those who are uninfected will not contract it. Testing the blood supply and doing some testing for purposes of epidemiological surveillance may be desirable, but this testing can be done anonymously. Limiting the amount of testing that is done also affords the greatest protection to individual privacy, thereby limiting the ostracism and stigmatization that so often, so needlessly, and so counterproductively accompany the spread of HIV and AIDS.

Contribution of Economic Tools to Policy Making

Good economic reasoning encourages policy making directed at underlying problems, not at superficial symptoms. Economics also offers a set of tools that are often extremely useful for rational policy making. These tools, known as cost–benefit analysis and cost-effectiveness analysis, are methods for evaluating the desirability of alternative policy options (Drummond, Stoddart and Torrance 1987). Both methods require us to estimate the costs of implementing alternative policies. Cost–benefit analysis also estimates the expected benefits corresponding to each alternative, and the optimal policy is the one that has the highest net benefit, that is, benefits less costs.

Cost-effectiveness analysis is closely related to cost–benefit analysis, except that it stops short of estimating the monetary benefits of particular policies. Instead, it calculates and compares the cost of alternative methods of achieving a particular qualitative outcome.

As a brief illustration, suppose we wish to compare the following eight programmes for HIV prevention and control: (1) mass education through national television and radio; (2) mass education through the distribution of a one-page AIDS information sheet to every household; (3) a special HIV and AIDS information programme for workers and tourists going abroad; (4) a special HIV and AIDS information programme for lorry drivers; (5) a programme to expand the provision for family planning services to unmarried individuals; (6) a programme to treat sexually transmitted diseases (STDs), which is important because STDs greatly increase the risk of HIV transmission; (7) a programme for screening the blood supply for HIV; and (8) a community-based programme aimed at reducing the demand for drugs and promoting harm reduction among injecting drug users in areas with relatively heavy drug use. Using cost–benefit analysis we would estimate the number of HIV infections that each programme would avert, and place a monetary value on those averted infections using estimates of the direct and indirect costs of the epidemic. We would then compare the estimated monetary value of averted infections and of any other expected consequences of each programme, such as control of STDs, fertility reduction, reduced drug use, lower crime rates, and so on, with the cost of each programme. Good programmes are those whose benefits exceed their costs, much like good investments, which are those that yield positive net returns.

In doing a cost-effectiveness analysis, we would not place a monetary value on the estimated number of averted HIV infections. We would simply calculate the cost per averted infection under each programme as a way to identify which of them offers the least expensive way to control the spread of HIV. Unlike cost–benefit analysis, which takes multiple programme impacts into account and indicates whether each programme is a good investment or not, cost-effectiveness analysis simply ranks alternative programmes in terms of their economic efficiency in achieving a particular outcome. As cost-effectiveness analysis does not require the monetization of programme benefits, it also requires fewer assumptions and calculations than cost-benefit analysis.

Cost-benefit and cost-effectiveness analyses provide a systematic, sensible and practical way of selecting among alternative policy options. Combinations of options may also be analysed, which is important if programmes complement each other. The analyses may be performed from the point of view of an individual, an organization, or society as a whole, and often yield different results depending upon whose point of view is adopted. Although these analyses are sometimes difficult to carry out because of data limitations and a variety of difficulties inherent in calculating and monetizing programme impacts, this is not always the case, as some recent cost-benefits of screening the blood supply for HIV demonstrate (Chapter 5 in this volume; Jianhua et al. 1995).

Considerable work remains to be done in applying the tools of cost-benefit and cost-effectiveness analyses to the evaluation of policies designed to promote HIV prevention and control. Especially interesting would be analyses of HIV and STD prevention programmes that involve expanding the distribution of condoms and of programmes for both mass and targeted education about HIV and AIDS, especially programmes designed to reach migrants. In the absence of a cure for HIV and AIDS, information about safe behaviour and the necessary motivation to practice it are the only options even remotely resembling a vaccine against HIV transmission. HIV can spread fast, but so too can information. Indeed, information delivered through community-based programmes and channels of influence appears to be the most potent ally available in the effort to control the further spread of HIV (Coates 1994).

Impact of AIDS on Economic Growth and Development

Leaders in the global campaign against AIDS have repeatedly expressed the opinion that the AIDS epidemic is likely to have a substantial—perhaps even a catastrophic—impact on the macroeconomics of developing countries (Philipson and Posner 1993; Bloom and Lyons 1993: Merson 1992; Panos Institute 1992; UNDP 1992). A variety of economic studies support these assertions. These studies indicate that in the hardest-hit countries of Africa, the HIV and AIDS epidemic may diminish the annual growth rates of national income by as much as two-thirds of a percentage point, and diminish the annual growth rate of national income per person by as much as one-third of a percentage point through the year 2010 (Cuddington 1992, 1993: 173–89; Cuddington and Hancock 1994; Over 1992). In relation to the growth rates of many of the world's economies, two-thirds of a percentage point is not as little as it may initially seem. Also, it adds up over time, which is important given that a biochemical vaccine against HIV infection and a cure for AIDS are nowhere in sight.

The economic simulation models and cost-of-illness calculations that support the prediction that AIDS will have dire macroeconomic consequences require many assumptions that are difficult to verify, but adopting a more direct approach to examining the impact of the epidemic on the growth rates of income per person is now feasible. We are in the second decade of the world AIDS epidemic, which has progressed relatively far in several countries, especially in Africa. For example, nearly 20 per cent of the adult populations of Uganda and Zambia are infected with HIV. In Zambia, the cumulative number of cases of full-blown AIDS has already reached 4 per cent of the adult population. With this range of HIV experience, from low-prevalence countries like China and Sri Lanka, to medium-prevalence countries like India, Myanmar and Thailand, to high-prevalence countries like Uganda and Zambia, we may examine whether countries that have experienced more severe AIDS epidemics have also experienced lower rates of economic growth, while controlling for other influences on economic growth and addressing the possible reciprocal influence of economic growth on the spread of the HIV.

Technical issues and other details aside, preliminary calculations based on data for fifty-one countries reveal that the AIDS epidemic has had only a small and statistically insignificant negative effect on income per person. These results resemble ones derived through similar analyses of the economic impacts of the world influenza epidemic of 1918–19 and the Black Death of the mid-1300s, both of which killed massive numbers of people in extremely short periods of time (details in Chapter 2 of this volume).

With these findings in hand, and given that countries like India already have first-generation estimates of the economy-wide costs of the epidemic, the amount of attention devoted to the macroeconomic impacts of the AIDS epidemic can be reduced. This will give policy makers and researchers an opportunity to focus greater attention on the impact of the epidemic on particular industrial and occupational sectors, on particular geographic regions, and on particular demographic groups, especially people living with AIDS, their families, women, migrants, the poor and other marginalized groups such as ethnic minorities, homosexuals and drug users. These are the areas that health policy makers, economists, international organizations, non-governmental organizations, and others concerned with the social and economic implications of the epidemic need to address most urgently. They involve complex issues that include matters of health, sociology, psychology, law, politics and economics. As research problems, they call for multidisciplinary approaches, mirroring their nature as multisectoral problems from the standpoint of policy design and implementation.

References

Bloom, D. and S. Glied. 1993. 'Who is bearing the cost of the AIDS epidemic in Asia?' In Bloom, D. and J. Lyons, eds., *Economic Implications of AIDS in Asia* United Nations Development Programme.

——1992. Projecting the number of new AIDS cases in the United States. *International Journal of Forecasting*, 339–65.

Bloom, D. and J. Lyons, (eds). 1993. *Economic Implications of AIDS in Asia.* United Nations Development Programme, New York.

Bloom, D. and A. Mahal. 1995. 'Economic Implications of AIDS in Asia', Draft.

——1995. 'Does the AIDS Epidemic Really Threaten Economic Growth?' Working Paper No. 5148. National Bureau of Economic Research Cambridge, Massachussetts.

Centre for International Research. *HIV/AIDS Surveillance Data Base.* United States Bureau of the Census, Washington D.C.

Coates, T. 1994. 'Communities and AIDS prevention: What works'. AIDS captions, May 2–4.

Cuddington, J. 1992. 'The Macroeconomic Impact of AIDS in a Dualistic, Labor-Surplus Economy with an Application to Tanzania'. Working Paper #92–12. Georetown University, Washington D.C.

Cuddington, J. 1993. 'Modeling and macroeconomic effects of AIDS, with an application to Tanzania'. *The World Bank Economic Review*, 7: 173–89.

Cuddington, J. and J. Hancock. 1994 'Assessing the impact of AIDS on the growth path of the Malawian economy'. *Journal of Development Economics. 4(3):*

Des Jarlais, D., S. Friedman, J. Sotheran, J. Wenston, M. Marmor, S. Yancovitz, B. Frank, S. Beatrice and D. Mildvan. 1994. 'Continuity and change within an HIV epidemic: Injecting drug users in New York City, 1984 through 1992'. *Journal of the American Medical Association,* 271, 121–7.

Drummond, M., G. Stoddart and G. Torrance. 1987. *Methods for the Economic Evaluation of Health Care Programmes. New York: Oxford University Press.*

Gharpure, H., N. Chanderkar, and S. Sengupta. 1992. 'Serosurveillance of HIV Infection in Migrant Workers: Socioeconomic Relationship'. Abstract No. B314 at the Second International Conference on AIDS in Asia and the Pacific, New Delhi, November 8–12.

Jianhua, Y., Yu Jingyuan, J. Tau, and Xu Yi. 1995. 'Blood screening in China: An economic analysis'. Draft. Beijing Institute of Information and Control, Beijing, China.

Lurie, P. and A. Reingold. 1993. *The Public Health Impact of Needle Exchange Programmes in the United States and Abroad.* University of California, Berkeley.

Merson, M. 1992. 'The AIDS Epidemic in Asia: The Reality, the Opportunity and the Challenge'. Keynote address, delivered at the Second International Congress on AIDS in Asia and the Pacific, New Delhi, November 8–12.

Nataraj, S. 'Locking up prostitutes'. In *The Third Epidemic: Repercussions of the Fear of AIDS.* The Panos Institute, London.

Over, Mead. 1992. 'The Macroeconomic Impact of AIDS in Sub-Saharan Africa'. Technical Working Paper No. 3. Washington D.C.: The World Bank, Technical Department, Population, Health, and Nutrition Division.

Panos Institute. 1992. *The Hidden Cost of AIDS: The Challenge of HIV to Development.* London: Panos Publications.

Philipson, T. and R. Posner. 1993. *Private Choices and Public Health: The AIDS Epidemic in an Economic Perspective.* Cambridge, MA: Harvard University Press.

Presidential Commission on the Human Immunodeficiency Virus Epidemic. 1988. Report. Washington DC.

Solon, O. and A. Barrozo. 1993. 'Overseas contract workers and the economic consequences of the HIV/AIDS in the Philippines'. In Bloom, D. and J. Lyons, *eds., Economic Implications of AIDS in Asia.* United Nations Development Programme, New York.

Stiglitz, J. 1988. *Economics of the Public Sector, second Edition.* New York: W.W. Norton.

Strang, J., D. Des Jarlais, P. Griffiths and M. Gossop. 1992. 'The study of transitions in the route of drug use, the route from one route to another'. *British Journal of Addiction* 87, 473–83.

United Nations Development Programme. 1992. 'The HIV Epidemic as a Development Issue'. New York: United Nations.

United Nations Development Programme. 1993. 'HIV/AIDS Situation in India'. Country report, presented at the UNDP/Asian Development Bank Workshop on the Economic Implications of the HIV/AIDS Epidemic in Selected DMCs, Manila, Philippines, September 5–8.

2

AIDS, Flu, and the Black Death: Impacts on Economic Growth and Well-being*

David E. Bloom and Ajay S. Mahal

Introduction

The World Health Organization (WHO) estimates that by late 1995 nearly 19.5 million people world-wide had been infected by the human immunodeficiency virus (HIV) that causes AIDS, with a cumulative total of 8.5 million cases of full-blown AIDS (WHO 1995). WHO also projects a significant future spread of HIV, with a cumulative global total reaching 30 to 40 million people by the year 2000 (WHO 1994a). Even more alarming is the projection by Mann, Tarantola, and Netter (1992) of 110 million cumulative cases of HIV infection world-wide by the year 2000.

Although biomedical and public health issues continue to dominate the agenda of AIDS researchers, recognition has grown in recent years that the epidemic is more than just a health problem. Throughout the world, relatively high rates of HIV infection among sex workers, injecting drug users, long-haul truck drivers, commercial blood donors, migrant workers, sailors, and fishermen

* An earlier version of this paper was presented at the Asian Development Bank. Financial support from the United Nations Development Programme is gratefully acknowledged. Mireille Jacobsen and Janhavi Dabholkar provided helpful research assistance. Alok Bhargava, Paul Gertler, Sherry Glied, Jeffrey Sachs, and participants in the economic development workshop at Harvard University and the health economics workshop at the National Bureau of Economic Research provided helpful comments.

provide compelling evidence of the interplay between economic forces and HIV transmission (see Barnett and Blaikie 1992; Bloom and Lyons 1993; Bloom and Mahal 1995; Mann, Tarantola, and Netter 1992; The Panos Institute 1992; Philipson and Posner 1993; World Bank 1992, 1993a). Moreover, research on the economic implications of the AIDS epidemic is increasingly being guided by models built around the observation that HIV is transmitted as a direct by-product of purposeful behaviour—not randomly, as in the case of most other infectious diseases (see Bloom and Glied 1989; Bloom and Mahal 1995; Kremer 1995; Philipson and Posner 1993).

Economic research also indicates that the per case medical care costs of AIDS are high relative to the costs of diagnosing and treating other serious illnesses (Bloom and Carliner 1988; Bloom and Lyons 1993; Hellinger 1993; The Panos Institute 1992). Added to these costs are the private income and social output losses associated with AIDS-related morbidity and mortality, which tend to be large because prime-age individuals are disproportionately represented among AIDS cases (Bloom and Mahal 1995; WHO 1994a). The costs are further magnified by the need to maintain sterile medical practices, blood testing, 'education for prevention' campaigns, and basic research on AIDS (Bloom and Carliner 1988; Bloom and others 1995; The Panos Institute 1992; Sisk 1988; World Bank 1992).

Many influential AIDS experts contend that the epidemic will have a substantial negative impact on national economic well-being. These experts fall into two groups. The first groups consists of those who infer this result from the combination of large projected numbers of prime-age seropositive individuals and the relatively high estimated cost of medical care for persons with AIDS. For example, Philipson and Posner (1993) assert that because of the epidemic's size, its distinctive economic character (in parts of Africa and, in the near future, in Asia as well) will be its substantial implication for such key indicators of macro-economic performance as economic growth, GNP and GNP per capita. The various United Nations agencies working on the economic and development implications of the epidemic express similar views. For example, the World Bank (1993a: 100) states that 'AIDS, affecting as its does mainly people in the economically productive adult years, had powerful negative economic effects on ... countries.' Similarly, the United Nations Development Programme (UNDP) claims that 'the extent of illness and death caused by the epidemic could deplete critical sectors of the labour force, ..., and adversely affect every sector of the economy. The consequences of the spread of the virus will be inexorable and awesome' (UNDP 1992: 1). The UNDP also argues that 'the AIDS epidemic imposes large costs on individuals and their families that will be translated into aggregate costs that could become large enough to create national economic crises' (Lyons 1993: 5). Finally, the former head of WHO's Global Programme on AIDS, Michael Merson, has said that the 'deaths of millions of able-bodied adults will ... rob society of their education, skills, and experience. The resulting productivity losses will... threaten the very process of development' (Merson 1992: 2).[1]

The second group of experts derive conclusions from data analyses guided by well-established economic models customized in various ways to fit the AIDS epidemic as it is projected to evolve. For example, Kambou, Devarajan, and Over (1992) simulate the impact of the AIDS epidemic using an eleven-sector computable general equilibrium model of Cameroon. They assume that the AIDS epidemic claimed the lives of 30,000 workers (or 0.8 per cent of the labour force) each year from 1987 to 1990, with deaths occurring disproportionately among the more skilled segments of the work-force. For example, they assume that 6 per cent of the skilled urban work-force died of AIDS each year, compared to 0.4 per cent of the unskilled rural labour force. In this simulation, the AIDS epidemic lowers the rate of growth of GDP by nearly 2 percentage points per year.

---

1.   As another example, Mann, Tarantola, and Netter (1992: 195) write that 'the adverse impacts of the AIDS epidemic will ... reduce the potential for economic growth. AIDS is distinct and ... its impact can be expected to be quite severe'. Similarly, Cohen (1993: 32) concludes that 'the economic and social costs of HIV are truly colossal. The epidemic, if unchecked, could transform the developmental performance of many countries'. Elsewhere, in the Panos Institute (1992: 116), the authors claim that 'HIV/AIDS has the capacity to seriously undermine the development prospects of many nations'.

Cuddington (1993) and Cuddington and Hancock (1994) use a standard neo-classical growth model to explore the effect of AIDS on economic growth. In this model AIDS-related morbidity and mortality decrease the size of the labour force. In addition, AIDS-related medical expenditures lower public and private savings, leading in turn to reduced investment in physical capital, and lower productivity. These studies focus on the epidemic's impact in Tanzania and Malawi, countries whose AIDS epidemics are among the most severe in the world. These studies indicate that AIDS will depress the annual growth rate of real GDP per capita by an average of 0.25 per cent (the mid-point of their low and high scenarios) through the year 2010, assuming that World Bank projections of the number of AIDS cases are realized.

Applying a related framework to data for sub-Saharan Africa, Over (1992) assumes that AIDS cases will be disproportionately concentrated among the more educated classes and also that 50 per cent of AIDS medical care costs will be financed by reduced savings (which translates into reduced investment and a slower rate of expansion of economic capacity). He concludes that the epidemic will depress growth rates of GDP per capita by roughly 0.15 percentage points per year (0.33 percentage points under a worst-case scenario), a sizeable amount in the context of sub-Saharan Africa's recent growth experience (that is, a 1.2 per cent average annual *decline* in income per capita from 1980 to 1991).[2]

Notwithstanding the consensus that emerges from these studies, there are good reasons to suspect that they overstate the seriousness and immediacy of the threat AIDS poses to economic growth. Firstly, the surplus labour in many developing countries could mitigate output losses that might otherwise be associated with AIDS morbidity and mortality.[3]

Secondly, although this has not yet been definitively established, a link between HIV infection and poverty appears to be emerging (see Bloom and Glied 1993; Over and Piot 1993). In-

---

2.   This result refers to the 'average' sub-Saharan country. If the simulations are confined to the ten African countries with the most advanced epidemics, the average negative effect on per capita income growth is 0.6 per cent per year.
3.   However, note that Cuddington (1992) finds little evidence that his results for Tanzania are sensitive to the presence of surplus labour.

deed, many studies have found that the more educated exhibit superior knowledge of HIV and AIDS and a greater willingness to take precautions against contracting HIV than the less educated (Ahituv, Hotz, and Philipson 1993; also see references cited in Philipson and Posner 1993). This link suggests that AIDS-related output losses, income losses, and medical expenditures will be relatively low on a per case basis, corresponding to the relatively low productivity, earnings, and utilization of medical services among the poor (Bloom and Glied 1993; Bloom and Mahal 1996; Griffin 1990; Philipson and Posner 1993).

Thirdly, normal social and economic adjustments will tend to mitigate the costs of the epidemic. For example, community-based organizations and extended family networks have emerged as mechanisms for coping with the requirements for medical treatment associated with the epidemic. These mechanisms, which have arisen in widely diverse settings, often provide health services more efficiently than the formal health care system (see Barnett and Blaikie 1992; The Panos Institute 1992; World Bank 1993a).

Fourthly, although AIDS-related medical care costs may be drawn disproportionately from personal savings in the short run, one would expect these costs to fall less heavily on savings in the longer run.

Finally, one might reasonably expect AIDS case projections to overstate the eventual number of cases, as individuals perceive and respond to the disincentives associated with the forms of behaviour that put them at high risk for contracting HIV (Bloom and Glied 1992; Philipson and Posner 1993). For example, a recent medium-scenario projection for Thailand of 1.4 million cumulative HIV cases by the year 2000 (Brown and others 1994) is considerably smaller than the 2 to 4 million cumulative cases that had been projected in 1992 (Viravaidya, Obremsky, and Myers 1993). Similarly, Bloom and Glied demonstrate that AIDS case projections constructed for the United States by various researchers in the 1980s overpredicted by 15 to 93 per cent the number of new AIDS cases in 1991 (Bloom and Glied 1992:344). They also show that the divergence of actual and projected AIDS cases is substantially attributable to reduced levels of high-risk behaviour. The same conclusion presumbly applies to the case of Thailand, as condom utilization among commercial sex workers increased from under 50 per cent in 1989 to 94 per cent in 1993, and the reported nation-wide incidence of sexually transmitted diseases (STDs) dropped precipitously from 6.5 to 1.6 per 1,000 population over the same period (Rojanapithayakorn 1994).

This study contributes to the existing literature on the impact of the AIDS epidemic on economic growth by estimating that impact directly from cross-country data on AIDS and economic growth, avoiding the pitfalls of simulation models and their reliance on assumptions that are often difficult to justify. As the AIDS epidemic is now in its second decade, and researchers have carried out comparable scientifically designed surveys on HIV prevalence in a number of countries, such an approach is feasible. To this end, we have assembled national-level data on HIV and AIDS and built a new data set that allows us to link them to economic data for fifty-one industrial and developing countries. Our analysis uses well-established empirical growth models to measure the nature and strength of statistical associations between the prevalence of AIDS and the rate of growth of GDP per capita, controlling for other factors possibly correlated with AIDS prevalence that might also influence growth. We examine the sensitivity of the results to alternative time-frames and indicators of the size of the AIDS epidemic. We also account for the possibility of simultaneity bias caused by the effect of economic growth on HIV transmission, as well as for possible nonlinearities in the relationship between HIV prevalence and economic growth.

Our main finding is that the AIDS epidemic has had a statistically insignificant effect on the growth rate of per capita income, controlling for other factors that influence economic growth. We also find evidence that this effect on income is qualitatively similar to that of the Black Death in England and France during the Middle Ages and of influenza in India during 1918–19.

Methodology

Data

Although many countries have reporting systems for HIV and AIDS, the figures obtained from them are more an indication of the amount of HIV testing that has been done, the capacity of different medical systems to detect HIV infection or AIDS, and the efficiency of disease reporting systems (for example, length of reporting lags and degree of under-reporting) than of the true extent of the epidemics (Bloom and Glied 1992; Chin 1995; Peterson and Sarda 1995; WHO 1994a). Indeed, the true number of HIV and AIDS cases is often estimated to be thirty to a hundred times the number of reported cases (Bloom and Mahal 1995; Peterson and Sarda 1995; WHO 1994b).

To monitor the extent and spread of HIV infection, many countries have established special HIV surveillance systems (Bloom and others 1995; Viravaidya, Obremsky, and Myers 1993; WHO 1994a, b). A number of these systems, especially those in developing countries, benefit from financial and technical assistance provided by WHO (Snell, Supran, and Tamashiro 1992). Under these sentinel surveillance systems, blood tests for HIV are performed for representative samples of groups that are thought to be at risk for HIV infection, for example, blood donors, injecting drug users, pregnant women, and commercial sex workers. Coupled with estimates of the size of these groups, the resulting data can be used to construct national estimates of HIV prevalence among adults (that is, the proportion of the adult population that is HIV-positive).

The HIV and AIDS data we analyse were assembled from several sources. We obtained national HIV estimates for adult HIV cases in African countries mainly from a report published by the United States Bureau of the Census' Center for International Research (U.S. Bureau of the Census 1994), and supplemented by other sources (Barnett and Blaikie 1992; WorldAIDS 1993; U.S. Bureau of the Census 1993). Estimates of the numbers of adult HIV cases in Asian countries are based on data provided either individually by national AIDS committees or by WHO regional offices. Adult HIV prevalence rates for countries in Europe and North America are drawn from Mann, Tarantola, and Netter

(1992) and WorldAIDS (1993). HIV estimates for the two Latin American countries in the sample are from WorldAIDS (1993). In all we have identified fifty-one countries for which reliable adult HIV prevalence estimates are available for the early 1990s (see Table 1 for the list of countries). As there are no more than a handful of countries for which HIV prevalence estimates are available for multiple years going back to the mid-1980s, a panel data analysis is effectively ruled out.

Direct measures of the number of AIDS cases are not available for any country in our sample, with the exception of the United States. However, using standard epidemiological models, one can estimate the numbers of AIDS cases from national estimates of HIV cases at a point in time, available information on the distribution of the lag between HIV infection and the onset of AIDS, and information on the time path of new infections in the country.

We used EPIMODEL, a standard package developed by James Chin (former chief epidemiologist of WHO's Global Programme on AIDS) and S.K. Lwanga, to estimate cumulative AIDS cases from HIV cases. Epimodel requires data on the year in which the HIV epidemic began (or, more precisely, when the number of HIV cases first exceeded 1 per cent in some sub-population), the number of HIV cases at some later point in time, and the year in which new cases of HIV infection are expected to reach their peak. (EPIMODEL assumes that the time series of new HIV infections follows a gamma function

$$\frac{t^{(\alpha-1)} e^{-}}{(\alpha-1)!}$$ (where t refers to time).

Depending upon the value of α, its single parameter, this function can take on a wide range of shapes, with higher integer values of α corresponding to more rapid increases in HIV incidence in the epidemic's early stages.[4] Using data on the progression from HIV infection to AIDS among members of the San Francisco cohort study, EPIMODEL forward calculates AIDS cases from the time

---

4. Chin and Lwanga (1991) report that $\alpha = 5$ provides a good fit to time series data on AIDS cases in countries with reasonably accurate reporting systems.

Table 1: Descriptive Statistics on Selected Variables

Variable	Fifty-one country sample[a]		Comparison sample of 128 countries	
	Average	Standard deviation	Average	Standard deviation
GDP Per capita, 1991 ($US)[b] (population weighted)	5,406	6,708	5,501	6,450
Average annual rate of growth of per capita GDP, 1980–92 (population weighted)	3.86	2.95	3.15	3.11
HIV prevalence per 1,000 adults, 1992				
Weighted[c]	6.00	23.28	n.a.	n.a.
Unweighted	29.74	51.49	n.a.	n.a.
Cumulative AIDS cases per 1,000 adults, 1980–92				
Weighted[c]	1.08	4.35	n.a.	n.a.
Unweighted	4.90	9.06	n.a.	n.a.
Cumulative AIDS cases per 1,000 adults, 1987–92				
Weighted[c]	0.92	3.66	n.a.	n.a.
Unweighted	4.24	7.72	n.a.	n.a.

a. Our sample includes fifty-one countries—in Africa: Burkina Faso, Burundi, Central African Republic, Congo, Cote d'Ivoire, Gabon, Gambia, Ghana, Kenya, Malawi, Mali, Nigeria, Tanzania, Uganda, Zaire, Zambia, Zimbabwe; in Asia: Bangladesh, China, Hong Kong, India, Indonesia, Republic of Korea, Myanmar, Nepal, Philippines, Singapore, Sri Lanka, Thailand; in Latin America: Brazil, Honduras; in Europe: Austria, Belgium, Denmark, Finland, France, Germany, Greece, Ireland, Israel, Italy, Netherlands, Norway, Spain, Portugal, Sweden, Switzerland, United Kingdom; in North America: United States, Canada; in Oceania; Australia.

b. These are PPP-adusted estimates of GDP per capita as reported in *Human Developement Report 1994 (*UNDP 1994).

c. Adult population sizes are used in constructing the weighted estimates.

series it generates on new HIV infections (Chin and Lwanga 1991).[5]

To estimate the year the epidemic began, we use WHO estimates of the year in which HIV established itself in each region, adjusted for cross-country differences within the region in either the year in which the first AIDS case was reported (Mann, Tarantola, and Netter 1992; U.S. Bureau of the Census 1993) or the first year in which more than 1 per cent of a sample of individuals in the country tested positive for HIV, depending upon the data available. EPIMODEL estimates of cumulative AIDS cases for 1992 are divided by each country's population to yield an estimate of national AIDS prevalence (see Chin 1994 and Chin and Lwanga 1991 for further details about EPIMODEL).

The data on HIV and cumulative AIDS prevalence are matched to economic and other social and demographic data for corresponding countries reported in Baron (1989); the 1989 PCGlobe database (see Kraas-Schneider 1989); the Heston-Summers data set (Version 5.5, Summers and Heston 1991); *Human Development Report* (UNDP 1994); *World Population Prospects* (United Nations 1993); *Social Indicators of Development Database* (World Bank 1993b); *World Tables 1993* (World Bank 1994); and *World Development Report* (World Bank, various issues).

We include data on rates of growth of per capita GDP and its determinants, such as indices of human capital (for example, average years of schooling and literacy rates), public-sector investment in defence and education, degree of openness (ratio of imports plus exports to GDP), and levels of per capita income. We also include data on tourist flows, indicators of health status, level and growth of urbanization, religious affiliation of the population in each country (the percentage Christian or Muslim), rates of growth of population and birth and death rates.

Empirical Model

The main goal of our analysis is to obtain a consistent estimate of β_1 in the context of the following model:

---

5. Gail and Brookmeyer (1988) show that this pattern of progression is well approximated by a Weibull distribution.

$$GDP_i = \beta_0 + \beta_1 AIDS_i + X_i\pi + \varepsilon_i \qquad (1)$$

$$AIDS_i = E\,(\alpha_k,\ HIV_i,\ FHIV_i,\ PHIV_i) \qquad (2)$$

$$HIV_i = \delta_0 + \delta_1\,GDP_i + Z_i\,(GDP_i)\,\delta_2 + R_i\,\delta_3 + \mu_i \qquad (3)$$

where   *GDP* is the rate of growth of real per capita gross domestic product;

AIDS is the annual average increase in the cumulative prevalence of AIDS;

X is a vector of variables that influence economic growth;

Z and *R* are vectors of variables that may influence HIV transmission patterns, some of which may depend upon the rate of growth of per capita GDP;

FHIV measures the number of years between when HIV first established itself in the country and when HIV prevalence is measured;

PHIV measures the number of years between when HIV first established itself in the country and when the peak number of new HIV cases is projected to occur;

E is the EPIMODEL map from HIV and FHIV to AIDS;

ε_i and μ_i are iid errors, each with zero mean;

β_0, β_1, π, and α_k (the gamma function parameter in EPIMODEL, which we allow to vary among country groups) are parameters (or vectors of parameters) to be estimated;

The subscript *i* refers to countries $(i = 1, \dots T)$;

The subscript *k* refers to country groups, which we define as the industrial countries of Europe, North America, and Oceania $(k = 1)$ and the developing countries of Asia, Africa, and Latin America $(k = 2)$.

Equation (1) introduces the average annual increase in the cumulative prevalence of AIDS into a standard reduced form specification that relates the growth rate of real per capita GDP to a number of variables whose relationship to this growth rate is well established in the empirical literature on growth (Barro 1991; Bloom and Freeman 1986, 1988; Levine and Renelt 1992; Mankiw, Romer, and Weil 1992). The AIDS variable is expected to capture the effect on growth of a smaller, and possibly less productive, work-force and of the diversion of social resources to caring for people with AIDS and the prevention of HIV transmission. The vector of control variables includes the initial level of per capita GDP; the lagged growth rate of real per capita GDP; and measures of the degree of openness of the economy, the stock of human capital, and the share of GDP devoted to public investment. In one specification, we include the rate of population growth, adjusted so that it does not reflect AIDS mortality. In another specification, we replace this variable with the average crude birth rate and the average crude death rate (also adjusted for AIDS mortality), whose influences on economic growth one would expect to be different (see Bloom and Freeman 1988; Coale 1986). The AIDS mortality adjustments are made so that the population variables do not capture any effects of AIDS on economic growth that might be operating through those variables.

Equation (3) allows for the possibility that the growth rate of GDP per capita influences the transmission of HIV. This mechanism could operate if commercially obtained sex were a normal economic good, positively associated with income and (in the long run) with income growth (see Over 1992). In addition, to the extent that income growth stimulates urbanization and the movement of people and goods, either domestic or international, it may promote HIV transmission via the influence of increased anonymity on the numbers of sexual partners and the demand for commercial sex. Income growth could also depress HIV transmission by leading to increased longevity and improved health, especially a lower rate of untreated STDs, which are a powerful determinant of the probability of HIV infection (Over and Piot 1993). Higher levels of educational attainment, another positive correlate of income growth, may also reduce the risk of HIV transmission through increased access to information.

We begin by calculating nonlinear least squares (NLS) estimates of the parameters of equation (1) and α. NLS estimates are necessary because of the nonlinear relationship between GDP and HIV, which can be seen by substituting equation (2) into equation (1):

$$GDP_i = \beta_0 + \beta_1 E(\alpha_k, FHIV_i, PHIV_i) + X_i \pi + \varepsilon_i \qquad (4)$$

We then account for possible simultaneity, using a nonlinear two stage least squares (NTSLS) procedure to estimate the parameters of equation (1) (see Amemiya 1985). Both the NLS and NTSLS estimates we compute, allow α to vary in integer steps from 3 to 11 and to assume different values for developing and industrial countries. We do this by conducting grid searches over the eighty-one possible combinations of α and selecting the estimates that maximize the values of R^2 for each model and estimator. Amemiya (1985) proves the consistency of this estimator.[6] We also test for simultaneity by comparing the NLS estimates of the parameters of equation (1) with the NTSLS estimates.

Results

Table 1 reports selected descriptive statistics for key variables used in our analysis. The statistics are reported for both the fifty-one countries in our sample and for a broader sample of a hundred and twenty-eight countries whose population and income data were reported in either the *Human Development Report 1994* or the *World Development Report 1994*. For the sample of fifty-one countries, the average cumulative AIDS prevalence from 1980 to 1992 is 4.9 per 1,000 adults (1.1 per 1,000 if weighted by adult population size in 1992) ranging from essentially zero in China to 39.6 in Zambia. HIV prevalence in 1992 averages 29.7 per 1,000 adults (6.0 per 1,000 if weighted by adult population size in 1992), ranging from a low of 0.01 in China to highs of 211.0 in Zambia and 191.0 in Uganda.

The fifty-one countries in our sample include countries from all major regions and represent 69 per cent of the total world population in 1992. The population-weighted average per capita income of these countries was $US 5,406 in 1991 (after adjusting for purchasing power parity [PPP]), slightly less than the average for the broader comparison set. Income growth for the fifty-one countries averaged 3.86 per cent from 1980 to 1992 (not using PPP-adjusted data), somewhat higher than the rate of 3.15 per cent

6.   Although the model technically treats the AIDS data as nonstochastic, the two stage least squares estimation procedure will also correct for classical error in the measurement of AIDS.

for the comparison set (both figures weighted by the size of the total population in 1992).

Table 2 reports NLS and NTSLS estimates of the parameters of equation (1). We computed the estimates in Table 2 allowing α to vary and to assume different integer values for developing and industrial countries.[7]

We first assess the impact of AIDS on income growth between 1980 and 1992. The year 1980 is roughly the point in time at which sizeable numbers of AIDS cases began to appear in a number of countries in the world. It is also a convenient starting-point given the availability of data on key economic variables. Although narrowing the range of years diminishes the information content of the data with respect to long-term trends in economic growth and magnifies the relative importance of business cycle fluctuations and random shocks, we also focus on income growth between 1987 and 1992 because AIDS became widespread throughout the world during these years.

The first column of estimates in Table 2 shows that income growth was lower in countries with larger increases in the cumulative prevalence of AIDS. The AIDS coefficient estimate is significant and sizeable, with each additional AIDS case per 1,000 persons per year being associated with a 0.86 percentage point reduction in the average annual rate of growth. The 1987–92 analysis exhibits a similar association. These results mainly reflect the fact that most of the seventeen African countries in our sample have both low growth rates and high AIDS prevalence relative to other countries in our data set.

The second and third columns in Table 2 examine the association between AIDS prevalence and income growth controlling for various possible influences on income growth. Following the literature on empirical growth models, we include as controls in the initial level of per capita income, a measure of 'openness' (that is, the ratio of exports plus imports to GDP), the ratio of public sector defence and education expenditures to GDP, the

---

7.   We also estimated the parameters of equation (1) with AIDS data constructed using Chin and Lwanga's preferred value of $\alpha = 5$ for all countries. As the estimates were qualitatively the same in all cases, they are not separately reported.

Table 2: The Impact of AIDS on the Growth Rate of Real GDP per Capita, 1980–92 and 1987–92

	1980–92					1987–92				
	NLS (1)	NLS (2)	NLS (3)	NTSLS (4)	NTSLS (5)	NLS (1)	NLS (2)	NLS (3)	NTSLS (4)	NTSLS (5)
Constant	1.96 (0.36)	3.13 (1.19)	6.89 (1.93)	3.41 (1.23)	7.22 (2.25)	2.18 (0.39)	5.08 (1.10)	7.44 (2.50)	4.67 (1.18)	7.61 (2.52)
Average annual change in cumulative AIDS cases per 1000 adults	−0.86 (0.19)	−0.02 (0.22)	0.19 (0.28)	−0.04 (0.36)	0.15 (0.40)	−0.48 (0.13)	−0.19 (0.17)	0.04 (0.22)	−0.07 (0.21)	0.18 (0.25)
GDP per capita (in $US '000s)		−0.21 (0.13)	−0.30 (0.15)	−0.21 (0.13)	−0.37 (0.19)		−0.29 (0.12)	−0.36 (0.14)	−0.29 (0.13)	−0.43 (0.18)
Rate of growth of real GDP per capita (lagged)		0.29 (0.15)	0.22 (0.16)	0.28 (0.16)	0.20 (0.19)		0.07 (0.16)	0.18 (0.15)	0.13 (0.20)	0.23 (0.18)
Govt. expenditures on education and defence as a proportion of GDP		0.34 (0.10)	0.27 (0.10)	0.34 (0.10)	0.29 (0.10)		0.22 (0.10)	0.13 (0.11)	0.18 (0.10)	0.12 (0.11)
Average schooling in 1980		0.05 (0.18)	−0.003 (0.193)	0.03 (0.18)	−0.01 (0.22)		0.002 (0.164)	−0.02 (0.21)	0.04 (0.18)	0.03 (0.24)
Ratio of imports plus exports to GDP		0.88 (0.37)	0.30 (0.33)	0.91 (0.36)	0.29 (0.10)		1.74 (0.52)	0.99 (0.57)	1.69 (0.56)	1.05 (0.65)

	(1)	(2)	(3)	(4)	(5)	(6)	(7)	(8)
Av. annual rate of pop. growth (AIDS-adjusted) per 1000 pop.	-0.19 (0.04)		-0.20 (0.04)		-0.20 (0.04)		-0.19 (0.06)	
Av. birth rate per 1000 pop.		-0.26 (0.06)		-0.30 (0.09)		-0.26 (0.07)		-0.30 (0.08)
Av. death rate (AIDS-adjusted) per 1000 pop.		0.06 (0.07)		0.16 (0.14)		0.13 (0.10)		0.20 (0.17)
α (industrial contries)	3	9	9	9	9	9	9	9
α (developing countries)	3	3	3	3	3	3	3	3
R^2	0.17	0.55	0.60	0.55	0.18	0.52	0.51	0.45
R^2 (first stage regression)		0.73	0.73				0.64	0.64

Notes

1. Heteroskedasticity-consistent standard errors are reported in parentheses below the coefficient estimates.

2. For the 1980–92 analyses with controls, we ran two sets of regressions, the first with the annual average increase in the cumulative number of AIDS cases (per 1,000 adults) over the period 1980 to 1992, the level of per capita GDP in 1980, the ratio of imports plus exports to GDP in 1980, the rate of growth of per capita GDP during 1970–80, and the rate of growth of population from 1980 to 1992 (after excluding mortality due to AIDS in that period). In the second, we replaced the rate of population growth variable by birth rates and death rates (per 1,000 population) during 1980–92 (death rates were adjusted to exclude mortality due to AIDS). For the 1987–92 analyses, we used the annual average increase in the cumulative number of AIDS cases (per 1,000 adults) over the period 1987–92, the level of per capita GDP in 1985, the ratio of exports plus imports to GDP in 1985, the rate of growth of per capita GDP during 1975–85, and adjusted rates of population growth, birth rates and adjusted death rates just as for the 1980–92 analysis.

3. For the two-stage least squares regressions reported here, the following variables served as instruments:

Notes to Table 2. Contd.

(i) For the regression of per capita GDP 1980–92:

Percentage of population Christain, percentage Muslim, life expectancy at birth (1980), number of doctors per 1,000 population (1980), number of tourists per 1,000 population (1980), growth rate of urban population from 1970 to 1980, percentage of population urban (1980), per capita income (1980), rate of growth of per capita income 1970–80, FHIV, government spending on education/defence as percentage of GDP (average for the years 1980–90), mean schooling 1980, rate of growth of population from 1970 to 1980, imports plus exports/GDP in 1980, and the adult literacy rate for 1980.

(ii) For the regression of per capita GDP 1987–92:

Percentage of population Christian, percentage Muslim, life expectancy at birth (1980), number of doctors per 1,000 population (1980), number of tourists per 1,000 population (1980), growth rate of urban population from 1970 to 1980, percentage of population urban (1980), per capita income (1985), rate of per capita GDP (1975–85), FHIV, government spending on education/defence as percentage of GDP (average for the years 1980–90), mean schooling 1980, rate of growth of population from 1970 to 1980, imports plus exports/GDP in 1985, and the adult literacy rate for 1980.

4. We compared specifications (2) and (4) and (3) and (5) in both panels. Under the null hypothesis, the test statistic is asymptotically distributed as chi-square with 3 degrees of freedom in the comparison of specifications (2) and (4), and chi-square with 2 degrees of freedom in the comparison of specifications (3) and (5).

1970–80 annual growth rate of per capita income, average years of schooling in 1980, and either the rate of population growth during 1980–92 or the average of the birth and death rates in 1980 and 1992 (see Barro 1991; Bloom and Freeman 1986, 1988; Levine and Renelt 1992; Mankiw, Romer, and Weil 1992). Both the population growth variable and the death rate variable are adjusted to remove the effects of AIDS mortality. This adjustment, which was derived using EPIMODEL with the final estimates of α, increased the average rate of population growth from 1.82 to 1.85 per cent per year and decreased the death rate from 10.47 to 10.17 per 1,000 population (based on the unweighted fifty-one country sample).

The most striking result in the second and third columns of estimates is that the introduction of controls drives the AIDS coefficient down substantially in (absolute) value and renders it insignificantly different from zero in both specifications. In other words, the raw negative association between economic growth and the change in AIDS prevalence is due to the fact that AIDS prevalence increased more in those countries with characteristics that are associated with slower growth, and not apparently to AIDS itself having an independent negative influence on economic growth. The results for the period 1987–92, reported in the second panel of Table 2, provide further confirmation of this basic result.

In analyses not reported in the tables, we also experimented with using HIV instead of AIDS prevalence, including cumulative AIDS prevalence as of 1980 or 1987 (depending on whether the dependent variable measures growth from 1980 or 1987), introducing controls for region, using population growth from 1970–80 instead of 1980–92, separating government expenditures on education and defence, and setting α equal to Chin and Lwanga's preferred value of 5 for all countries. Our central finding about the epidemic's insignificant effect on income growth was not altered in any of these analyses. We also estimated a specification that is quadratic in the change in cumulative AIDS prevalence, but found no evidence of a statistically significant departure from linearity.

Note also that the estimates of the coefficients of the control variables in specification (2) are generally consistent with estimates reported elsewhere in the empirical growth literature. For example, because the rate of growth of per capita income is negatively related to the past level of per capita income, the estimates suggest convergence in levels of income per capita. The estimates also suggest that both openness and government investment promote economic growth and that rapid population growth or a high birth rate depress economic growth. However, as estimates of the schooling coefficient are consistently small and insignificantly different from zero, the estimates do not support the hypothesis that growth is promoted by having a higher initial stock of human capital. In keeping with the findings of Bloom and Freeman (1988) and Coale (1986), the estimates reveal a positive but statistically insignificant association between the adjusted death rate and growth.

The fourth and fifth specifications in Table 2 reports NTSLS estimates of the effect of AIDS prevalence on average income growth. We instrument both the annual average increase in cumulative AIDS prevalence and the adjusted rate of population growth (or the birth and adjusted death rates) with the following variables in both the 1980–92 and 1987–92 analyses: 1989 percentages of the population that are Christian and Muslim, life expectancy in 1980, urbanization in 1980, the growth rate of the urban population from 1970 to 1980, the physician-to-population ratio in 1980, the ratio of international tourists to population in 1980, the adult literacy rate in 1980, and FHIV.[8]

In principle, the NTSLS estimates account for the possible reciprocal influence of income growth on HIV transmission and AIDS. However, accounting for possible simultaneity has remarkably little effect on the coefficient estimates, with the NTSLS estimate of the AIDS coefficient remaining statistically insignificant in all analyses. Indeed, specification tests are unable

8.   The results were not substantially different when FHIV was excluded from the list of instruments. See Bloom and Mahal 1996 for the results of further analyses conducted using different specifications and slight variations in the methods used to construct the population data, and for some additional test results.

to reject the null hypothesis of no simultaneity for any of the comparable specifications in Table 2.[9]

Although none of the estimated coefficients of the change in cumulative AIDS prevalence variables reported in specifications (2) through (5) in Table 2 are significantly different from zero, it is instructive to assess their magnitude, especially in relation to the effects estimated in previous literature (for which there are no standard errors). For example, projections constructed using EPIMODEL indicate that cumulative AIDS prevalence in Tanzania will increase by 5.29 per 1,000 adults per year between 1991 and 2010. Using this figure, the 1980–92 NTSLS specification in Table 2 suggests that projected changes in cumulative AIDS prevalence in Tanzania will depress its annual growth rate of income per capita by 0.21 percentage points ($= 5.29 \times - 0.04$). Note, however, the considerable variability, from $- 0.21$ to $+ 1.01$, in the growth effect of AIDS across the 1980–92 specifications in Table 2. Although the 'best estimates' of the effect of AIDS on growth rates of income per capita reported in Cuddington (1992, 1993) and Over (1992) tend to fall below this range, their results rest upon the relatively high AIDS projections made by the World Bank in the late 1980s (see Bulatao 1990; Over 1992).[10]

Comparing AIDS with Other Epidemics

Additional perspective on the foregoing results may be gained by comparing them with the economic impacts of other epidemics that claimed many lives. In this connection, the AIDS epidemic, which has no effect on non-labour factors of production and no debilitating effect on the productivity of uninfected people, is most

9. The test statistics for a comparison of specifications (2) and (4) and (3) and (5) in panel 1 are 1.22 and 0.49, respectively. For panel 2 the corresponding test statistics are 7.10 and 0.46. Under the null hypothesis of no simultaneity, these statistics have chi-square distributions with 8 and 9 degrees of freedom, respectively. The critical values for these statistics at the 5 per cent level of significance are 15.5 and 16.9 respectively.

10. For example, Bulatao's projections of cumulative AIDS prevalence for Tanzania increase at an annual rate of 10 per 1,000 adults from 1991 to 2010. This figure is nearly double the corresponding rate of increase we project using EPIMODEL with more recent data on HIV prevalence.

naturally compared with the Black Death that swept Europe during the Middle Ages, and with the 1918–19 influenza epidemic in India.

The Black Death was a combined epidemic of the bubonic and pneumonic plagues that spread throughout western Europe during 1348–50 (although we include later plague epidemics in our analysis as well). During that period, an estimated 24 per cent of western Europe's population died, more than two-thirds of which represented excess mortality (Russell 1948). The two types of plague, which are different forms of the same bacterial infection, were transmitted from rodent to human populations by fleas. The bubonic plague is not infectious among humans, although it can lead to the pneumonic plague as a complication. The latter is infectious among humans and was nearly always fatal before antibiotics. Overall, the fatality rate for both types of plague cases during the Black Death is believed to have reached 90 per cent (Bres 1986). Some evidence indicates that older individuals were disproportionately highly susceptible to the plague, and that the poor were more exposed to infection because of unfavourable sanitary conditions. Nonetheless, there is little reason to believe that either the age or income differentials were large (Hirshleifer 1987; Russell 1948).

Although data on per capita income or output are not available, medieval historians report a rapid rise in various wage indicators in both England and France during the course of, and immediately following, the Black Death (see Hirshleifer 1987; Robbins 1928; Russell 1948; Slicher van Bath 1963). Whether these increases reflect mainly a shrinking supply of labour (see Hirshleifer 1987), an upward long-run trend in real wages, or a highly inelastic demand for labour in the very short run is, however, unclear.[11]

To help interpret the reported wage increases, we examine average annual percentage changes in real wages for unskilled British agricultural labourers working on the estates of the bishops of Winchester during six sub-periods between 1310 and 1449, that is, 1310–29, 1330–69, 1370–89, 1390–1409, 1410–29, and 1430–

---

11. Indeed, one account of the sharply higher wages describes them as 'panic or compulsion' rates of pay (Robbins 1928:463).

Table 3: Economic Impacts of Other Epidemics

Dependent variables	Regressors			Number of observations:
	Constant	Rate of growth of population	Indicator variable for plague periods	
Black Death				
Average annual rate of real wage growth, England, 1310–1449, for twenty year periods[a]	0.70 (0.43)	0.12 (0.65)	—	6
Twenty-five year rates of real wage growth, France, 1313–1488[b]				
Workers *nourri*	0.12 (0.17)	—	0.10 (0.32)	7
Workers *non-nourri*	0.09 (0.14)	—	0.09 (0.25)	7
Influenza				
Percentage changes in acreage sown per capita, for provinces in India, 1916–17 to 1919–20[c]	−3.00 (1.33)	−0.25 (0.28)	—	13

Note:
Heteroskedasticity-consistent standard errors are reported in parentheses below the coefficient estimates.

a. Averge annual rates of growth of real wages in England were calculated from data reported in Hirshleifer (1987) on the average wages of unskilled agricultural workers employed on the estates of the bishops of Winchester for twenty-year periods from 1300 to 1459. In calculating a wage growth series, we assigned the average wage for the period to the mid-point of the interval. The wages were deflated using the price of wheat. Population growth was derived from data reported in Russell (1948) and and Hirshleifer (1987). Because the Black Death occurred so close to the endpoint of one of the twenty-year intervals under consideration, we grouped the periods 1330–49 and 1350–69 into one.

49. The wage data are deflated by the price of wheat. We measure the association between the real wage changes and changes in the population of England during the corresponding sub-periods. The population changes reflect the effects of the major plagues that occurred in 1348–50, 1360–1, 1369, and 1374, which resulted in an estimated excess mortality of 16.6 per cent, 12.7 per cent, 10.0 per cent and 8.6 per cent respectively (see Hirshleifer 1987: 100, Table 2.2 drawn from Russell 1948: 263).

The first row of figures in Table 3 reports estimates of a simple regression of the growth rate of (wheat-price deflated) wages on population growth. Although the positive intercept indicates long-term real wage growth, the coefficient of the population growth variable is small and insignificantly different from zero. Thus, one cannot reject the null hypothesis that real wages did not exhibit a differential rate of growth during the periods of the major medieval plagues in England.

Data reported in Robbins (1928) permit some analysis of the effect of the plague on wages in France. Two series of nominal daily wages are available, for workers *nourri* (fed) and workers *non-nourri* (not fed), for quarter-century periods from 1301 to 1500. Deflating these series by the price of poultry converts them to real wage series. Regressing the quarter-century changes in each deflated series on a constant and a dummy variable taking the value one during 1338–62 and 1363–87—major plague periods in France—provides evidence on an insignificant positive trend in both wage series, with a small and statistically insignificant increase during the major plague periods.

---

b. Wage growth in France was calculated from data reported in Robins (1928) on the average nominal wages of workers *nourri* and of workers *non-nourri,* for twenty-five-year periods from 1301 to 1500. To calculate the series on wage growth rates, the average wage was assigned to the mid-point of the intervals. The wages were deflated using data on the price of poultry, also reported in Robbins (1928). Plague epidemics occurred in France during 1348–51, 1361, 1363, 1369, and 1371 (Robbins 1928: 454).

c. Changes in acreage per capita in thirteen Indian provinces were calculated from data on changes in acreage sown (Schultz 1983; Sen 1967) and changes in agricultural population during the period 1916–17 to 1919–20 from data reported in Sen (1967).

Although these wage change analyses are admittedly crude because of severe data limitations, they nonetheless provide no evidence that real wages departed significantly from their long-term trend during periods of great plague mortality in England and France.

The influenza epidemic of 1918–19 provides another opportunity to examine the effect on income of a sharp increase in mortality. In India, where the world-wide epidemic was most severe, influenza claimed an estimated 20 million lives, or 6.2 per cent of India's total population and 8.3 per cent of the working-age population in agriculture (Schultz 1983). Mortality rates among the working-age population in agriculture varied between 2 and 15 per cent across provinces. Data on death rates in the 1918–19 cropping season and on changes in acreage sown and the size of the agricultural population from the 1916–17 season to the 1919–20 season—which were comparable in terms of climatic conditions—are reported in Schultz (1983) and Sen (1967), who debated their use in testing the surplus labour hypothesis.

The Indian data permit us to examine the effect of a sharp and unanticipated decline in population on output per capita. The data reveal declines in acreage sown per capita in seven out of thirteen provinces between 1916–17 and 1919–20. However, the regression of acreage sown per capita on the estimated change in the agricultural population provides no evidence that the decline in acreage sown was significantly greater in provinces that experienced sharper population declines. These cross-provincial results are thus qualitatively similar to those on the wage effects of the Black Death in Europe.

Summary and Conclusion

The results of our cross-country analysis provide little support for the widespread claim that the AIDS epidemic will slow the growth rate of income per capita. Although the epidemic is already quite advanced in a number of countries, after controlling for standard influences on growth (and possible simultaneity), we find no evidence that the economies of these countries grew at a significantly slower pace between 1980 (1987) and the early 1990s than those of other countries in which changes in the cumulative prevalence of AIDS was lower. Although our point estimates vary quite widely, from negative to positive, across specifications, nearly all of the estimates fall well below their estimated standard errors. This finding is consistent with several crude analyses we performed of the impact on the growth rates of either real wages or output per capita of two other major epidemics: the Black Death during the Middle Ages and the influenza epidemic of 1918–19. Indeed, taken as a whole, the results of this paper suggest that the average standard of living is remarkably robust with respect to major epidemics, with income per capita following the dashed line in Figure 1 more closely than the solid line.

Our findings suggest that there is more flash than substance to the claim that AIDS impedes national economic growth. Further research aimed at explaining this finding in terms of labour supply and demand elasticities, relative shifts in labour supply and demand caused by AIDS morbidity and mortality, the emerging link between AIDS and poverty, and economic and institutional adjustment that dampen the adverse economic impacts of the epidemic would be extremely useful. Further work is also needed to assess whether our main conclusion applies to the impact of AIDS on the broader concept of economic development. Along these lines, Bloom, and others (1995) suggest that it does not, mainly because AIDS has a large negative impact on life expectancy, a major component of the UNDP's human development index on which their analysis focuses. Thus, the AIDS epidemic may well prove to have significant implications for development, even though its implications for per capita income are not significant.

Although we find little support for the often-made argument that HIV and AIDS prevention and control programs will yield benefits via a higher rate of income growth, our study does not deny the existence of other benefits. Indeed, much ongoing research suggests that the most serious economic consequences of the AIDS epidemic are to be found in particular industrial and occupational sectors, in particular geographic regions, and among particular demographic groups, as has been discussed in the concluding section of the preceding chapter. These topics appear to be the most promising areas for further research, along with

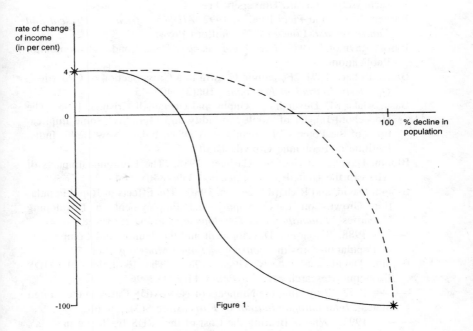

Fig. 1: Hypothetical Relationships Between Population Declines and Income Changes

greater application of cost–benefit and cost–effectiveness analyses to programmes and policies that address the care of persons living with AIDS, and the prevention of further HIV transmission.

References

Ahituv, Avner, V. Joseph Hotz, and Tomas Philipson. 1993. 'Will the AIDS Epidemic be Self-Limiting? Evidence on the Responsiveness of the Demand for Condoms to the Prevalence of AIDS'. Discussion

Paper No. 93–3. Chicago: University of Chicago, Population Research Center.

Amemiya, Takeshi. 1985. *Advanced Econometrics*. Cambridge, Massachussetts: Harvard University Press.

Barnett, Tony, and Piers Blaikie. 1992. *AIDS in Africa: Its Present and Future Impact*. London: The Guilford Press.

Baron, Raymond. 1989. *Travel and Tourism Data*. London: Euromonitor Publications.

Barro, Robert. 1991. 'Economic Growth in a Cross Section of Countries' *Quarterly Journal of Economics* 106(2): 407–45.

Basu, Alaka M., Devendra B. Gupta, and Geetanjali Krishna. 1995. 'The Household Impact of Adult Morbidity and Mortality: Some Implications of the Potential Epidemic of AIDS in India'. New Delhi, India: Institute of Economic Growth. Draft.

Bloom, David, and Geoffrey Carliner. 1988. 'The Economic Impacts of AIDS in the United States'. *Science* 239(4840): 604–10.

Bloom, David, and Richard Freeman. 1986. 'The Effects of Rapid Population Growth on Labor Supply and Employment in Developing Countries'. *Population and Development Review* 12(3): 381–414.

————— 1988. 'Economic Development and the Timing and Components of Population Growth'. *Journal of Policy Modeling* 10(1):57–82.

Bloom, David, and Sherry Glied. 1989. 'The Evolution of AIDS Economic Research'. *Health Policy* 11(2):187–96.

————— 1992. 'Projecting the Numbers of New AIDS Cases in the United States'. *International Journal of Forecasting* 8(3):339–66.

————— 1993. 'Who is Bearing the Cost of the AIDS Epidemic in Asia'. In David Bloom, and Joyce Lyons, eds., *Economic Implications of AIDS in Asia*. New Delhi, India: United Nations Development Programme.

Bloom, David, and Joyce Lyons, eds. 1993. *Economic Implications of AIDS in Asia*. New Delhi, India: United Nations Development Programme.

Bloom, David, and Ajay Mahal. 1995. 'The Economic Implications of AIDS in Asia'. Draft. New York: Columbia University, Department of Economics.

————— 1996. 'Does the AIDS Epidemic Threaten Economic Growth?' *Journal of Econometrics*. Forthcoming.

Bloom, David, Neil Bennett, Ajay Mahal, and Waseem Noor. 1995. 'The Impact of AIDS on Human Development'. Draft. New York: Columbia University, Department of Economics.

Bres, P. 1986. *Public Health Action in Emergencies Caused By Epidemics*. Geneva: World Health Organization.

Brown, Tim, Chirapun Gullaprawit, Werasit Sittitrai, Sombat Thanprasertsuk, and Aphichat Chamratrithirong. 1994. 'Projections for HIV in Thailand 1987–2005: An Application of EPIMODEL'. Draft. Bangkok, Thailand: National Economic and Social Development Board Working Group.

Bulatao, Rodolfo. 1990. 'The Demographic Impact of AIDS in Tanzania'. Washington, D.C.: World Bank. Background paper prepared for the Tanzania AIDS Assessment and Planning Study.

Chin, James. 1990. 'Current and Future Dimensions of the HIV/AIDS Pandemic in Women and Children'. *The Lancet* 336:221–4.

———— 1994. 'A Beginner's Guide for Understanding and Using Epimodel—Version 2'. Berkeley, CA: University of California, School of Public Health.

———— 1995. 'Estimation and Projection of HIV Infections and AIDS Cases'. Berkeley, California: University of California, School of Public Healthy.

Chin, James, and S.K. Lwanga. 1991. 'Estimation and Projection of Adult AIDS Cases: A Simple Epidemiological Model'. *Bulletin of the World Health Organization* 69:399–406.

Coale, Ansley. 1986. 'Population Trends and Economic Development'. In Jane Menken, ed. *World Population and U.S. Policy.* New York: W.W. Norton & Company, Inc.

Cohen, Desmond. 1993. 'The Economic Impact of the HIV Epidemic'. New York: United Nations Development Programme, HIV and Development Programme. Working Paper.

Cuddington, John. 1992. 'The Macroeconomic Impact of AIDS in a Dualistic, Labor-Surplus Economy with an Application to Tanzania'. Washington, D.C.: Georgetown University, Department of Economics. Working Paper No. 92–12.

———— 1993. 'Modeling the Macroeconomic Effects of AIDS, with an Application to Tanzania'. *The World Bank Economic Review* 7(2): 173–89.

Cuddington, John, and John Hancock. 1994. 'Assessing the Impact of AIDS on the Growth Path of the Malawian Economy'. *Journal of Development Economics* 4(3):363–8.

Gail, Mitchell, and Ronald Brookmeyer. 1988. 'Methods for Projecting the Course of the Acquired Immunodeficiency Syndrome Epidemic'. *Journal of the National Cancer Institute* 80(12): 900–12.

Griffin, Charles. 1990. *Health Financing in Asia.* Washington, D.C.: World Bank. Report No. 8553-ASI.

Hellinger, Fred. 1993. 'The Lifetime Cost of Treating a Person with HIV'. *Journal of the American Medical Association* 270(4): 474–8.

Hirshleifer, Jack. 1987. *Economic Behaviour in Adversity.* Chicago: University of Chicago Press.

Kambou, Gerard, Shantayanan Devarajan, and Mead Over. 1992. 'The Economic Impact of AIDS in an African Country: Simulations with a Computable General Equilibrium Model of Cameroon'. *Journal of African Economies* 1(1):109–30.

Kraas-Schneider, Frauke. 1989. *Bevölkerungsgruppen und Minoritäten. Handbuch der ethnischen, sprachlichen und religiosen bevölkerungsgruppen der Welt.* Stuttgart: Franz Steiner Verlag.

Kremer, Michael. 1995. 'Integrating Behavioral Choice into Epidemiological Models of AIDS'. Cambridge, Massachussetts: Massachussetts Institute of Technology, Department of Economics. Draft.

Levine, Ross, and David Renelt. 1992. 'A Sensitivity Analysis of Cross-Country Growth Regressions'. *American Economic Review* 82 (September): 942–63.

Lyons, Joyce. 1993. 'Introduction'. In David Bloom and Joyce Lyons, eds., *Economic Implications of AIDS in Asia.* New Delhi, India: United Nations Development Programme.

Mankiw, Gregory, David Romer, and David Weil. 1992. 'A Contribution to the Empirics of Economic Growth'. *Quarterly Journal of Economics* 107(2):407–37.

Mann, Jonathan, Daniel Tarantola, and Thomas Netter. 1992. *AIDS in the World.* Cambridge, Massachussetts: Harvard University Press.

Merson, Michael. 1992. AIDS in Asia and the Pacific: The Reality, the Opportunity, and the Challenge'. Keynote address at the Second International Congress on AIDS in Asia and the Pacific, New Delhi, India, November.

Over, Mead. 1992. 'The Macroeconomic Impact of AIDS in Sub-Saharan Africa'. Technical Working Paper No. 3. Washington, D.C.: World Bank, Africa Technical Department, Population, Health, and Nutrition Division.

Over, Mead, and Peter Piot. 1993. 'HIV Infection and Sexually Transmitted Diseases'. In Dean Jamison, W. Henry Mosley, Anthony Measham, and Jose Bobadilla, eds., *Disease Control Priorities in Developing Countries.* Washington, D.C.: Oxford University Press.

Panos Institute, The. 1992. *The Hidden Cost of AIDS: The Challenge of HIV to Development.* London: Panos Publications.

PCGlobe, Inc. *The PCGlobe Database,* Tempe, AZ.

Peterson, Georg, and Rabin Sarda. 1995. 'The HIV and AIDS Epidemic in the Western Pacific'. Manila, Philippines: World Health Organization, Regional Office for the Western Pacific. Draft.

Philipson, Tomas, and Richard Posner. 1993. *Private Choices and Public Health: The AIDS Epidemic in an Economic Perspective.* Cambridge, MA: Harvard University Press.

Pitayanon, Sumalee, Sukhontha Kongsin, and Wattana Janjareon. 1994. *Economic Impact of HIV/AIDS Mortality on Households in Thailand.* Research report presented at the Asian Development Bank/United Nations Development Programme Finalization Meeting on Economic Implications of HIV/AIDS, Manila, Philippines, August 2–4.

Robbins, Helen. 1928. 'A Comparison of the Effects of the Black Death on the Economic Organization of France and England'. *Journal of Political Economy* 36 (August): 447–79.

Rojanapithayakorn, W. 1994. 'The One Hundred Percent Condom Programme in Thailand: An Update'. Abstract No. 478C, The Tenth International Conference on AIDS, Yokohama, Japan, August 7–12.

Russell, Josiah. 1948. *British Medieval Population.* Albuquerque, New Mexico: The University of New Mexico Press.

Schultz, Theodore. 1983. *Transforming Traditional Agriculture,* 2nd ed. Chicago: University of Chicago Press.

Sen, Amartya. 1967. 'Surplus Labor in India: A Critique of Schultz's Statistical Test'. *Economic Journal* (March): 154–61.

Sisk, Jane. 1987. 'The costs of AIDS: A Review of the Estimates'. *Health Affairs* 6(2):5–21.

Slicher van Bath, B.H. 1963. *The Agrarian History of Western Europe. A.D. 500–1850.* London: Edward Arnold Publishers.

Snell, J., E. Supran, and H. Tamashiro. 1992. 'WHO International Quality Assessment Scheme for HIV Antibody Testing: Results From the Second Distribution of Sera'. *Bulletin of the World Health Organization* 70(5): 605–13.

Summers, Robert, and Alan Heston. 1991. 'The Penn World Table (Mark 5): An Expanded Set of International Comparisons'. *Quarterly Journal of Economics* (May): 327–68.

UN (United Nations). 1993. *World Population Prospects.* New York: United Nations, Department for Economic and Social Information and Policy Analysis.

UNDP (United Nations Development Programme). 1992. 'The HIV Epidemic as a Development Issue'. New York: United Nations Development Programme. Pamphlet.

———— 1994. *Human Development Report 1994.* New York: Oxford University Press.

U.S. Bureau of the Census. 1993. *HIV/AIDS Surveillance Database.* Washington, D.C.: Center for International Research.

———— 1994. *The Impact of HIV/AIDS on World Population*. Washington, D.C.: Government Printing Office.

Viravaidya, Mechai, Stasia Obremsky, and Charles Myers. 1993. 'The Economic Impact of AIDS in Thailand'. In David Bloom and Joyce Lyons, eds., *Economic Implications of AIDS in Asia*. New Delhi, India: United Nations Development Programme.

World Bank. 1992. *Tanzania: AIDS Assessment and Planning Study*. Washington, D.C.

———— 1993a. *The World Development Report*. Washington, D.C.: Oxford University Press.

———— 1993b. *Social Indicators of Development Database*. Washington, D.C.

———— 1994. *World Tables 1993*. Washington, D.C.: Oxford University Press.

WHO (World Health Organization). 1992. 'AIDS/HIV Infection in Southeast Asia'. New Delhi, India: Regional Office for Southeast Asia.

———— 1994a. *The HIV/AIDS Pandemic: 1994 Overview*. Geneva: WHO, Global Programme on AIDS.

———— 1994b. *The Current Global Situation of the HIV/AIDS Pandemic*. Geneva: WHO, Global Programme on AIDS.

———— 1995. *The Current Global Situation of the HIV/AIDS Epidemic*. Geneva: WHO, Global Programme on AIDS.

WorldAIDS. 1993. *DataFile 1993*. London: Panos Publishers.

3

The Economic Impact of HIV/AIDS Mortality on Households in Thailand

Sumalee Pitayanon, Sukontha Kongsin, and Wattana S. Janjareon

Introduction

The Thai economy experienced impressive growth and underwent a series of structural shifts during the last two decades. Real gross domestic product (GDP) grew by an average rate of 7 to 8 per cent per year, which is high by any standards. The industrial sector expanded rapidly, with the manufacturing sector's share in GDP rising from 14 per cent in 1969 to 28 per cent in 1992, surpassing the share of the agricultural sector, which dropped from 32 to 12 per cent during the same period. Exports also grew substantially, from 15 per cent of GDP in 1970 to 24 per cent in 1980 and 36 per cent in 1992. Per capita income rose from $US 117 per year in 1969 to $US 1,990 per year in 1992, taking Thailand off the list of developing countries and making it one of the 'newly industrializing countries'.

Underlying this impressive growth and structural change is a serious imbalance between the rural and urban sectors. Even though it is declining, rural poverty is still substantial: the latest estimates indicate that in 1988 the incomes of 21 per cent of the rural population were below the poverty line (Krongkaew, Tinakorn, the Suphachalasai 1992). Income inequality has increased, with the income share of the top 20 per cent of the population increasing from 49 per cent in 1975–6 to 55 per cent in 1988–9, and the share of the lowest 20 per cent declining from

6 to 4.5 per cent during the same period. The group with the lowest income is concentrated in rural areas.

Adding to the rural population's economic woes was the arrival of HIV/AIDS in the mid-1980s, and its rapid spread in Thailand's rural areas in recent years. A report by the Ministry of Public Health (MOPH 1995) indicates that more than 60 per cent of AIDS cases are among labourers and agricultural workers, who fall mainly in the low income group. About half of the reported cases are from the northern provinces, mainly the rural areas of Chiangmai, Chiangrai, Lampang, Lamphun, and Payao, with Chiangmai having the largest number of reported cases as of 31 January 1995.

Because HIV/AIDS infects mainly adults during their sexually active years and is inevitably fatal, the socio-economic implications of HIV/AIDS for development are immense. At the family level, the death of an adult during his or her sexually active years means the loss of a family member of prime working age whose foregone income can adversely affect the welfare of surviving family members, especially if the deceased was also the family's main breadwinner. This impact will be even worse if the family is a low-income family, because such families generally possess few resources, and are thus less able to cope with increased medical care costs and other related expenses, in addition to the foregone earnings of the ill family member. Hence, HIV/AIDS not only increases mortality, but also immiserates the poor and widens income inequality between the haves and the have-nots.

The main objective of this study is to measure and analyse the economic impact of an adult HIV/AIDS-related death on a rural Thai household based on a primary data survey of rural households in Chiangmai province in northern Thailand, where the number of reported HIV/AIDS cases is among the highest in Thailand. Specifically, the study measures the size and significance of the economic impact of an adult AIDS-related death on the household after all coping strategies have been employed. In addition, it investigates whether the economic impact of an adult AIDS death is different from the impact of an adult death resulting from another cause. To aid policy makers, the study also examines whether any link exists between adult AIDS mortality and low income and poverty in Thailand's rural areas. Finally, the study analyses the ability of households with different socio-economic characteristics to cope with the adverse economic impact of an adult AIDS death so as to identify those least able to cope and most in need of government assistance. The methodology employed in this study is similar to the World Bank studies in Africa by Ainsworth and Rwegarulira and Ainsworth and Over, which are reviewed and presented in Gertler (1993).

As this is the first study, based on hard evidence of the economic impact of an HIV/AIDS-related death on a family in Thailand, it provides useful information to the government and other agencies on the 'spillover effects' of an HIV infection and its direct threat to households' welfare and survival. The evidence suggests that AIDS interventions can no longer focus primarily on the infected individual and ways of preventing additional infection, but must also address the growing needs of those who are uninfected but affected, that is, the infected person's family and extended family, friends, and the community as a whole, because we now know that the epidemic's toll will be measured not only in terms of lives lost, but also in terms of the progressive circle of reduced functioning rippling through families, communities, and regions. This will be reflected not only in lost economic productivity, but in increasing social burdens, such as caring for children orphaned by the epidemic (John Kreniske n.d.).

The Current HIV/AIDS Situation in Thailand

AIDS was first reported in Thailand in 1984. By 1994 the cumulative number of reported AIDS patients totalled 15,665, of which 7,299, or 47 per cent, were reported in 1994 and January 1995. In addition, 6,691 people were reported as being infected with HIV. As these figures are based on a voluntary reporting system, whereby health institutions and physicians are encouraged to report cases anonymously to the public health authorities, the under-reporting of AIDS cases is a problem in Thailand, as in most countries.

Although the reported number of HIV/AIDS patients in Thailand may not be alarming, this number is expected to rise sharply in the near future. The Ministry of Public Health (MOPH) has estimated that the actual number of cumulative HIV cases at the end of 1993 was between 500,000 and 600,000. By the year 2000, if behavioural patterns do not change, this number will rise to 1.38 million and the cumulative number of people with full-blown AIDS will be around 480,000. The total number of AIDS death until the year 2000 will be 450,000. The number of babies infected with HIV through their mothers is estimated to reach about 63,000 by the year 2000. This number includes approximately 47,500 babies with full-blown AIDS.

The various transmission routes of AIDS in Thailand have varied in importance at different stages of the epidemic. Early cases of reported AIDS were generally confined to homosexual men returning from abroad. This was followed by an explosive spread of HIV infection among injecting drug users in 1987 and 1988. The virus then spread to male and female sex workers and their clients, with the result that heterosexual transmission became increasingly important. By 1991, many provinces had started reporting cases of perinatal transmission. Thailand initiated blood screening in 1985, and since 1989 every unit of donated blood has been screened for HIV. Currently, sexual intercourse accounts for more than 75 per cent of AIDS cases, infection among injecting drug users for 7.3 per cent, and transmission from infected mothers to the babies for 7.1 per cent.

In terms of prevalence rates, the highest rates are among injecting drug users (34.3 per cent), followed by lower-cost prostitutes (27.0 per cent), men with other sexually transmitted diseases (STDs) (8.5 per cent), higher cost prostitutes (7.7 per cent), pregnant women (1.8 per cent), and recipients of donated blood (0.7 per cent). Prevalence rates have increased among all these groups since 1989, especially among prostitutes (male and female), male outpatients with STDs, and more recently, pregnant women. However, HIV infection among intravenous drug users has levelled off since 1989.

More than 80 per cent of HIV patients are aged between fifteen and forty-four. The male to female ratio is about 7.5 to 1. As mentioned earlier, agricultural workers and labourers, especially in the country's five northern provinces, make up the bulk of the cases.

The Survey

Data Collection

The data used in this study were generated from a field-based survey of households with recent experience of an HIV/AIDS-related death in five districts of Chiangmai province in northern Thailand where, as mentioned earlier, the number of HIV/AIDS cases and deaths is among the highest in Thailand. The selection of households was based on hospitals' records of HIV/AIDS-related deaths during 1992 and 1993. In this way we eliminated households where the cause of death was unconfirmed. Because our study focuses on the potential economic impact of HIV/AIDS-related deaths on the family, only households in which the deceased were of working age were included.

From the hospital records we first grouped households by their district of origin. We then chose the five districts with the highest number of reported HIV/AIDS-related deaths, and classified their households by sub-district of origin. We only used sub-districts with at least three HIV/AIDS-related deaths for our study, and based on this criterion, selected twenty-seven sub-districts. Having weighted these sub-districts by their proportion of reported deaths from HIV/AIDS, we randomly selected 100 households for interviews (see Table 1). As we expected that some households might not co-operate and we might not be able to locate others, we prepared a list of substitute households to use in such cases. Because the total number of reported HIV/AIDS deaths in each chosen district was not large, all the cases from the hospital records were included either for interviewing or as substitutes. We interviewed a total of 116 households.

In addition to the households with recent experience of an HIV/AIDS-related death, our survey also included 100 households where a non-HIV/AIDS-related death had occurred, and 108 households where no death had occurred, as a control group. We obtained a list of non-HIV/AIDS deaths during 1992 and 1993 in the same districts and sub-districts as our target group from hospital records. As the reported number was small, we asked our interviewers, who were public health officers in charge of the sub-districts surveyed, to randomly select additional households

Table 1: Households Studied by Location and Type

District	Sub-district	Households with recent HIV/AIDS death				Control Group		
		Total reported by hospitals	Selected sample	Substitutes	Total interviewed	Household with recent non-HIV/AIDS death		Households with no death interviewed
						Reported by hospitals	Interviewed	
1	2	3	4	5	6	7	8	9
Mae Rim	Don Kaew	6	3	3	3	1	3	3
	Salong	5	3	2	3	1	3	3
	Rim Tal	6	3	3	3	2	3	3
	Mae Ram	4	3	1	3	1	3	3
	Kee Lhek	3	3	0	3	2	3	3
	San Pong	5	3	2	3	1	3	3
	Muang Kaew	6	4	2	4	0	3	4
	Rim Nua	7	3	4	4	0	3	3
	Total	72	25	17	26	8	24	25
San Sal	San Na Meng	5	4	1	4	2	3	4
	Mae Fak Mal	10	7	3	7	2	6	7
	Nong Jom	7	4	3	5	1	4	4
	Nong Hann	3	3	0	3	3	3	3
	Mae Fak	5	3	2	4	2	3	3
	Total	30	21	9	23	10	19	21

(Contd)

Table 1 (*Contd*)

1	2	3	4	5	6	7	8	9
San Kampang	San Kampang	10	7	3	7	1	6	7
	Ton Pao	5	4	1	4	0	4	4
	Huay Sal	6	4	2	5	3	4	4
	Total	21	15	6	16	4	14	15
Haang Dong	Nong Ku-wal	4	3	1	3	1	3	3
	Koon Dong	5	3	2	4	0	3	3
	Nam Prae	6	4	2	4	1	3	4
	Haang Doong	6	4	2	5	3	3	4
	Nong Tong	5	5	0	3	2	3	3
	Sob Mae Ka	1	1	0	3	1	3	3
	Total	27	20	7	22	8	18	20
Fa-ang	San Sal	5	4	2	5	0	4	4
	Wieng	19	10	9	10	3	8	10
	Mon pin	10	5	5	6	0	5	5
	Mae Soon	7	4	3	4	0	4	4
	Mae Ngon	5	4	2	4	1	4	4
	Total	48	27	21	29	4	25	27
	Grand Total	168	108	60	110	34	100	108

in their sub-districts where a non-HIV/AIDS-related death had occurred since 1992 (to make up the numbers). The interviewers
also randomly selected 108 households in the same communities
with no deaths during 1992–4.

Our main survey tool was a structured questionnaire. We also
incorporated a few open-ended questions to obtain additional
qualitative information. To validate the information obtained from
the household respondents, we asked community leaders in the
districts and sub-districts covered in the survey a set of open-
ended questions. Finally, to cross-check the information given by
adults, we designed a separate set of questions for children in the
households surveyed.

Household interviews were conducted in March 1994 in co-
operation with local public health workers in the districts and sub-
districts covered by the study. Household respondents were the
heads of households or others who could provide the information.

Because our survey was based on the records of hospitals under
the jurisdiction of the Ministry of Public Health and the interviews
were conducted in districts of the province with the highest
reported number of HIV/AIDS cases, our findings must be interpreted with caution. The exclusion of other hospitals and districts
raises questions about whether our findings are representative of
the rest of the province and of the northern area of Thailand as
a whole. However, a comparison of the characteristics of those
who had died of AIDS in the northern areas of the country with
similar cases in Chiangmai province shows few major differences
(Table 2). The two main differences are in sex and average age
at death. These can be explained by the scope of our study, which
limited the sample to working adults, and thus excluded children
and women who did not work outside the home. As for the cause
of infection, the smaller proportion of deaths related to sexual
intercourse in our study is due to a large number of non-responses
to this question.

Methodology

The measurement of the economic impact of HIV/AIDS mortality
on households in this study was based on three methods of
analysis: the calculation of the direct and indirect costs of death,

Table 2: AIDS and ARC Mortality in Chiangmai Province, and the study

Category	Northern Thailand (Sept 1984–Aug.1993)	Chiangmai Province (Sept. 1984–Aug.1993)	Study (March 1994)
AIDS and ARC Mortality	783 (100%)	238 (100%)	118 (100%)
Sex			
Male	670 (86%)	204 (86%)	113 (96%)
Female	113 (14%)	34 (14%)	5 (4%)
Average age (years)	28	28	30
Marital status			
Single	405 (52%)	133 (56%)	61 (52%)
Married	313 (40%)	70 (29%)	39 (33%)
Other	60 (8%)	30 (13%)	18 (15%)
Area			
Non-municipal	771 (99%)	235 (99%)	118 (100%)
Municipal	11 (1%)	2 (1%)	0
Cause of infection			
Intravenous drug uses	26 (3%)	7 (3%)	3 (3%)
Sexual intercourse (heterosexual)	646 (82%)	166 (70%)	46 (39%)
Perinatal	85 (11%)	44 (18%)	0
No response	31 (4%)	16 (7%)	67 (57%)
Occupation			
Labourers	257 (33%)	95 (40%)	46 (39%)
Agri workers	268 (34%)	40 (17%)	20 (17%)
Sales & service workers	64 (8%)	16 (7%)	15 (13%)
Commercial sex workers	16 (2%)	2 (1%)	2 (2%)
Other	116 (15%)	58 (24%)	20 (17%)
Unknown	66 (7%)	27 (11%)	13 (11%)

Note: Northern Thailand includes Chiangmai, Chiangrai, Lampang, and Payao provinces.
ARC: AIDS-related complex
Source: Ministry of Public Health data and authors' survey.

the investigation of household coping strategies, and the determination of the real economic impact of death from HIV/AIDS.

Direct and Indirect Costs of Death

We calculated the direct and indirect costs of an HIV/AIDS-related death on a household using standard cost–benefit analysis. The direct costs of death included out-of-pocket medical care expenditure, travel expenses relating to medical care, and the costs of funeral rites. The indirect costs of death were calculated from the foregone earnings of the deceased.

To calculate foregone earnings, we started by working out the total number of lost work years by subtracting the age of the deceased from the average age of retirement, which we assumed to be sixty. For annual income foregone for those with a regular income we used a 5 per cent discount rate. We then multiplied the annual foregone earnings by the number of lost work years to obtain total foregone earnings. For those who had also held a supplementary job before their illness and death, we included the supplementary income in the calculations. Finally, in addition to the lost income of the deceased, we calculated the lost earnings of other household members who had to leave work to take care of the sick person, and thus arrived at the figure for the household's total foregone earnings.

Household Coping Strategies

We analysed household coping strategies based on a simple model of household economic decision-making. In this model, families are concerned about their welfare along many different dimensions, for example, consumption, health status, education, and number of children, as well as the welfare of their extended family and unrelated community members.

Families have resources with which to pursue their welfare. These resources include human capital (the number of family members, their education, and their earning capacity) and physical capital (savings, durable goods, productive assets, and land). They can use both human and physical capital to generate income for making purchases subject to environmental constraints, which include the prices and quality of available goods and services such as food, housing, medical care, and schooling. Decisions about how to pursue welfare result in welfare outcomes, for example, consumption, health status, and schooling of children.

When individuals suffer from an AIDS-related illness and ultimately die, their families are affected by an immediate reduction in their resources and welfare. The infected individual's earning ability is reduced, and eventually the household loses all of that individual's earning capacity. However, families do not react passively. Rather, they act to minimize the impact on their overall welfare. When individuals first become ill, they work less and may seek medical care. The lost income from the reduced time spent working and the increased medical expenses mean that fewer resources are available for the rest of the family to meet their needs. As a result, other family members may reorganize their time to minimize the income loss and smooth out consumption. A particularly costly reallocation of time is pulling children permanently out of school, which lowers their future earning capacity. Some households may sell assets to pay for medical care and smooth consumption, which might compromise their future earning capacity.

When the sick individual dies, families permanently reorganize their labour supply, time allocation, and expenditure patterns. While families that experience an AIDS-related illness and death are greatly affected, many other households are affected indirectly. For example; extended families who help each other out in times of need may transfer resources to those directly affected, orphaned children may be fostered with relatives, and elderly parents may go back to work or be supported by the households of other adult children. A large number of deaths within extended families and community support networks reduces the viability of these social support networks to help people cope with unanticipated economic and health shocks.

Determination of the Real Economic Impact of Death from HIV/AIDS

We determined the real economic impact of an HIV/AIDS-related death on a household, in particular, the impact on household income and changes in household's consumption levels, using regression analysis. The two economic variables were regressed with a number of socio-economic factors associated with the death of an adult family member from HIV/AIDS or some other cause. Because we obtained too many responses to the variables used in the regression, the number of cases with complete data became too small, rendering the multiple regression test insignificant. In place of the multiple regression analysis we used a simple regression to detect whether an HIV/AIDS-related death causes an impact on household income, and consumption change, that is different from that of a non-HIV/AIDS-related death.

We also made extensive use of descriptive statistics and frequency distribution, particularly for the analysis of the comparative differential impact of an AIDS and a non-AIDS death.

Results

This section presents the socio-economic background of the surveyed households and the results of our analysis of the economic impact of HIV/AIDS mortality on households and household coping strategies.

Socio-economic Characteristics of Households Experiencing an HIV/AIDS-Related Death

Rural households experiencing an HIV/AIDS-related death were mainly the lowest income and least educated group, and were engaged in agricultural work and labour (Table 3). The average yearly income of the households experiencing an HIV/AIDS death was 66 per cent of the income of the households experiencing death from other causes, and 53 per cent of the income of the households that had not experienced a death. More than half of the households that had experienced an HIV/AIDS-related death had incomes lower than the average of $US 2,238 per year, a level already considered low by national standards. In 1992, the average yearly income per household for Thailand as a whole, adjusted by the consumer price index for March 1994, was $US 3,615 ($US 2,454 for rural areas). If the 1988 World Bank poverty line of $US 275 per person per year for rural areas in Thailand was to be adjusted by the rural price index for March 1994 and for the presence of three people in the average household, about

Table 3: Socio-economic Characteristics of Survey Households

Characteristic	Household with HIV/ AIDS death	Household with non-HIV/ AIDS death	Household with no death
Annual household income ($US)	2,238	3,370	4,188
Percentage under poverty line	25	20	15
Percentage of household heads with education higher than primary school	1	9	8
Occupation of household head (per cent)			
White-collar worker	13.1	14.1	31.8
Agricultural worker	47.5	38.0	57.6
Production, construction, transport worker	16.4	14.1	10.8
Labourer	23.0	19.7	0
Assets (per cent)			
Own house	8	5	4.6
Own land	13	15	8.0
Average size of land owned (sqr wah)	958	1,141	1,128
Self-described economic status in community			
Well & very well off	21	27	34
Moderately well off	36	39	49
Poor	29	25	15
Very poor	13	9	2

Source: Authors' survey.

one-fourth of the households in our sample that had experienced an HIV/AIDS-related death would be below the poverty line. This proportion was more than 20 per cent for those households that had experienced a non-HIV/AIDS-related death and 15 per cent for those households that had not recently experienced a death.

Economic Impact of an HIV/AIDS-Related Death on a Rural Household

The economic impact of an HIV/AIDS-related death on a rural household analysed in this study includes the costs of death calculated in money terms, the impact on family labour supply and production, and the impact on children and the elderly, as well as social discrimination against the infected person and his or her family.

Direct and Indirect Costs on an HIV/AIDS-Related Death on a Rural Household   The economic impact of an HIV/AIDS death on a rural household measured in terms of direct and indirect costs per death was substantial, and was greater than the impact of a death from other causes that occurred in the community during the same period.

The direct medical care cost for each HIV/AIDS patient was measured at approximately $US 1,000, which was equivalent to about six months' worth of the average household's income (Table 4). This was slightly greater than the average medical care cost of the non-HIV/AIDS patient. In terms of total direct costs to a household, there was little difference between HIV/AIDS-related deaths and non-HIV/AIDS-related deaths (10 per cent), with the cost of the non-HIV/AIDS-related death being slightly greater than the cost of the HIV/AIDS-related death because the households spent more on funeral rites.

The largest part of the economic costs of an HIV/AIDS-related death is the foregone income of the deceased. Calculating from regular work income alone, this amount totaled $US 28,592, and was approximately 30 per cent more than the foregone income of the individual who died from a non-HIV/AIDS-related cause. This large difference in foregone income is because those who died from AIDS were generally younger than those who died from other causes; thus the number of work years lost were greater. For

Table 4: Direct and Indirect Costs of an HIV/AIDS-related Death and a Death due to Other Causes ($US)

Cost	HIV/AIDS-related death	Non-HIV/AIDS-related death
Direct Costs		
Medical treatment	973	883
Travel expenses	63	53
Funeral expenses	1,537	1,874
Total direct costs	2,574	2,810
Indirect costs		
Income loss of care provider	102	78
Income loss of the deceased (regular job; per annum)	1,880	1,788
Income loss of the deceased (regular + supplementary job; per annum)	2,902	2,234
Income foregone by the deceased (regular job, per annum)	28,592	22,020
Income foregone by the deceased (regular + supplementary job; per annum)	47,550	28,241
Total Indirect Costs		
Without supplementary job	28,694	22,098
With supplementary job	47,652	28,319
Total Direct and Indirect Costs of Death		
Without supplementary job	31,268	24,908
With suplementary job	50,226	31,102

Source: Authors' survey.

the deceased who also held a supplementary job (14 per cent) before their death, the loss of income to the household was large.

The lost income of the care-provider constitutes only a small proportion of the indirect costs because of low earnings in rural areas· and because they tended to care for the sick person only part of the time.

Impact on Family Labour Supply and Production   The negative impact of an HIV/AIDS-related death on the household labour supply for family production was substantial, and affected about 52 per cent of households that engaged in such economic activities (25 per cent of survey households had a family business) (Table 5). The production loss was almost 50 per cent, leading to about a 47 per cent loss in household income. This impact may have been so substantial partly because most of those who died of HIV/AIDS were men of prime working age. Because the size of the average household was small, the death of a such a household member had a substantial negative impact on family production. Data limitations meant that we could not examine the extent of this impact on household by type of industry or any other household socio-economic characteristics.

An HIV/AIDS-related death appears to have a slightly greater impact on a household from lost labour supply than a death from other causes. Lost income as a result of production loss was around 45 per cent for a household that experienced a non-HIV/AIDS-related death compared to 47 per cent for a household that experienced an HIV/AIDS-related death. Although the proportion of households stating that the death had a serious impact on household production was higher among the households that had experienced a non-HIV/AIDS-related death (42 per cent compared to 35 per cent) the proportion of such households among those that had experienced a non-HIV/AIDS-related death that felt seriously affected by this income loss was nevertheless lower than the proportion of households that had experienced an HIV/AIDS-related death (22 per cent compared to 33 per cent). This difference could be because a larger proportion of women had died in those households with a non-HIV/AIDS-related death, while very few women had died in the households with a death due to

Table 5: Other Socio-economic Impacts of HIV/AIDS-Related Death and Non-HIV/AIDS-Related Death on Households

Impact	HIV/AIDS related death	Non-HIV/AIDS related-death
Family labor supply and family production		
Percentage of households engaging in family production	25.0	31.0
Percentage of households stating serious impact on household production	35.0	42.0
Size of impact on household production (per cent)	49.4	49.3
Percentage of households stating serious decrease in household income from lost production	33.0	22.0
Size of household income decrease from lost production (per cent)	47.5	45.2
Children		
Number of affected young children	48	69
Percentage being cared for by a parent	63.0	62.0
Percentage being cared for by a grandparent	21.0	19.0
Percentage being cared for by other relatives	10.0	13.0
Percentage being cared for by an orphanage or temple	6.0	4.0
Elderly		
Percentage of households with elderly care burden on the deceased before death	47.0	27.0
Number of elderly being cared for by deceased before death	84	36
Percentage of households with elderly looking after themselves	43.0	44.0
Percentage being cared for by spouse or children of the deceased	15.0	21.0
Percentage being cared for by other relatives	37.0	33.0
Percentage being cared for by community or a temple	2.0	n.a.

(Contd)

Table 5 *(Contd)*

Social discrimination against infected person		
Discriminated against	48.3	n.a.
Not discriminated against	37.1	n.a.
No response	14.6	n.a.
Social discrimination against other household members		
Discriminated against	16.6	n.a.
Not discriminated against	64.7	n.a.
No response	19.6	n.a.

n.a.: not applicable.

AIDS. Although the women participated in family production, their contribution may have been less than that of male family members because they had to spend part of their time doing household chores and looking after children. Although such work obviously has an economic value, calculating such a value is beyond the scope of this study.

Impact on Children   While HIV/AIDS is currently spreading mostly through the adult population, children are likely to be greatly affected as well, especially in a situation where HIV/AIDS is spreading through heterosexual activity. Children are at risk of contracting the virus from their mothers and, if they survive, of being orphaned. Surviving uninfected children are likely to be worse off than children of uninfected parents. The reduction in resources available to the family and its likely disintegration mean that fewer resources will be available to invest in such children's health and education.

Adult ill health or death has a negative effect on the health of other family members, especially children. This is partly because the children could become infected, but mostly because of the increased burden that adult ill health or death places on other family members, thereby reducing their ability to perform adequate health and child care activities. The extent to which children can be fostered with other relatives will mitigate the effects on them. However, foster children are typically worse off than children who are not in foster care (Gertler 1993).

In our survey, forty-eight young children were in households in which an adult had died of HIV/AIDS-related causes. If we assume one child per household, this number represents approximately 40 per cent of the total number of households. More than half of these children were being cared for by a parent, one-third by other extended family members such as grandparents or other relatives, and 6 per cent were being cared for by an orphanage or temple. Unfortunately, we were not able to find out what proportion of these children were themselves infected with HIV.

The distribution of care-providers for children affected by an adult death in those households that had experienced a non-HIV/AIDS-related death was not much different from the households that had experienced an HIV/AIDS-related death, except that a smaller proportion of these children were in an orphanage or temple. The larger number of affected young children (sixty-nine) in those households where the death had not been from HIV/AIDS was mainly because a greater proportion of the deceased were married men or women.

Impact on the Elderly   Thailand does not currently have a public social security program to support the elderly. Only those people who worked for the government or large private enterprises have pensions. Care for elderly parents is largely provided by their adult children in the form of money for living expenses. Mortality from AIDS is thus likely to create a large number of elderly people without any source of support.

In our study, we found that 47 per cent of the households that had experienced an HIV/AIDS-related death had a problem with caring for elderly family members after the death. Forty-three per cent of such elderly people were left to look after themselves, extended family members cared for 52 per cent, and the community and temples cared for 2 per cent, while the remaining 3 per cent provided no information. This problem was less prevalent among households that had experienced a death from other causes, and none of their elderly were being cared for by the community or a temple. However, a large proportion of these households also had the elderly left looking after themselves.

Social Discrimination   One outcome for households with an HIV/AIDS-related death which was not encountered by the households with a non-HIV/AIDS-related death was social discrimination. Several of the discriminatory practices had an adverse effect on the household economy. Our study shows that despite an attempt to keep the cause of death a family secret, almost half of the households felt the impact of this social discrimination, which carried on even after the death of the sick family member, although it was less severe.

The discriminatory practices that had an adverse impact on the household economy included social pressure to leave a job, former customers no longer ordering goods from the family business, no new customers, and employees quitting the household business (Table 6). The percentage of households affected by these practices was small because only a few of the households surveyed were in business for themselves, and because of attempts to keep the infection a secret from employers.

However, keeping the infection a secret from neighbours may be more difficult at the village level where most people know

Table 6: Types of Social Discrimination Faced by Households with a Family Member with HIV/AIDS (percentage of households)

Type of social discrimination	During illness	After death
Affecting household economy		
Household member forced to leave job	7.5	13.0
No customers	5.0	7.0
Departing employees	6.0	7.0
No goods orders for family business	7.5	7.0
Others		
No association	33.0	27.0
Forced to leave community	7.5	7.0
Children forced to leave school	5.0	7.0
Children prevented from playing with other children	28.0	27.0

each other. Thus, social discrimination in the form of villagers not associating with people from infected households or not allowing their children to play with children from infected households was more prevalent. Social pressure on infected households to leave the community or to withdraw their children from school, though not widesread, reflects a serious lack of understanding among the public about the way HIV is spread.

Household Coping Strategies during HIV/AIDS Illness and after Death
To cushion the adverse effect of increased medical care costs for the sick person, declining household income from lost earnings, lost labour supply for family production, and the stresses of social discrimination, the household may use a number of strategies to cope. The effectiveness of each strategy and its impact on households' current and future welfare depends on their socio-economic characteristics. For instance, households that have greater economic resources should experience a smaller adverse impact than households that have fewer resources. The following sections examine various household coping strategies and households' ability to cope in relation to their socio-economic characteristics. To detect the real impact of an HIV/AIDS-related death on households' ability to cope, we compared households' where such a death had occurred with those that had experienced a non-HIV/AIDS-related death.

Adjustment of Household Resources For households that have accumulated savings, the most natural way to respond is to use this available resource. Although the use of household savings will have the least adverse impact on the current welfare of other household members, future household investment will certainly be negatively affected. Furthermore, the opportunity cost (lost interest) associated with dissaving must also be considered as a component of the indirect costs of the illness on the household.

In our survey, about 60 per cent of the households that had experienced an HIV/AIDS-related death had savings to finance their increased costs (Table 7). On an average, each household spent $US 863 from its savings on care and treatment for the

Table 7: Household Coping Strategies During Illness and After Death

Strategy	Households with HIV/AIDS-related death	Households with non-HIV/AIDS-related death
(1)	*(2)*	*(3)*
Dissaving		
% households using savings	60	53
Average savings used ($US)	862.6	684.12
Consumption expenditure reduction		
% of households reducing expenditure	52	50
% change in household food consumption	42	25
% of households seriously affected	29	30
Sales of household assets		
% of households selling assets	19	12
% of households selling land	44	38
% of households selling livestock	8	23
% of households selling a vehicle	28	–
Reallocation of household members' time (% of household members)		
No change	56	48
Work harder to substitute for lost income	20	15
Need to find a job	2	2
Helped with the family business	2	4
Left job to help take care of the sick person	1	1
Changed to new job for higher income	1	1
Reduced work to help family	2	1
Found supplementary job	1	1
Left school for work	1	1

(Contd)

Table 7: *(Contd)*

(1)	(2)	(3)
Substitution of lost labour in family production (%)		
Employed substitute labour	10	3
Other members worked harder	3	6
Members left school for family work	13	13
No response or not appropriate	74	77
Borrowing and source thereof (%)		
Households borrowing	11	20
Households brrowing from banks	9	29
Households borrowing from a moneylender	23	21
Households borrowing from relatives	46	25
Households borrowing from co-operatives & revolving funds	23	25
Average amount borrowed ($US)	2740.8	981.4
Transfers-in		
Households receiving transfers-in (%)	15	7
Amount of transfers per month ($US)	28.16	44
Amount of transfers per year	328.48	596
Non-family institutions and health care costs (% of households)		
Received government employees' health care benefits	9	6
Received benefits from private health insurance	3	3
Received health care benefits for private-sector employees	4	3
Received benefits from government health card scheme	14	10
Received benefits from FMP programme	10	14
Received benefits from social security programme	5	5

Source: Authors' survey.

person with HIV/AIDS. This amount was approximately 88 per cent of the average total health care expenses of the sick person from the time he or she fell ill until death. Households had to finance the rest of the health care and other expenditures from other sources.

For households that had assets, selling assets was another way to cushion the household's rising expenses and falling income. The sale of certain assets, such as jewellery, may have little impact on the household's welfare, but selling assets such as land, live-stock, and vehicles, which were used in family production, may result in a negative impact on both current and future family production.

Of the households we surveyed, 19 per cent of the households that experienced an HIV/AIDS-related death opted for this strategy. The asset most often sold was land, followed by vehicles and livestock. Although the households used much of the money raised in this way to finance increased health care costs, they also used part of the money to maintain other household consumption.

Households that had few or no resources to fall back on saw a reduction in current household expenditure on consumption as a way out. If this reduction is large, it will adversely affect the nutrition and health of household members and their ability to work. Of the households that had experienced an HIV/AIDS-re-lated death, 52 per cent adopted this strategy, of which 29 per cent admitted that the reduction had had a serious effect on their welfare. We estimated that on an average, their consumption of food and beverages, the largest consumption expenditure item, fell by 42 per cent.

Information gathered from the children that we interviewed separately confirmed this changed household consumption pattern: 45 per cent of the children felt that their current household con-sumption level was somewhat lower or much lower than before the HIV/AIDS death, and 53 per cent indicated that their household's economic status in the community was somewhat or much better before the HIV/AIDS death than at the present time.

Many households tried to cope by reallocating the time household members spent on various activities. Most of the re-al-location involved other members taking on more work than previously to make up the lost income, helping with the family business to substitute for the lost labour, reducing the time spent at work to help the family, needing to find work, changing to a new job that paid more, needing to find supplementary work, or quitting a job to help with family chores and take care of the sick person. A sizeable proportion of those members affected by this coping strategy were the elderly parents of the deceased. In addition, the children of the deceased as well as other school-aged members of the households were in some cases withdrawn from school to start work and to help the family restore its income and family production levels. While withdrawing young children from school so that they can work may help the family restore its income, it will affect the earning ability of these children in the future.

Apart from adjusting household members' time to help in family production, 10 per cent of the households that experienced an HIV/AIDS-related death, or 40 per cent of the households that had a family business, hired substitute labour to replace the ill and deceased person. With rising household expenses and falling income, the additional expenditure on hiring substitute labour could result in a shortage of production capital for the household, leading to an adverse impact on family production in the future.

Borrowing Despite households' adjustment and use of existing resources to cope with the situation, a number of the households that experienced an HIV/AIDS-related death had to turn to borrowing as a way out. The cost of borrowing in the form of interest charged adds to the households' burdens. Eleven per cent of the households surveyed borrowed money during this time of hardship.

Most of the households borrowed from informal credit sources, such as relatives or moneylenders, where interest charged is normally high. They also turned to co-operatives or local revolving funds, where interest is lower. They were less likely to use formal credit institutions such as banks.

The amount of household borrowing ranged from $US 360 to $US 9,547, or an average of $US 2,750. Although relatives were the most common source of funds, the average amount of borrowing from this source was rather small, averaging $US 360 per case, while the average amount borrowed from moneylenders was $US 8,000.

Transfers-in   During difficult times households may also receive monetary support from relatives or members of their extended family living away from home. In our study, 15 per cent of the households affected by an HIV/AIDS-related death received transfers-in from outside. This proportion may seem small, but if we consider that rural households in Thailand are generally poor and earn little, their ability to provide extended family members with cash may be limited. However, of those who received transfers-in, the average amount received was $US 28 per month or $US 328 per year. The people who provided the money were mainly adult children of the household head working away from home, or the siblings of the head of the household.

Non-family Institutions and Health Care Costs   About 45 per cent of all households that experienced an HIV/AIDS-related death received subsidies in some form from a non-family institution. Because private health insurance and employers' health benefits in Thailand do not cover HIV/AIDS-related illness, claims under these schemes were often made by reporting the cause of death as non-HIV/AIDS-related. If the actual cause of death had been reported, more of the financial burden for medical care would have fallen on households.

Among the households that received some kind of financial support for medical care, about 10 per cent got free medical services from the Free Medical Services for the Poor Programme (FMP Programme), a programme the Ministry of Public Health provides in rural areas; 14 per cent received benefits under the ministry's Health Card Programme, a government-run voluntary health insurance scheme whereby special membership cards are sold at a subsidized price to people in rural areas seeking higher quality medical treatment than that provided by the FMP programme. About 9 per cent received subsidies from the civil service or a public enterprise as part of their employment welfare benefits. A much smaller proportion registered claims with their private health insurance carrier, received social security, or obtained welfare benefits from a private employer.

Coping Strategies of Households that Experienced a Non-HIV/AIDS-Related Death

The coping strategies of households that experienced a non-HIV/AIDS-related death were somewhat different from those of households that had to cope with an HIV/AIDS-related death. To begin with, although the percentage of households that reduced their consumption and were seriously affected by this cut was similar to the corresponding percentage for households with an HIV/AIDS-related death, the size of the impact in terms of cuts in expenditure on food and beverages was lower for the non-HIV/AIDS households (25 per cent compared to 42 per cent).

As concerns the use of existing family resources, although the pattern was quite similar, that is, most households relied on their savings first, followed by the sale of assets and transfers-in from relatives, the proportion of the non-HIV/AIDS households using this method was lower than that of the HIV/AIDS households. More of the non-HIV/AIDS households turned to borrowing (20 per cent versus 11 per cent), but the amount the average HIV/AIDS household borrowed was much higher than what a non-HIV/AIDS household borrowed ($US 2,750 versus $US 981). Note also that about 92 per cent of HIV/AIDS households borrowed from non-bank sources, while 70 per cent of the non-HIV/AIDS households chose this route.

Extended family support to non-HIV/AIDS households was also similar to that provided to HIV/AIDS households, but the extent of the support differed: only 7 per cent of the non-HIV/AIDS households received transfers-in from relatives compared to 15 per cent of the HIV/AIDS households, but the amount received was much higher.

In terms of external support, a larger proportion of the non-HIV/AIDS households obtained free hospital care and treatment under the FMP Programme: 14 per cent compared to 10 per cent of the HIV/AIDS households. As for government subsidies under the Health Card Programme, 10 per cent of non-HIV/AIDS households received these benefits compared to 14 per cent of the

HIV/AIDS households. Just as for HIV/AIDS households, the proportion of non-HIV/AIDS households under health insurance schemes (3 per cent), receiving subsidies from social security (5 per cent), or eligible for employer-provided benefits from the public sector (6 per cent) or the private sector (3 per cent) was small because of the limited coverage currently provided by such schemes.

Ability to Cope and Types of Households that Experienced a Death due to HIV/AIDS
The ability of households to cope is generally correlated with their socio-economic characteristics, mainly income, educational attainment, and employment status. Households with higher incomes, better educational attainment, and higher-status occupations are often viewed as better able to cope with HIV/AIDS-related illness and death because these characteristics are generally associated with the ability to accumulate assets. Moreover, better-educated households are generally more informed, which enables them to adjust more readily.

Household Income and Ability to Cope   Table 8 shows the impact of HIV/AIDS-related illness and death and of non-HIV/AIDS-related illness and death on household consumption broken down by income level. Generally, a larger number of lower-income households experiencing an HIV/AIDS-related illness and death felt that their consumption level was seriously affected. This proportion ranged from 22 to 66 per cent for households with incomes lower than $US 1,200 per year compared to 18 to 37 per cent among those with higher incomes. The pattern was similar among households that experienced a non-HIV/AIDS-related death; however, more of the lower-income households felt that the illness and death had a serious impact on their consumption, with the figures ranging from 33 to 69 per cent.

As concerns the sources of funds to cope with the situation, these were more limited for the low-income households than for the high-income households, both for households that experienced an HIV/AIDS-related death and those that experienced a death from other causes. Apart from those entitled to subsidies from their employers, most relied mainly on their savings, transfers

Table 8: Economic Impact of Adult HIV/AIDS-related and Non-HIV/AIDS-related Deaths

Type of Household and Impact	Annual Income in Bahts							
	1–3000	3001–5000	5001–10000	10001–30000	30001–50000	50001–80000	80001–100000	>100000
1. Households with HIV/AIDS-related deaths								
Consumption								
Proportion feeling serious impact on consumption	22	66	–	47	37	25	22	16
Source of Hospital Treatment								
% receiving free treatment from welfare	–	–	–	11	18	12	13	–
% receiving subsidies from health card	–	–	–	11	–	6	–	–
% receiving subsidies from employers & insurance	10	33	–	5	6	6	25	7
% using own/relatives' funds	40	33	100	50	55	53	37	71
Source of Household Health Care								
% using savings	80	50	75	52	64	62	88	82
% selling assets	–	50	–	29	36	23	11	–
% borrowing	20	–	25	19	–	15	–	18
Care of Children after Death								
% under care of extended family	29	–	–	29	14	25	60	–
% under care of orphanage or temple	29	–	–	5	–	–	–	–

(Contd)

Table 8: *(Contd)*

Type of Household and Impact	Annual Income in Bahts							
	1–3000	3001–5000	5001–10000	10001–30000	30001–50000	50001–80000	80001–100000	>100000
2. Households with non-HIV/AIDS-related deaths								
Consumption								
% feeling serious impact on consumption	33	33	66	69	25	25	40	–
Source of Hospital Treatment								
% receiving free treatment from welfare	25	20	–	–	13	6	–	27
% receiving subsidies from health card	–	–	–	–	–	–	20	–
% receiving subsidies from employers & insurance	–	–	–	8	7	12	40	7
% using own/relatives' funds	50	20	33	67	47	44	20	40
Source of Household Health Care								
% using savings	56	33	100	60	62	57	80	87
% selling assets	–	17	–	–	8	21	–	13
% borrowing	33	50	–	40	31	21	20	–
Care of Children after Death								
% under care of extended family	33	25	40	12	24	14	40	22
% under care of orphanage or temple	–	12	–	5	5	–	–	–

from relatives, and borrowing. Although a number of higher-income households also resorted to borrowing, the ability to borrow depends on collateral and the ability to pay back the loan, which poorer households do not have.

External support in terms of government subsidies for health care costs did not seem to reach the poorest households, even though these are the main targets of the government assistance programme in rural areas. Among the households that experienced an HIV/AIDS-related death, the lowest income group did not benefit from either the FMP Programme or the Health Card Programme. Those who benefitted from the programmes were concentrated among the middle and higher income groups. Moreover, a number of the middle and higher income households also received subsidies from their employers, while most of the lowest-income households were agricultural workers and labourers who were not eligible for such benefits. Among the households that experienced a non-HIV/AIDS-related death, government assistance in terms of free medical treatment under the FMP Programme and the Health Card Programme did appear to reach the very poor, but high-income households also benefitted from these subsidies. The higher income groups were more likely to have received other external subsidies from employers, health insurance, and social security.

As for the impact on children, those from higher-income households that experienced an HIV/AIDS-related death were all taken care of by extended family members, while children from the poorest households were more likely to be left to the care of an orphanage or temple. A similar pattern was evident among the households that experienced a non-HIV/AIDS-related death.

Household Educational Level and Ability to Cope   In this study household educational attainment refers to the educational attainment of the head of the household. Generally, education enhances earning ability. Thus, households with a highly-educated head are generally viewed as having more resources to turn to in times of need. Furthermore, well-educated household are believed to have more information to help them adjust to the sickness and death of a family member with less hardship to their members.

Despite limited data and a very small variation in terms of household educational attainment (which is not surprising given that most people in rural Thailand receive only a primary school education), Table 9 suggests that households with low education levels suffered more from cuts in consumption than households with more education. This is shown more clearly among the households that experienced a non-HIV/AIDS-related death.

Children and the elderly who were left without support from the extended family were mainly from the least-educated households. These households were also more likely to withdraw family members from school or work to help with family chores, and to borrow money.

Households Occupation and Ability to Cope   Given the concentration of households in agriculture and manual labour, analysing ability to cope by household occupation was difficult. However, the data indicated that among the households that experienced an HIV/AIDS-related death, agricultural households had the highest proportion seriously affected by a cut in consumption (46 per cent), followed by white-collar workers (44 per cent), as shown in Table 10. Households engaged in blue-collar work were less seriously affected (33 per cent), while labourers were the least affected (7 per cent). This pattern was somewhat different for the households that experienced a non-HIV/AIDS-related death, as the labourers had largest proportion seriously affected (62 per cent), followed by other blue-collar workers (43 per cent), white-collar workers (36 per cent), and agricultural workers (31 per cent).

For the households that experienced an HIV/AIDS-related death, the children of all but the white-collar workers were taken out of school to work, help with household chores, and take care of younger children and the sick person. An analysis of the effects on the children of households that experienced a death due to other causes was not possible because of insufficient data.

As concerns sources of finance for households that experienced an HIV/AIDS-related death, those engaged in white-collar work had fewer family resources to finance health care costs, and thus a larger proportion of this group (29 per cent) had to turn to borrowing. The proportion of households in other occupations that

Table 9: Economic Impact of Adult HIV/AIDS-Related Death and Non-HIV/AIDS-Related Death by Educational Attainment

Type of Household and Type of Impact	Education level					
	Primary/ lower primary	Upper primary	Lower secondary	Upper secondary	Higher education	No response
1	2	3	4	5	6	7
1. HIV/AIDS Death Household						
Consumption						
Proportion feeling serious impact (%)	30	–	–	–	–	31
Proportion feeling small impact (%)	20	20	100	–	–	28
Proportion feeling no impact (%)	44	80	–	–	–	36
Care of Children after Death						
Proportion under care of extended family (%)	24	–	–	–	–	22
Proportion under care of orphan-home & temple (%)	8	–	–	–	–	–
Care of Elderly						
Proportion looking after themselves (%)	40	–	–	–	–	37
Proportion under care of extended family (%)	50	–	–	–	–	58
Proportion under care of community & temple (%)	3	–	–	–	–	–
Time Reallocation of Children						
Proportion that had to find job (%)	1	–	–	–	–	2
Proportion that left school for work (%)	2	–	–	–	–	–
Time Reallocation of Young Relatives						
Proportion that had to find job (%)	1	7	–	–	–	–
Proportion that left school for work (%)	2	–	–	–	–	–
Proportion that left school to look after children & sick & housechores (%)	7	–	–	–	–	–

(Contd)

Table 9: *(Contd)*

	1	2	3	4	5	6	7
Household Debt							
Proportion having debt		22	20	–	–	–	21
2. Non-HIV/AIDS Death Household							
Consumption							
Proportion feeling serious impact (%)		38	25	–	–	–	25
Proportion feeling small impact (%)		28	13	50	100	–	16
Proportion feeling no impact (%)		28	63	50	–	100	50
Care of Children after Death							
Proportion under care of extended family (%)		22	25	–	–	–	23
Proportion under care of orphan-home & temple (%)		–	–	–	–	–	6
Care of Elderly							
Proportion looking after themselves (%)		48	–	–	–	50	36
Proportion under care of extended family (%)		48	100	–	–	50	64
Proportion under care of community & temple (%)		–	–	–	–	–	–
Time Reallocation of Children							
Proportion that had to find job (%)		2	4	–	–	–	1
Proportion that left school for work (%)		–	–	–	–	–	1
Time Reallocation of Young Relatives							
Proportion that had to find job (%)		–	–	–	–	–	–
Proportion that left school for work (%)		–	–	–	–	–	–
Proportion that left school to look after children, sick and house-chores (%)		1	–	–	–	–	–
Household Debt							
Proportion having debt		25	25	–	100	–	13

Source: Survey (March 1994).

Table 10: Economic Impact of Adult HIV/AIDS-Related Death and Non-HIV/AIDS-Related Death by Occupation

Type of Household and Type of Impact	Occupation				No response
	White-collar workers	Agricultural workers	Blue-collar workers		
			Production, construction, transportation	Labourers	
HIV/AIDS Death Household					
Consumption					
Proportion feeling serious impact (%)	44	46	33	7	20
Time Reallocation of Young Relatives					
Proportion left school for work (%)	–	4	–	–	–
Proportion left school to help house-chores & took care of younger children & sick (%)	–	2	66	10	11
Source of Finance of Health Care					
Proportion using own saving (%)	36	51	50	44	42
Proportion selling assets (%)	7	15	20	13	14
Proportion borrowing (%)	29	9	–	7	5
Proportion receiving transfers from relatives (%)	7	7	–	7	13
Proportion using government services (%)	21	–	20	7	6
Proportion using health insurance (%)	–	4	–	7	–
Proportion using employer (%)	–	7	–	–	3
Proportion using health card (%)	–	7	10	19	11
Proportion using social security (%)	–	2	–	–	6

(Contd)

Table 10: *(Contd)*

Type of Household and Type of Impact	White-collar workers	Agricultural workers	Occupation		No response
			Blue-collar workers		
			Production, construction, transportation	Labourers	
Non-HIV/AIDS Death Household					
Consumption					
Proportion feeling serious impact (%)	36	31	43	62	15
Time Reallocation of Young Relatives					
Proportion left school for work (%)	–	–	–	–	–
Proportion left school to help house-chores & took care of younger children & sick (%)	–	–	–	–	2
Source of Finance of Health Care					
Proportion using own saving (%)	50	38	60	47	46
Proportion selling assets (%)	7	9	14	13	11
Proportion borrowing (%)	21	16	29	20	11
Proportion receiving transfers from relatives (%)	–	9	–	7	7
Proportion using government services (%)	7	3	–	–	9
Proportion using health insurance (%)	14	–	–	–	2
Proportion using employer (%)	–	5	–	–	2
Proportion using health card (%)	–	15	14	–	9
Proportion using social security (%)	–	3	14	13	2

had to borrow money was much lower: 9 per cent for agricultural workers and 7 per cent for labourers. This pattern was different for the households that experienced a non-HIV/AIDS-related death, as the largest proportion borrowing was among blue-collar workers in the production, construction, and transport sectors (29 per cent), followed by white-collar workers (21 per cent), labourers (20 per cent), and agricultural workers (18 per cent).

Regression Analysis
In addition to the foregoing analyses, we also employed regression analysis to investigate whether an HIV/AIDS-related death actually makes a difference to the economic condition of the affected household. Two key economic variables explored were household income and household consumption change. The socio-economic factors included in the regression model as the determining factors of household income and household consumption change after death were household size, sex of the deceased, age of the deceased at death, household status of the deceased, cause of death, occupation of the deceased before death, and educational attainment of the deceased. Logarithmic values of household income and household consumption change were then regressed with these determining variables, most of which were dummy variables.

These regressions were not successful because of the limitations mentioned earlier (see page 64). We therefore attempted a simple regression of the level of household income and the level of household consumption change with the cause of death, that is, HIV/AIDS-related or non-HIV/AIDS-related, with the results as shown in Table 11. The two simple regression tests indicate that an adult HIV/AIDS-related death causes a greater negative impact on household income and larger consumption change to the household than an adult death not related to HIV/AIDS.

Further experimentation with simple regression analysis of other socio-economic factors connected with HIV/AIDS and non-HIV/AIDS deaths indicates that no other factors can explain the variation in household income level. This could be because of the small sample of households as well as the relatively slight variation in the socio-economic characteristics of the deceased. How-

Table 11: Regression Analysis of Socio-economic Factors for Households that Experienced an HIV/AIDS-Related Death

Regression 1

Dependent variable = household income

Variable	Coefficient	t-statistic
Constant	10.073	37.631
HIV/AIDS-related cause of death	−0.653	−1.741*

$R^2 = 0.0272$; F-statistic = 3.031; N = 110.
* significance of .05.

Regression 2

Dependent variable = household income

Variable	Coefficient	t-statistic
Constant	2.961	18.865
HIV/AIDS-related cause of death	0.589	2.631*

$R^2 = 0.115$; F-stat. = 6.924; N = 55.
* sig. level = .01

Regression 3

Dependent variable = household income

Variable	Coefficient	t-statistic
Constant	10.938	5.083
HIV/AIDS-related cause of death	−1.136	−2.173*
Occupation: professional, technical, & managerial	0.351	0.138
Occupation: clerical, sales, service workers	−0.385	−0.117
Occupation: agricultural workers	−1.081	−0.177
Occupation: production, construction, transportation workers	−1.269	−0.588
Occupation: labourers	−1.785	−0.841
Sex	0.003	1.236

$R^2 = 0.141$; F-stat. = 1.547; N = 74.
* sig. level = .05

(Contd)

Table 11: *(Contd)*

Regression 4

Dependent variable = household income

Variable	Coefficient	t-statistic
Constant	10.073	37.631
HIV/AIDS-related cause of death	−0.653	−1.741*
Primary education	−1.800	−0.855
Lower secondary education	−1.872	−0.877
Upper secondary education	−0.668	−0.286
Sex	0.0002	0.981

$R^2 = 0.104$; F-stat. = 1.583; N = 74.
* sig. level = .05

Regression 5

Dependent variable = household income

Variable	Coefficient	t-statistic
Constant	10.938	5.083
Sex	−6.917	−0.467
AIDS-related death	0.389	1.399*
Occupation: clerical, sales, service workers	1.653	1.750**
Occupation: agricultural workers	0.994	0.909
Occupation: production, construction, transportation workers	1.507	1.3678
Occupation: labourers	1.153	1.075
Primary education	−0.191	−0.212
Lower secondary education	0.272	0.295

$R^2 = 0.329$; F-stat. = 2.027; N = 42.
* sig. level = .10; ** sig. level = .05

ever, on the household consumption change regression, apart from the HIV/AIDS-related cause of death variable, another socio-economic factor that contributes to the variation in the level of household consumption change is the occupation of the deceased, especially if the deceased was either a clerical, sales, or service worker or a production, construction, or transportation worker.

Although our regression analysis was not satisfactory because of data limitations, the results shown in Table 11 suggest that an adult HIV/AIDS-related death contributes to a larger variation in household income and household consumption change than death from other causes.

Policy Implications

This study has demonstrated several important features of the economic impact of an adult HIV/AIDS-related death on a rural household in Chiangmai province, northern Thailand. We found that this impact is sizeable and significant despite all the coping strategies adopted by such households. The study also shows the existence of a link between AIDS and low income, lack of education, and poverty. This link was revealed by households' differential susceptibility to AIDS depending on their income, the size of the economic shock associated with AIDS mortality, and the ability of households at different economic levels to cope with this shock. In other words, the poorest and least educated are the most susceptible to AIDS and the economic shock they suffer is greater than that experienced by higher-income and better-educated households. Furthermore, they are also the least able to cope because they have fewer household resources and limited access to non-family institutions to help spread the costs of medical care.

This finding confirms earlier work by Bloom and Glied (1993) and Thant (1993). According to Thant, the HIV/AIDS epidemic in South-east Asia is spreading in a non-random pattern, and the poor are more at risk than those who are economically better off. Thus the costs of the epidemic will fall disproportionately on the poor. Bloom and Glied found that as in India and Indonesia, the costs of AIDS in Thailand were concentrated heavily on individuals with AIDS, and their families, because of the limited role of non-family institutions in helping to spread the costs. Because HIV/AIDS is disproportionately affecting low-income households, the medical care costs of HIV/AIDS are likely to increase economic inequality in Thailand and contribute to the further immiserization of the poor.

Our study also showed that the economic impact of an adult AIDS death is more severe than an adult death from other causes because HIV tends to infect relatively younger adults in their prime working years, which means that the household foregoes more income than would be case for the death of an older adult. Our regression analysis, though limited in scope, supports the evidence provided by the other (descriptive) statistical analyses, that is, that an adult HIV/AIDS-related death causes a greater change in household income and a larger percentage change in the household consumption level than a non-HIV/AIDS-related death. In addition, the social discrimination practised against those infected with HIV/AIDS, and members of their households, to which households that experienced a non-HIV/AIDS-related death were not exposed, caused their lives to be made even more miserable, and the household economy to be more adversely affected. Because HIV/AIDS infects mostly lower-income and less-educated households with fewer resources, and hence less ability to cope, AIDS implies more than just an increase in mortality. The spillover effect of AIDS will lead to the further immiserization of the poor and worsen the distribution of income between the haves and the have-nots.

Because the current Thai government views poverty alleviation and improved income distribution as one of the most important and urgent issues to be addressed, the economic impact of an adult AIDS death on rural households deserves attention. Appropriate government interventions to help those most affected and most in need should also be developed where they are absent, and strengthened where they exist.

Government measures to alleviate rural poverty have been in place in Thailand since the early 1980s as part of the national development plan. These measures involve an integrated effort by six ministries: the Ministry of Public Health, the Ministry of Education, the Ministry of Agriculture and Co-operatives, the Ministry of Industry, the Ministry of the Interior, and the Ministry of Labour and Social Welfare. The following sections briefly discuss how some of these measures could be strengthened or extended to alleviate the plight of rural households affected by an adult AIDS death.

Provision of Basic Welfare
The Social Welfare Department, part of the Ministry of Labour and Social Welfare, is responsible for providing basic necessities to households experiencing a sudden crisis, such as flood and fire victims and poverty-stricken households in need of food, clothing, and temporary shelter. As the government's welfare budget is relatively small, the Social Welfare Department generally works in co-operation with non-governmental organizations (NGOs) both at the national and at the local level.

In the case of poor households affected by AIDS, an attempt to keep the cause of illness secret may reduce their chances of receiving assistance, especially if they were not welfare recipients before. In such cases, a special effort to widen and strengthen existing government welfare assistance measures for the poor and the needy is called for to ensure coverage for such households. One way to help identify such households is to have HIV/AIDS counsellors available in hospitals and to encourage NGOs to help with this effort.

Currently, the Ministry of Labour and Social Welfare has a cash assistance programme for low-wage enterprise workers who are infected by HIV and can no longer work. The main objective of this assistance is to help the victims and their families find an alternative occupation. Short courses of occupational training are also provided for those members of the household who wish to become self-employed. Several NGOs offer similar types of assistance in areas where HIV/AIDS is widespread.

With the HIV/AIDS epidemic spreading rapidly, the demand for such assistance will increase substantially. The ability of government agencies to cushion the suffering of those affected, and the question of how to encourage NGOs to participate more in assistance programmes will become major issues for the government when dealing with rural poverty and the rural development programme.

Education Subsidies

In Thailand, the first six years of education are compulsory and provided free of charge. Yet households incur other costs in relation to schooling, for example, they must pay for clothing, books, stationery, and travel. The most impoverished households find these costs a heavy burden and may decide not send their children to school at all.

The withdrawal from school of young children, especially girls, and the need for them to work to help restore the household's income and pay for the family's medical care costs will intensify the problem of young girls from rural northern Thailand becoming prostitutes. This in turn exacerbates the spread of AIDS. Providing education subsidies in the form of full scholarships to young children in the most needy households, particularly those with an adult infected with HIV/AIDS, as well as providing training so that they can find a reasonably well-paid job, should be considered a major tool in the fight against AIDS and poverty in rural areas.

Currently, several government agencies and NGOs are providing 'skills training programmes' for young girls in villages that are known to be heavily involved in commercial sex and where HIV infection is prevalent. In addition, a number of private organizations offer full scholarships to rural children to enable them to attend secondary school. Finally, beginning in 1996, the government will provide free lower secondary schooling to all children.

Whether these subsidies will be effective in keeping young children in school and away from the sex trade is a matter for further evaluation. The large number of young rural girls involved in commercial sex despite so many years of rural development efforts is mainly due to the lack of reasonably paying jobs even for those girls with skills training and a school education. Employment generation and a fair distribution of income in rural areas would help alleviate this situation.

Credit Market

In most of rural Thailand, households still borrow mostly from informal sources, generally local moneylenders and relatives. The interest charged by informal sources of credit, especially moneylenders, is very high compared to other sources, but the borrowing process is uncomplicated. Other local credit sources where interest is lower and the borrowing procedure is simple are local co-operatives and revolving funds. However, the amount of funds available from these sources is generally small. With the rapid spread of HIV/AIDS in rural Thailand, demand for credit to finance rising medical care expenditures, to restore household income and consumption, and to maintain household production activities will rise substantially from their already high level. The government needs to implement a policy to enlarge existing sources of credit in rural areas to serve rural households hit by adult HIV/AIDS-related deaths. Recently, the government discussed a plan to set up a credit fund with low or no interest to help households affected by HIV/AIDS in communities where the disease is widespread, but the implementation process is proceeding extremely slowly.

Farm Input Subsidies
Assistance provided to households that operate their own farms could be in the form of farm input subsidies and free loans of farm tools or machinery to replace lost labour. The free exchange of labour during the farming season among surviving members of households affected by an HIV/AIDS-related death in the same community should also be encouraged to reduce the costs of hiring substitute labour.

Currently, only a few informal groups of widows of men who have died of AIDS exist in Chiangmai and other provinces in northern Thailand where HIV/AIDS is widespread. The groups' main purpose is to help each other. Such groups could encourage the free exchange of labour during the farming season to help restore household farm production.

Care of Orphans and the Elderly
In Thailand, the extended family plays an important role in taking care of young children and older people left without an immediate family because of the death of their parents or adult children. Our study confirms this role of the extended family. With the rapid spread of AIDS in recent years, the number of young children, whether infected with HIV or not, who will become orphans, and

older people who will be left to fend for themselves, will increase substantially.

To strengthen the role of the extended family, a government assistance package may be required, because the ability of extended family members to care for distant relatives may be limited, especially in low-income households. For example, in low-income households where the adults who could take care of young children and the elderly need to work during the day, a community centre where children and old people could be taken care of during that time may be needed. For low-income households that have adults who could take care of the children and the elderly at home, assistance in the form of food subsidies or help with other expenses may be necessary. Those households caring for infected children with few or no symptoms should be taught how to look after these children and be provided with free medical supplies. Orphanages and homes for the elderly should be used only when extended family members can no longer cope.

However, our study revealed that a sizeable number of older people are being left to fend for themselves, without the help of their extended family. With the size of the average household becoming smaller because of the success of the family planning programme, the need for young adults to move to urban areas to find work, and the increasing number of adult AIDS deaths, the plight of the elderly in rural areas will become worse.

The recent move by the Ministry of Public Health to issue a free medical care card to all those aged sixty and above in rural areas and in low-income urban communities is one way to cope with the problem. In addition to free medical care, other assistance programmes are needed to help older people with their day-to-day activities, such as shopping, cooking, and house cleaning. A programme of visits by volunteer social workers to the homes of older people could be developed, along with community nursing homes for the aged.

Subsidies for Medical Care Costs

As mentioned earlier, the government provides assistance to the rural poor for medical care costs in two ways: the FMP Programme and the Health Card Programme. The free medical service cards under the FMP Programme are issued to people below a specified minimum income level (cash and non-cash), who are screened and approved by a committee of village leaders. The Health Card Programme is a cross between a health insurance scheme and a club membership. The cards are sold at a highly subsidized cost to people in rural areas who have sought special maternal and child care and regular medical treatment in addition to what they would have received under the public health system. Membership can be on an individual or on a family basis. All cards are valid for one year and there is a ceiling on the number of episodes of illness that will be treated during that year, and on the free medical benefits received for each episode.

Although basic health care services in Thailand are considered satisfactory, the evidence suggests that the FMP Programme does not reach the lowest income households experiencing an HIV/AIDS-related death. Those who receive free medical treatment tend to belong the middle and higher income groups. The Health Card Programme is not as popular, and is not as widely used by lower-income households as expected.

A thorough evaluation of the FMP Programme and its screening and selection process, as well as a study of factors hindering widespread acceptance of the Health Card Programme in rural areas should be undertaken so that government measures already in effect to alleviate the plight of the poor actually reach their target group.

Other Policy Implications
In addition to broadening and strengthening existing government programmes aimed at alleviating rural poverty so as to cover those rural poor adversely affected by HIV/AIDS, other policy implications arising from our study concern protecting the employment and human rights of people living with AIDS and their families and providing accurate medical information to protect them from fraudulent practices.

As our study shows, discrimination against those infected with HIV/AIDS, as well as their family members, is widespread in Thailand. This leads to many victims losing their jobs, or their family business losing customers and employees. Consequently, their economic problems are intensified. A government policy to protect AIDS sufferers' human rights by safeguarding the confidentiality of their health records and protecting their right to continue working while their health permits them to do so should be developed and implemented. However, this policy should be supplemented by a government campaign to educate the public about HIV and AIDS and get across the message that discrimination against those with the disease is wrong.

As concerns fraud, fear has led many AIDS victims to turn to traditional healers and various kinds of herbs in the search for a cure. 'News' about magical drugs and healers is widespread among AIDS victims, and the prices of these so-called drugs and healers are generally high. Given the difficulty of stopping desperate people with a terminal illness and no hope for a cure through conventional medicine from seeking alternative sources of care, it is the government's job to provide those infected with accurate information to protect them from losing more of their money to unscrupulous 'healers'.

Conclusion

The policy suggestions arising from the results of our study have been outlined earlier and are intended to give policy makers some guidelines on possible ways of dealing with the socio-economic impact of HIV/AIDS-related deaths at the household level. Our intention was also to explore existing government assistance measures aimed at the rural poor, and to seek ways to broaden and strengthen these measures to cover households seriously affected by an adult HIV/AIDS-related death. To save money, new measures should be introduced only when necessary. Furthermore, we suggest that these policies be implemented alongside current preventive measures and not viewed as substitutes for such measures. Preventing the further spread of AIDS is still the best policy for fighting the disease. However, in a country like Thailand, where the incidence of AIDS has been increasing rapidly over the past few years and is expected to rise substantially by the year 2000, the socio-economic implications of an HIV/AIDS-related death on the household, the community, the region, and finally the nation, will be immense. It is the government's job to foresee these adverse consequences and find ways to plug the holes in the social safety net before they become huge tears in the fabric of Thai society as the full force of the AIDS epidemic is unleashed.

Our study is the first piece of research in Thailand based on hard survey data that provides Thai policy-makers with information about the economic impact on a household of an adult HIV/AIDS-related death. As with most pioneering work, our study is not without flaws. Apart from the budgetary and time constraints that seriously limited the scope of our survey, the fact that AIDS is still a sensitive and controversial subject, and therefore hard to discuss openly with household members, made our interviews difficult. To alleviate the confidentiality problem, we used local public health workers as the survey enumerators. Despite intensive training, we found that lengthy questions that asked for many details about households' economic conditions which would be useful for economic impact analysis were too complicated for both the interviewees and the interviewers, who were not trained as professional enumerators on socio-economic surveys (unlike the staff of the National Statistical Office, whom we had initially planned to employ as our enumerators). This resulted in many questions not being answered. Time constraints also prevented us form checking and correcting answers. Future surveys on the socio-economic impact of HIV/AIDS need to correct these deficiencies.

Furthermore, future research on this or similar topics should include sample cases in private hospitals and other hospitals outside the jurisdiction of the Ministry of Public Health (for example, military and university hospitals) to present a complete picture. A comparative study of urban households would also be useful to ascertain whether rural-urban differences exist in the economic impact of HIV/AIDS-related deaths. Because our data are mainly cross-sectional and retrospective, data bias from an inability to recall past information may exist in our analysis results. A longitudinal study of affected households from the time an adult member becomes ill with HIV/AIDS until the time of death should be attempted to obtain more accurate information on the impact of an adult HIV/AIDS-related death on a household's socio-economic condition.

References

Bloom, David E., and Serry Glied. 1993. 'Who Is Bearing the Cost of the AIDS Epidemic in Asia?' In David E. Bloom and Joyce V. Lyons, eds., *Economic Implications of AIDS in Asia.* New Delhi, India: United Nations Development Programme.

Gertler, Paul J. 1993. 'AIDS and the Family: Economic Consequences and Policy Responses in Asia'. Study on the Economic Implications of the HIV/AIDS Epidemic in Selected DMCs: Inception Workshop, Manila, Philippines, September 8–10.

Kreniske, John. n.d. 'HIV Transmission and Economic Development'. New York: Columbia University, HIV Center for Clinical and Behavioral Studies.

Krongkaew, Medhi, Pranee Tinakorn and Suphat Suphachalasai. 1992. 'Rural Poverty in Thailand: Policy Issues and Responses'. *Asian Development Review* (Asian Development Bank) 10(1): 199–225.

MOPH (Ministry of Public Health). 1994a. *National AIDS Programme: Progress and Programme Update.* Bangkok, Thailand.

———— 1994b. *Policy on AIDS Prevention and Control.* Bangkok, Thailand.

———— 1995. 'HIV/AIDS Situation in Thailand: Update 31 January'.

Thant, Myo. 1993. 'The Economic Implications of AIDS in Southeast Asia: Equity Considerations'. In David E. Bloom and Joyce V. Lyons, eds., *Economic Implications of AIDS in Asia.* New Delhi, India: United Nations Development Programme.

4

The Household Impact of Adult Morbidity and Mortality: Some Implications of the Potential Epidemic of AIDS in India

Alaka M. Basu, Devendra B. Gupta and
Geetanjali Krishna

Introduction

Although the number of identified cases of full-blown AIDS in
India is still small—as of 1 January 1995 1,017 cases had been
reported to the Ministry of Health and Family Welfare—all indirect estimates (National AIDS Control Organization (NACO)
1993) suggest that this figure is a gross under-representation of
the actual number of AIDS sufferers in the country, which health
experts believe to be between 5,000 and 10,000. It is estimated
that some 2–3 million people are currently HIV-positive, which
implies a massive increase in AIDS cases in coming years and,
given our knowledge about the changing rate at which the virus
spreads through a population, this reservoir of cases is growing
rapidly. World Health Organization (WHO) estimates suggest that
India currently had about 1.6 million HIV-positive cases in 1993
and 20,000 cases of full-blown AIDS, and that by the end of the
century the number of HIV-positive cases will have risen to between 5 and 10 million (NACO 1993).

These are grim numbers, even if the large size of India's
population is taken into account. They are even more menacing
given the limited resources available to deal with the problem.

However, while the country and the world at large are aware of the enormity of the problem, a reading of the literature reveals less awareness of the need to deal with two separate dimensions of it. The first dimension, and that which current policy is most explicitly taking into account, is the need to slow down the spread of the virus and to reduce as many risk factors as possible; but given the number of people already believed to be infected, a second dimension of the AIDS problem needs to receive much more attention from policy makers than it has to date. This is the need for a strategy to deal with the inevitable impact of the disease on those currently infected and their families and on those who will become infected, albeit at a slower rate if preventive strategies are effective. Moreover, when policy makers do consider this aspect of the problem, they do so more often as a justification for pumping more resources into prevention than for increasing the allocation for interventions that mitigate the adverse impacts of the disease.

Even when policy makers do show specific concern about the potential and actual impact of AIDS, this concern is usually limited in its scope. For example, India's national AIDS control strategy does mention strategies to cope with the effects of AIDS, but these strategies are almost entirely concerned with two possible impacts: the psychological impact of the disease that often results in the social ostracization of sufferers and their families, and the impact in terms of the high costs of medical treatment. Thus, proposed strategies focus on providing counselling services, and on upgrading the health sector to meet the new demands that will be made on it.

While both these impacts are substantial and cannot be ignored, other economic and social costs are equally devastating and are not yet being seriously addressed. These costs are unique to AIDS because of the unique profile of those affected by HIV and AIDS, who are predominantly of working age and have a relatively high proportion of economic, social and emotional dependants. The incapacitation and death of such a person imposes costs that go well beyond the reduced welfare of the person actually infected.

Recently, investigators have attempted to estimate some of the economic costs of an AIDS epidemic for the nation and for different sectors of the economy, based largely on studies sponsored by the United Nations Development Programme (UNDP) (see for example Bloom and Lyons 1993). While this is a necessary exercise, one should note that AIDS carries with it other relatively hidden costs that are potentially even more drastic. These are the costs to the households of AIDS sufferers, costs that, in developing countries at least, such households themselves must currently bear. If the expected rise in AIDS infection and mortality does occur, affected households will find such costs increasingly difficult to meet. This points to the need for an urgent review of current strategies to help individuals and their families cope with the consequences of the disease.

At the same time, as has already been mentioned, the resources required for such 'coping interventions' are likely to be woefully limited. Therefore the authorities will have to establish priorities if such interventions are not to be spread too thinly. Dealing adequately with all possible impacts of the disease on a household and on all affected households is impossible. What is needed is thus a much greater understanding of the most important impacts of AIDS-related morbidity and mortality on households, as well as the influence of socio-economic differences on such impacts. While health experts recognize the differences in risk that exist and the consequent need to tailor preventive strategies to specific risk situations, they are much less aware of the implications of differential impacts of the disease.

While such recognition of the heterogeneity of populations is implicit in attempts to distinguish categories such as the poor or women as more vulnerable, income and gender are only two of the possible classifications in a country as demographically, socially, economically, and culturally diverse as India. For example, the cultural context is especially important. Not only does it often define, or at least strongly influence, behavioural propensities, it also affects the outcomes of such behaviour in ways that standard microeconomic models cannot capture. Caste is a simple example. Several very clear differences in economic behaviour are sufficiently institutionalized to be identified with caste even if they have an original material basis.[1]

This study has one major and one relatively minor focus. The overall focus is on the hypothesis that even in the general community (as opposed to in certain well-defined high-risk groups, such as commercial sex workers or drug injectors), there is much socio-economic variation, which in turn translates into variation in AIDS-related variables. The major focus is on demonstrating such variation in the impact of an eventually fatal illness such as AIDS on the sufferers' households. In the process, the study tentatively identifies some of the more vulnerable groups in terms of both impact and the ability to cope with this impact. The minor focus is on the variations in the risk of acquiring HIV, both because of variation in the level of ignorance about the illness and because of knowing or unknowing variation in high-risk behaviour.

All these hypotheses are examined here using the results of a pilot field study in Delhi. The study focuses on the possible impact on households of a rise in the morbidity and mortality of men aged between nineteen and thirty-nine. Became the study is limited to mortality from any cause and not just AIDS, it is a description of the minimum impact of a rise in AIDS-related morbidity and mortality; that is, AIDS itself has adverse consequences in addition to those common to adult deaths in general. While the bulk of the information about the impact is therefore somewhat

---

1. The labour force participation of women is one such behaviour. The lower castes have traditionally had, and continue to have, more economically active women than many of the upper castes, even when poverty levels are controlled. In turn, in the present context, this cultural propensity should influence the ability of lower-caste households to cope with a male death in ways that are profoundly different from those of a higher-caste household of similar economic means because of the differential impact of the death. At the same time, the lower castes, partly because of their longer history of diffidence, face other costs that make them more vulnerable to adult illness. For example, they may be less able to take advantage of modern medical services, even when these are in principle free. The implications of serious illness are therefore correspondingly more severe. They are also more severe because of women's traditional care-giving roles. If women's income is crucial to household survival, as it often is in poor lower-caste households, then the removal of such women from the labour force to care for the ill will increase household poverty.

hypothetical, it is complemented with case studies of households that had lost an adult member in the last two years preceding the survey.

In addition, while primary respondents in this study are male, we recognize that women will make up an increasing proportion of all AIDS sufferers, and that the economic and social impact on households of a rise in AIDS-related female morbidity and mortality can be as profound as, and sometimes even more profound than, that of AIDS-related male morbidity and mortality. To support this recognition empirically, we also did a series of case studies of households that had lost an adult female in the last two years.

Data and Field Methodology

This is an exploratory study. In addition to describing some key findings, it has also tried to develop a methodology suitable for replication on a wider scale. In the process we discovered several approaches that work and some that do not. This section also discusses the latter to inform others about possible problems in research of this nature.

The study reached two main methodological conclusions. The first is that on a subject as sensitive and complicated as AIDS, a proper understanding will be possible only if the large-scale survey method is complemented by collecting qualitative data, not just in the course of the survey, but also through a few in-depth anthropological studies. The second is that while an awareness of the disease and an understanding of high-risk behaviour requires one to focus primarily on AIDS as a separate infection (as was indeed done during the field survey) where the impact of the infection is concerned, one needs to develop more general analytical strategies. This is partly because there are as yet too few identified cases of AIDS to allow one to draw generalizations about the potential impact through an analysis of these cases alone.

We have used two methods to overcome this handicap. First, we focus on the hypothetical case. That is, we try to understand the economic impact on households of a major illness and possible death from this illness in a hypothetical way by getting respondents to visualize the possible impact of themselves being thus incapacitated. However, being fully aware of the biases inherent in such a hypothetical approach, biases that later turned out to be not as serious as we had initially expected, we supplemented this information with a few case studies of households that had actually experienced the death of an adult member.

The second modification was the use of major illness and death in general as a proxy for AIDS-related morbidity and mortality. This was decided after much pre-testing, which suggested that not only were respondents unable to relate our hypothetical questions to AIDS as a specific disease (sometimes because they had not even heard of the disease), they often objected to being asked to even visualize themselves in the situation of having such a disease. In the India cultural context, not only do norms govern polite behaviour, people also have strong feelings about questions being ill-intentioned if they relate to unpleasant possible events. For example, asking a man to think of himself as an AIDS patient can be misconstrued as implying that he will or should get AIDS.

We thus felt that using severe illness as a proxy for AIDS infection was a suitable middle path because it elicited better co-operation from the respondents. We also thought it was justifiable because AIDS patients do not suffer from some unique symptoms and outcomes of HIV infection. The immediate cause of suffering and death is some other recognizable illness. Moreover, this study was concerned with the economic impact of AIDS on households, as opposed to the social and psychological impacts, which do depend on the nature of the illness and the cause of death.[2]

The questionnaire used in the survey was developed after detailed discussions among the principal investigators and the field and other staff involved in the study. It went through an extended round of pre-testing in the field among men of varied socio-economic and cultural backgrounds. However, given the shortage of time available for the study, even after this pre-testing many

---

2. The social and psychological impacts can, of course, impinge on the economic functioning of households, so in this sense we are underestimating the potential household impact of an AIDS epidemic. Nevertheless, our findings indicate that the gravity of the situation as well as the variations in impact are reasonably well captured by studying severe illness and death in a productive adult even without identifying HIV as the underlying cause.

of the questions were left open-ended as we did not think it possible to anticipate all possible responses. In any case, we wanted to introduce a qualitative element into the data collection, so interviewers were encouraged to record verbatim the additional things that respondents had to say during the interview. This qualitative information has been a great help in interpreting the quantitative findings from the study.

The survey respondents form a representative sample of men in the selected age-group in Delhi. In other words, the sample drew from all parts of the city, from slums to upper-income neighbourhoods. The original sample frame that was used to select the respondents was a larger recent survey of the city. We identified all households in this earlier study sample that had men aged nineteen to thirty-nine and chose a quarter of these for interviews. We ended up with a sub-sample of 600 households. In the end we interviewed 500 men. The rest were unavailable for a variety of reasons, including having moved elsewhere or being unwilling to respond. Of the 500 interviews, eleven were rejected as being improperly conducted and five were excluded as they were largely incomplete. This left us with a final sample size of 484.

In addition to the survey, we did a series of case studies of households that had actually experienced an adult death in the last two years. Our larger sample frame had sixty-two such cases, and we did detailed case studies of thirty-three of these so as to understand some of the costs to the household of the adult's death, and the coping strategies employed. An interesting aspect of these case studies is that they included ten cases in which the dead household member had been female. From this group we were able to draw some tentative conclusions about the costs to households of an adult female contracting a serious illness and eventually dying, something that strategies to meet the forthcoming AIDS epidemic will have to keep in mind.

While the overall response to the survey was extremely satisfactory, some of the questions were more difficult to ask than others. Naturally, the questions about sexual behaviour were the most awkward to elicit responses to, and this probably explains in part the low level of risky sexual activity recorded in the survey. Note, however, that in most cases where answers were suspect, the respondent had not been interviewed in complete privacy. The presence of an onlooker known to the respondent, especially when this onlooker happened to be a parent of the respondent, naturally caused some difficulty but was often difficult to prevent, particularly in the city's poorer sections.

One way around some of this awkwardness was for us to ask respondents about the behaviour of their peers rather than their own. We did this and obtained much better responses than we got for the sexual proclivities of the respondents themselves, but we believe that even these are underestimates. We also tried to distinguish between high-risk lifestyles and high-risk behaviours.

Some respondents had problems with the hypothetical questions and needed a lot of time to be able to articulate their role in the family economy and the impact of the possible marginalization of this role, but on the whole this turned out to be a relatively easy section to canvas, although we would suggest several modifications if the survey were replicated elsewhere.

The problems of collecting socio-economic information through household surveys are adequately covered in the literature and we will not repeat the findings here, except to say that income always poses the greatest challenge (for a brief but comprehensive coverage of this issue see Basu 1992). We used several measures of economic status and cross-checked these with each other for internal consistency. These measures included the kind of work the respondent did, the ownership of assets, expenditure patterns, and detailed questions on income from a variety of sources.

Results

The following sections present survey findings on high risk behaviours and on the potential impact of adult mortality, with emphasis on the second issue.

Awareness of AIDS

NACO has become the conduit for a massive information, education, and communication campaign to make people aware of AIDS. This campaign involves various government departments as well as a host of non-governmental agencies and individuals with the skill to develop information packages.[3] The result is that while information, education, and communication activities accounted for about 15 per cent of Government of India funds for the National AIDS Control Programme in 1987–92, this figure rose to 34 per cent in 1992–3 (NACO 1993).

How effective has this information, education, and communication strategy been? According to several small AIDS-awareness studies conducted by various voluntary organizations, the general public is still quite ignorant of and complacent about the way in which HIV and AIDS may impinge on their lives. Not only is people's information about the disease incomplete and inaccurate, there is a widespread confidence (common to most other parts of the world) that only 'others' are at risk of contracting the disease (NACO 1993).

Our own data tell a slightly different story. Of course, like the other studies so far, this is partly because it is based on a specific sample that may not be representative of the situation in the country as a whole. Because the survey was conducted in Delhi, one would expect general awareness about the disease to be relatively high given that Delhi's population is exposed to a barrage of information about the AIDS threat, both through the mass media and through agents working at a more interpersonal level. At the same time, the socio-economic profile of Delhi's population is considerably better than the national average. This should also increase greatly the access to and receptivity of the city's people to the various information, education, and communication messages about AIDS that they are bombarded with.

At a superficial level, the overall figure of 81 per cent (see Table 1) for the proportion of the survey sample that has heard of AIDS is quite respectable, but it becomes less comforting when one takes into account all the above-mentioned advantages of the survey population. It becomes still less reassuring when one looks

3.   Universities and schools have been active in spreading the message of low-risk behaviour, national television and radio broadcast information, and employers are helped to spread knowledge and information about preventive strategies among their employees. Funds are available relatively easily to individuals and institutions committed to developing effective AIDS-awareness programmes for dissemination through a range of media.

at socio-economic differentials in such awareness levels. And it becomes even less satisfactory when one finds out exactly what people know about AIDS and the socio-economic differences in such knowledge.

Table 1 presents some of the socio-economic variation in the awareness of the existence of AIDS. The economic situation of the household seems to exert a consistently strong effect on such awareness with all differences being in the expected direction. Economic status as measured by income, by quality of housing material, and by asset ownership is clearly related to AIDS awareness: the better off the household, the more likely it is that the respondent will have heard about AIDS. In addition, Table 1 shows that educational differences in awareness levels are also high and demonstrate that the illiterate respondent is completely cut off from many important sources of information.

The social constraints on acquiring information about the illness seem to be less consistent. For example, the kind of family the respondent belongs to seems to matter little in determining his level of awareness, but his marital status seems to matter much more. Respondents who have never been married are much more likely to have heard about the infection than those who have been married. While one could speculate that this result is due partly to the younger age (and therefore perhaps also higher educational level) of the sample of unmarried men, this does not seem to be a complete explanation if one looks at differences in awareness by age, where the results show that older respondents seem to have as much knowledge as the youngest group in the sample. The difference in awareness by marital status seems more likely to be the result of the different social worlds inhabited by the married and the unmarried. The latter tend to have more interaction with the outside world and, by extension, greater exposure to information and knowledge.

As for the sources of this information, Table 2 highlights the overwhelming role of television. The major influence of this medium reflects the extent to which it has entered Delhi households, even those that are poor by any other criterion, as well as the appeal of this medium in general, so that even those who do not themselves own a television set are regularly exposed

Table 1: Socio-economic Differentials in the Awareness of AIDS

Socio-economic status of male respondents	Percentage aware of AIDS	
	Respondents	Women in respondents' households
Total sample	81	40
Age (years)		
19–24	87	35
25–34	76	42
35+	87	48
Household income per month (Rs)		
Upto 3,000	66	23
3,001–7,000	87	36
7,001+	97	66
Type of house[a]		
Kucha	39	0
Semi-pucca	68	10
Pucca	84	43
Car ownership		
Yes	91	92
No	80	35
TV ownership		
Yes	85	44
No	65	13
No. of years of education		
None	39	5
1–7	71	17
8–12	81	31
13+	96	66

(Contd)

Table 1: *(Contd)*

Socio-economic status of male respondents	Percentage aware of AIDS	
	Respondents	Women in respondents' households
Occupation		
Professional and white-collar workers	94	52
Self-employed	82	47
Manual/unskilled	68	23
Unemployed	89	46
Marital status		
Ever married	74	37
Never married	91	46
Household structure[b]		
Nuclear	79	41
Stem	84	31
Joint	82	48
Caste and religion		
Hindu upper caste	88	49
Hindu middle caste	79	35
Scheduled caste	67	15
Muslim	66	22
Other Religions	90	62
Region of origin		
North India excluding Delhi	73	37
Delhi	86	41
Rest of India	86	45

a. Kuccha: constructed of temporary materials. Semi-pucca: partly constructed of temporary materials. Pucca: solid structure.
b. Nuclear: single person, married couple, one parent with or without unmarried children. Stem: two conjugal units of different generations with or without unmarried children. Joint: two or more conjugal units of the same generation with or without married units of other generations.
Source: Authors' survey.

Table 2: Socio-economic Differentials in the Source of Knowledge about AIDS

Socio-economic status	*Percentage aware of AIDS through*					
	Radio	T.V.	Newspaper/ magazine	Posters	Government and community workers	Friends/ relatives
Total sample	28	83	65	31	13	29
Age (years)						
19–24	30	84	64	31	10	33
25–34	30	85	68	32	10	28
35+	13	72	50	25	15	18
No. of years of education						
None	32	53	16	5	5	47
1–7	15	63	27	29	12	27
8–12	28	82	59	26	10	32
13+	32	94	87	40	17	24
Household income per month (Rs)						
Up to 3,000	19	69	39	22	3	36
3,001–7,000	23	87	67	35	14	29
7,001+	35	95	81	38	14	20
Occupation						
Professionals and white-collar workers	30	87	74	38	20	30
Self-employed	22	93	70	27	13	20
Manual/ unskilled	27	70	45	30	8	34
Unemployed	37	91	80	29	10	27

Source: Authors' survey.

to television programmes through the community nature of television watching. For example, although 27 per cent of the sample households did not possess a television set, only 12 per cent of the households said they did not watch television.

Table 2 also reveals the declining role of radio, but this finding may be specific to the city of Delhi, or at least to a large metropolis in general. Evidence is available that shows that radio continues to play an important entertainment and educational role in the more remote parts of the country and among those who are relatively deprived economically.

The written word is naturally elitist in its outreach when it comes through the newspaper or magazine. What is surprising is how limited its effect is when presented in the form of the numerous posters and slogans that dot the city's public spaces. This is not a function of illiteracy alone. Even the literate (as well as the relatively highly-educated) respondents seem to have little faith in such mass poster campaigns as an important source of knowledge and information about AIDS.

What about the finer details of AIDS awareness? Merely knowing that an illness exists is not enough. To be able to modify their behaviour appropriately, people need to know how the virus is transmitted from one person to another, the most effective forms of behaviour that help in avoiding infection, and so on. In addition, people require information on these matters if they are to organize their lives in a way that does not impinge on the social and emotional well-being of victims of the illness, that is, they need information so that they can deal with people with AIDS and understand that they should not be discriminated against, and so on.

Once again, a survey conducted in Delhi is not a representative test of the constituents of AIDS awareness, but it does provide a good example of how even the residents of a city as advanced and privileged as the capital of the country are beset by misinformation, and how large socio-economic variations exist in the extent of knowledge.

Table 3 looks at the level of misinformation about the modes of transmission of AIDS. The drop in awareness levels compared to Table 1 is sharp and does not reflect well on the AIDS aware-

Table 3: Socio-economic Differentials in the Awareness of How AIDS is Spread

Socio-economic status of male respondents	Percentage who think that AIDS is spread by						
	Hand-shaking	Hug-ging	Kiss-ing	Sharing cothes	Sharing eating utensils	Step-ping on urine/ stools	Mos-quito/ fly/bed bug bites
Total sample	61	59	46	55	53	52	50
Marital status							
Ever married	49	49	37	46	45	44	43
Never married	77	73	58	67	64	63	59
No. of years of education							
None	5	5	0	5	5	0	5
1–7	27	29	22	25	24	22	24
8–12	57	54	43	53	51	52	47
13+	81	79	61	71	69	66	65
Caste and religion							
Hindu upper caste	72	69	50	60	58	56	51
Hindu middle caste	53	50	40	46	45	46	48
Scheduled caste	38	40	31	36	31	33	28
Muslim	43	48	33	33	38	33	33
Other religions	64	71	53	57	61	46	53
Region of origin							
North India excluding Delhi	43	43	30	40	37	20	40
Delhi	71	67	56	64	62	61	55
Rest of India	77	89	56	61	61	50	61
Household structure							
Nuclear	62	60	48	56	53	53	50

(Contd)

Table 3: *(Contd)*

Socio-economic status of male respondents	Percentage who think that AIDS is spread by						
	Hand-shaking	Hug-ging	Kiss-ing	Sharing cothes	Sharing eating utensils	Step-ping on urine/ stools	Mos-quito/ fly/bed bug bites
Stem	54	54	40	52	47	48	42
Joint	61	58	42	54	52	48	49
Occupation							
Professionals and white collar workers	72	70	56	63	62	62	59
Self–employed	72	70	57	69	66	62	65
Manual/unskilled	37	39	28	34	35	35	32
Unemployed	75	64	49	59	54	56	47
Household income per month (Rs)							
0–1,000	40	30	30	40	40	40	30
1,001–3,000	42	43	31	35	35	35	32
3,001–7,000	63	60	45	53	51	51	47
7,001+	75	75	56	67	63	60	63
Type of house							
Kuccha	0	0	0	0	0	0	0
Semi–pucca	47	47	34	41	34	38	44
Pucca	65	63	49	59	56	56	52
TV ownership							
Yes	67	65	50	60	58	56	55
No	39	39	28	36	31	36	28
Car ownership							
Yes	79	94	55	76	76	65	69
No	61	58	46	54	52	52	48

Source: Authors' survey.

ness campaign that has the stated goal of letting people know what kinds of behaviour they need not be scared of. If only about half of those who know that AIDS is a disease also know that it cannot be spread by activities such as hugging or sharing clothes and utensils, then the remaining half is not likely to behave sympathetically toward the carriers of HIV infection. Perhaps the fault lies in the use of the wrong media for such information. Posters and pamphlets are an important part of the current strategy to disseminate accurate information about AIDS, but as Table 2 shows, posters and pamphlets are low on the list of important sources of AIDS information.

Socio-economic differences in the extent of such misinformation are consistent with the hypothesis that knowledge depends on economic factors such as income, but also depends on a number of socio-cultural factors, such as age, marital status, and state of origin. The young, unmarried male from Delhi is much more correctly informed than his more conservative, older, married counterpart from other parts of northern India.

High-Risk Behaviour

Unsafe heterosexual sex is believed to be the most common mode of transmission of HIV infection in India (NACO 1993 estimates that about 75 per cent of India's AIDS cases were transmitted through this route). However, blood transfusion and the sharing of unsterilized needles are also important carriers of the infection, currently estimated as being responsible for the transmission of 12 and 6 per cent respectively of all cases (NACO 1993), and may be proportionately more important among some groups of the population.

Injections given in a normal medical setting should not ordinarily be an important source of HIV infection but this may change as the total amount of infection in the country increases. Injections may also be an important vehicle of HIV transmission among certain categories of the general population (not to say among specific high-risk groups such as drug users). In particular, one would expect the combination of poverty and ignorance to increase the risk of acquiring the HIV infection through the use of unsterilized needles, aided by the increasingly common tendency to demand and be given injections for a range of illnesses, even when they are not called for.[4] Several studies have demonstrated the tendency to equate injections with treatment. The same studies have shown that the private health sector is the bigger culprit in this case than the public health sector and that the poor are the bigger victims. For example, one study in the Jalgaon district of Maharashtra (Duggal and Amin 1989) found that in its sample, 72 per cent of diarrhoea patients, 67 per cent of those with coughs and colds, 87 per cent of malaria patients, 61 per cent of those with measles, and 76 per cent of patients with heart ailments received injections. In our study, more than 60 per cent of respondent households had members who had needed an injection or an intravenous drip in the last two years (and even this may be an underestimate), and in only about half of these cases did the respondent know with certainty that the medical staff had used a disposable needle. (Whether so-called disposable needles are ever completely disposed of or are repackaged and find their way back into hospitals or drug stores is another issue and one that has been a matter of some concern in the popular press in recent times.)

These are high levels of injection use and high levels of risk by any reckoning. They become even more worrying when one tries to disaggregate the population to identify the groups most at risk. For example, our study found that the proportion of disposable needles used rises sharply as income rises, which is what one would have expected. What is more disheartening is that so many of the poor do not even know the difference. Not only does this finding reflect their greater exploitability, it also reveals that they have not thought it necessary to find out if they got a sterile needle. The state must honour such implicit faith in the medical system through both the public and private health sectors, quite apart from trying to increase patients' awareness of these issues (see Ramasubban 1991).

The giving and taking of infected blood is believed to be another important source of HIV transmission, but overall levels

4. For a discussion of the value attached to injections in developing countries see Wyatt 1984.

of such blood exchanges were small in the sample used for this study. The process may have risks associated with the needle used aside from the risk associated with contaminated blood. By this reasoning, blood donors as well as transfusees are at risk. It is revealing that once again, ignorance about the kind of needle used for a blood transaction is so rampant: 31 per cent of donors and as many as 65 per cent of recipients did not know what kind of needle had been used.[5]

One comes now to high-risk behaviours, which are under the direct control of individuals. However, unlike in the case of the clearly higher vulnerability of the poorer segments of society to indirect risks of transmission, relative risks cannot be so neatly categorized. Of course, this is partly because data on sexual behaviour are not so easy to come by in a one-shot survey. But even when respondents are reporting on the behaviour of their peers, whatever little pattern is apparent in such risk behaviour would seem to indicate that the better off are more vulnerable than poorer groups (Table 4). However, this seems to be more than balanced by the reverse socio-economic differential in the practice of safe sex: the economically better off are much more likely to have 'friends' who use condoms during their visits to prostitutes.

Premarital and extramarital sexual activity similarly display no consistent patterns, but other small-scale intensive studies suggest that our figures are underestimates of the actual amount of such activity. In any case, the importance of this factor as a mechanism for spreading HIV infection is not clear. Most such activity seems to be monogamous. Even in the study, most of the respondents who admitted to having a relationship outside their marriage clarified that it had been in the past or was with one woman only.

Thus the connection between poverty and HIV/AIDS is not, at least at the first sight, as obvious as that between poverty and poor health in general. In many parts of the world, at least during the initial stages of an AIDS epidemic, the better-off groups in the population seem to be more susceptible to the infection than

5.   There is also an interesting demonstration of relative power in this situation. The giver (the blood donor) is in a much better position to demand conditions (a sterile needle) from the health care system than the taker (the blood receiver).

Table 4: Some Indicators of Lifestyle-Related Risks (Percentage of respondents)

Socio-economic status of male respondents	Smoke	Drink	Know drug users	Have friends who visit prostitutes	Whose friends visit prostitutes and use condoms	Visit prostitutes	Have a current sexual relationship	Travel out of town for work
Total sample	53	38	9	6	20	0.6	5	13
Household income per month (Rs)								
0–3,000	58	42	11	3	1	0.5	5	7
3,001–7,000	49	38	8	7	18	0	2	14
7,001+	48	30	8	8	27	2.0	9	21
Occupation								
Professional and white-collar workers	50	45	6	8	33	0	4	24
Self-employed	47	35	7	8	33	2.0	4	16
Manual/unskilled	61	44	11	4	0	0.5	4	7
Unemployed	44	11	15	4	25	0	8	3
No. of years of education								
None	76	55	60	2	0	0	0	8
1–7	62	47	17	7	17	0	5	3
8–12	51	13	8	5	23	1.0	5	9
13+	45	28	6	7	27	0	6	22

(Contd)

Table 4: (*Contd*)

Socio-economic status of male respondents	Smoke	Drink	Know drug users	Have friends who visit prostitutes	Whose friends visit prostitures and use condoms	Visit prostitutes	Have a current sexual relationship	Travel out of town for work
Age (years)								
19–24	39	22	10	7	27	0	6	9
25–34	58	43	9	5	17	1.0	5	15
35+	56	61	9	2	0	0	0	15
Marital status								
Ever married	60	48	8	4	15	0.7	2	14
Never married	41	21	10	8	25	0.5	9	11
Household structure								
Nuclear	55	41	10	7	26	0.7	6	14
Stem	48	37	10	1	0	0	2	10
Joint	49	32	7	6	12	0	5	16
Others	53	26	10	5	0	3.0	5	5
Caste and religion								
Hindu upper caste	51	36	8	6	28	1.0	5	17
Hindu middle caste	59	44	9	6	9	0.7	4	15
Scheduled caste	56	54	6	8	25	0	5	7
Muslim	56	3	22	3	33	0	6	0
Other religions	32	23	6	3	20	0	3	13

Source: Authors' survey

poorer groups because they can afford the kind of high-risk life-style that increases their susceptibility. However, this conclusion leads to a false sense of complacency about AIDS in poor countries and poor households. All available evidence indicates that the profile of AIDS sufferers is changing rapidly, with increasing numbers of cases among those nations and individuals least able to prevent or deal with the spread of the disease. Moreover, the connection of poverty with AIDS is more disastrous when one looks at the impact of AIDS as opposed to the determinants of infection.

A brief case study of one of the survey respondents helps illustrate the higher risks some categories of people face. Nem Singh is married and was the only truck driver in our sample. He admits to having irregular relationships with women other than his wife. He has visited commercial sex workers and has not used any protection when doing so. After such visits he has occasionally experienced difficulties in urinating. He does not use any protection during sexual relations with his wife because they want another son (they already have four children). He does not know about AIDS.

The global picture today is also of a massive spread of HIV and AIDS among the more disadvantaged. Two features of disadvantage seem to be important: absolutely poverty and social and economic inequality. Other socio-cultural, and perhaps biological, factors are also implicated in the spread of AIDS: in particular, there is some suggestion in the literature that poverty and malnutrition increase people's biological susceptibility to the infection (see for example Head 1992), and more than a suggestion that poverty significantly reduces the length of the virus incubation period (see for example Ainsworth and Over 1994; Gilks 1993).

The Household Impact of Adult Morbidity and Mortality

While the economic impact on a society or a country of a massive rise in adult morbidity and mortality of the kind predicted for the AIDS epidemic in India is rightfully a matter for concern, information about sectoral or societal impacts cannot be used to derive the impact of such illness and death on households, especially in poor countries with high levels of unemployment and under-employment. This section therefore explores some of the possible economic impacts of AIDS on households through more direct information obtained from actual households. It proposes two hypotheses. First, that the death of an adult of productive age inflicts a cost on the household that cannot be captured by any simple measures such as loss of income. Therefore, if the projected rise in HIV/AIDS in India does take place, one would expect an increase in household suffering that the current research and policy on the health and mortality of children and older people has not even begun to address. The significant factor here is adult mortality, whether or not the immediate underlying cause is AIDS. However, because AIDS-related morbidity and mortality is likely to have many additional ramifications that mortality from other causes may not have (including an economic impact generated by discrimination), our findings are a description of the minimum impact that AIDS mortality would have on households.

The second hypothesis is more interesting. This states that the costs to a household of the death of an adult member vary considerably, as does its ability to meet these costs. Such variation obviously exists along standard socio-economic lines, and poverty is of course a major determinant of the way AIDS will affect households. However, to understand fully the variation in the impact of mortality, and therefore to devise more targeted strategies to neutralize this impact will require an analysis that goes beyond standard indices like income to include a number of social and cultural attributes that are less amenable to change, and that have a strong bearing on the way households respond to crises.

Very broadly, the direct household costs of an HIV/AIDS infection are incurred at two different times, first, during the active stages of the infection, and second, after the patient's inevitable death. The costs in the first period can be of two kinds: medical and non-medical. The non-medical costs consists of the indirect expenses associated with ill health, such as special foods, transport, the opportunity costs of the care-givers' time, and the direct costs of the lost income of the sick household member. All estimates suggest that the last of these is the most important in terms of both amount and relevance (see for example Bloom and

Glied 1993; UNDP 1992), largely because it extends into both the time periods mentioned. The direct impact of lost income is the primary focus of this study, and we devote relatively little space to the possible impact of the medical expenses associated with AIDS as a separate category.

Overall Impact

Medical Care Given that this is a hypothetical study, arriving at estimates of the real costs of an infection such as AIDS to different households is difficult. However, we do have estimates of the medical costs to society from other sources such as Bloom and Glied (1993), and by any reckoning these are large because the drugs used to treat AIDS are extremely expensive, and because the period during which the patient exhibits symptoms can be long. In the present context, it is important to determine the household's role in meeting these costs. To determine this, extrapolations must be made from information about the role of households in meeting medical costs in general, with the understanding that even if the household's responsibility for treating AIDS patients remains proportionately the same as its responsibility for treating ill health in general, the absolute costs of this responsibility will be enormous.[6]

An indirect way of ascertaining the household's economic responsibility for health care is to look at how much responsibility other agencies, such as the state, can assume. First, there is the government's health care system. This has been described elsewhere (for current position, see the Ministry of Health and Family Welfare's latest yearbook), and here we will reiterate only that in principle, government-funded health services are available to everyone, have no user charges, and cover the full range of preventive and curative health care. The reality is, of course, somewhat different. Access to health care varies depending on a number of socio-economic indicators, and is reflected in a great

---

6. At the same time, as Feachem and others (1991) point out, the household share of medical expenditure varies depending on the ailment; thus remember that this section offers only broad generalizations.

variation in user rates across location and for different kinds of health problems.[7]

The private health sector is also vast and widespread, but its quality is uneven. What is surprising about the private system is how much family health care it accounts for. According to Berman (1991), of all expenditures on health care, 60 per cent is borne by households, and Nandraj (1994) believes that the private health sector accounts for 4 to 5 per cent of India's gross domestic product.

As Table 5 shows, we found that only a small proportion of households have access to any kind of insurance, including medical insurance. In addition, the holding of insurance varies sharply with differences in class. Table 5 also shows who actually bore the costs of the most recent hospitalization in the household. The household's role in meeting these expenses could not be displayed any more starkly: either the respondent or his family members seem to have virtually exclusive responsibility for meeting the costs of hospital medical care. No wonder Duggal and Amin (1989) have estimated that household expenditure on health care is four to five times the level of state expenditure on health care. If households have to bear the major responsibility for the costs of AIDS treatment, one can easily envisage the pauperization of households that experience the illness. The state's responsibility for providing efficient and cheap medical care cannot be overemphasized.

Social Security　How important is the role of the state in helping households meet some of the enormous burden that illness or premature death imposes on them? Although total and proportional expenditure on social security by the government has grown steadily over the years, there does not as yet exist any comprehensive social security system: that is, one for which all individuals are eligible. Thus if the projected rise in AIDS incidence does

---

7.　For example, estimates indicate that as of 1990–1, the government has spent 67 per cent of its health care resources on the urban sector (which has only 26 per cent of the population) and 33 per cent on the rural sector (Reddy 1994). In terms of per capita allocation, the urban sector received 5.8 times more than the rural sector.

Table 5: Household Susceptibility to Risk: Households' Insurance Status

Socio-economic status of male respondents	Percentage of sample with insurance	Who pays the premium			Who paid last hospital bills				
		Self	Employer	Other	Self	Other family members	Loan	Employer	Other
Total sample	21	83	8	6	52	29	2	9	5
Age (years)									
19–24	11	78	5	17	29	51	2	11	4
25–34	25	85	7	4	59	21	2	7	5
35+	33	80	13	0	72	11	0	17	0
Marital status									
Ever married	23	84	7	4	63	18	3	7	5
Never married	17	81	9	9	26	52	0	13	4
No. of years of education									
None	2	100	0	0	53	11	5	16	11
1–7	12	86	14	0	48	28	8	8	4
8–12	14	87	6	6	55	30	1	6	5
13+	38	81	8	8	48	32	0	12	3
Occupation									
Professional and white collar workers	42	78	16	2	54	27	0	14	4
Self-employed	28	91	0	6	54	30	2	7	2
Manual/ unskilled	8	93	0	7	52	25	4	8	5
Unemployed	8	60	0	40	39	39	0	9	9
Household income per month (Rs)									
0–3,000	9	70	11	6	21	7	2	3	2
3,001–7,000	22	87	5	2	53	33	0	4	5
7,001+	40	82	9	9	44	35	0	19	2

Source: Authors' survey.

take place, this marginal role of the state will have tragic consequences for households' ability to cope.

Table 5 indicates that only 21 per cent of respondents have access to any kind of formal insurance. Low as this figure is, it is tremendously high compared to secondary evidence on the situation in the country in general (see Basu, Gupta, and Krishna 1994). Moreover, employers paid for only 8 per cent of policies. The respondents themselves bore the costs of an overwhelming proportion of premium payments (83 per cent).

The other kind of employer-provided social security operates through such schemes as pensions and gratuities paid primarily upon retirement, but also often paid upon disability or death, both of which would increase with the onset of an AIDS epidemic. Once again, such schemes cover only a small proportion of the population, but what is perhaps more important is that the extent to which such benefits would mitigate the household impact of a rise in AIDS is not clear. For example, the disability pension schemes offered by the government apply mainly to disabilities acquired in the course of duty, and to include AIDS in this category of disability, even for special groups such as armed forces personnel posted far from their wives, will need a great deal of legal skill. Similarly, the value of most benefit schemes depends heavily on the length of time employees have served in the government. As the AIDS epidemic is expected to hit younger individuals disproportionately, they will more often be those with fewer years of service.

Finally, there is the informal sector, which includes the bulk (about 90 per cent) of the work-force, and which has no access to employer benefits in any formal sense. This sector can expect state support only in some parts of the country and only in specific ways, few of which seem likely to be able to deal with the household impact of a potential AIDS epidemic. Noteworthy exceptions include the midday meal scheme in Tamil Nadu and the pension schemes (for widows and the aged) of the Kerala government, both of which, if widespread enough, can go a long way toward mitigating the rise in dependency ratios that would accompany increased adult morbidity and mortality.

Other Coping Mechanisms Given the state's marginal role in the lives of most people, especially when dealing with unanticipated crises such as those arising from ill health and premature death, our data suggest that households have worked out their own ways of dealing with such crises, with varying degrees of success. Given a lack of universal and satisfactory intervention by the government, these coping mechanisms need to be identified in a search for policies that complement, rather than replace, existing household strategies.

The first column of Table 6 shows that while 34 per cent of respondents felt that their households would be able to cope fairly well with their incapacitation for some time, either because of sufficient means or because the respondents' role in the family economy was marginal, they often went on to add that this coping would require a cut in some kinds of expenditures. The most commonly-mentioned target of such an expenditure cut (mentioned by 43 per cent of respondents) was 'luxury foods' (meaning items such as meat and eggs). It is revealing that good food is so often considered the most expendable form of consumption, even though good food forms only an occasional part of the average household's diet.

As we would have expected, many households felt that they would need to explore additional sources of money in the event of the respondent not being able to work. In other words, family survival was already so precarious that the scope for reducing expenses any further was limited. Nine per cent of households would have to return to their place of origin where their families would provide the support lacking in Delhi.

Table 7 examines some of the other sources of funds that the household would have to explore if the respondent were to fall seriously ill. The first row is particularly revealing in that it shows that savings and assets play such a small role in households' capacity to cope with a sudden disaster. The most common recourse is to loans. Most of the literature on the credit market in India maintains that government loans form a negligible proportion of all transactions in the country. The relatively well-off family member, the local moneylender, the landlord, or the employer

Table 6: Socio-economic Differentials in Coping with Inability to Work

Socio-economic status of male respondents	Percentage who think their household would			
	Carry on as usual for some time	Carry on with expenditure cuts	Need other sources of income	Return to family/ village
Total sample	34	34	49	9
Age (years)				
19–24	46	19	32	5
25–34	29	39	55	10
35+	17	54	68	11
Household income per month (Rs)				
0–1,000	20	27	54	26
1,001–3,000	20	31	64	14
3,001–7,000	35	40	44	9
7,001+	56	30	33	0
Car ownership				
Yes	62	28	28	0
No	32	35	50	9
TV ownership				
Yes	37	35	47	2
No	21	30	57	30
No. of years of education				
None	20	31	67	22
1–7	28	28	59	19
8–12	30	41	53	5
13+	45	28	35	4

(Contd)

Table 6: *(Contd)*

Socio-economic status of male respondents	Percentage who think their household would			
	Carry on as usual for some time	Carry on with expenditure cuts	Need other sources of income	Return to family/ village
Occupation				
Professional and white-collar workers	33	41	50	8
Self-employed	48	34	46	5
Manual/unskilled	24	39	62	12
Unemployed	39	6	14	2
Marital status				
Ever married	26	41	62	9
Never married	47	35	14	5
Household structure				
Nuclear	29	30	43	12
Stem	30	46	63	5
Joint	60	22	41	0
Others	18	58	74	3
Caste and religion				
Hindu upper caste	35	31	47	5
Hindu middle caste	34	37	52	8
Scheduled caste	30	31	52	13
Muslim	22	40	59	25
Other religions	48	35	29	3
Region of origin				
North India excluding Delhi	25	36	54	18
Delhi	41	33	44	2
Others	29	48	63	–

Source: Authors' survey.

Table 7: Other Sources of Income to be Tapped if Respondent is Incapactiated (percentage of respondents)

Socio-economic status of male respondents	Loans	Savings	Assets	Other household members would seek work
Total sample	57	14	4	23
Age (years)				
19–24	60	17	2	17
25–34	60	13	5	26
35+	56	18	3	24
Household income per month (Rs)				
0–3,000	67	5	3	22
3,001–7,000	52	15	6	26
7,001+	36	41	3	21
No. of years of education				
None	78	9	0	12
1–7	58	8	5	25
8–12	57	11	6	25
13+	47	29	0	22
Occupation				
Professional and white collar workers	42	28	5	26
Self-employed	44	20	6	29
Manual/unskilled	68	7	3	20
Unemployed	91	0	0	0
Marital status				
Ever married	50	13	5	24
Never married	58	19	2	18

(Contd)

Table 7: *(Contd)*

Socio-economic status of male respondents	Loans	Savings	Assets	Other household members would seek work
Household structure				
Nuclear	60	12	5	20
Stem	48	19	5	27
Joint	49	19	2	30
Others	75	7	0	18
Caste and religion				
Hindu upper caste	48	22	4	25
Hindu middle caste	69	5	1	23
Scheduled caste	41	16	11	34
Muslim	81	10	0	5
Other religions	56	22	11	11
Region of origin				
North India excluding Delhi	61	14	3	21
Delhi	54	16	6	23
Others	54	0	0	38

Note: This table excludes those respondents who said they would be able to carry on as before.
Source: Authors' survey.

are much more likely to be tapped for such help, usually at exorbitant rates of interest.[8]

This finding indicates that a much more effective credit system is needed to deal with the periodic crises that regularly plague the lives of so many people in the developing world. Currently, elite groups corner most of such credit, which is usually supplied to

---

8. The curious thing is how rarely people default on repaying such informal loans; yet one reason outsiders such as the state are believed to be wary of entering the credit market is because of their fear of default.

deal with people's development goals rather than with crisis. There is also a case for replacing some of this tendency to take loans with more widespread and effective systems of risk insurance that go beyond paying for medical costs: the non-medical costs of an AIDS case will rise as the disease reaches its last stages and results in death. Moreover, such insurance will have to contain a strong social welfare component: that is, it must be priced low enough and publicized sufficiently, in order to make it accessible to the most vulnerable groups of society, especially now that it appears that these groups have another major risk to deal with, that of acquiring the HIV infection.

Table 7 also finds that an important household solution to the disability or death of a productive male would be for other household members to enter the labour force, but this is easier said than done. Even a policy of helping the household members of an ill or dead breadwinner to find employment (such as the policy available to central government employees) can work only as long as the household has other employable members available.

A definition of 'employable' has, moreover, to go beyond indicators such as age and education. Several important constraints on the availability of potential workers are not related to their age and skills, but to their cultural attributes. In the Indian context, gender is important in this respect. Many groups have strong cultural and social inhibitions about letting women enter the labour force, especially if the work is outside the home or the family business. In the study sample, for example, only 16 per cent of the wives of respondents were working. A large proportion of the non-working wives were stated to be unemployed because for them to seek work was considered unsuitable. Indeed, our qualitative responses recorded a large number of married men using phrases such as 'family honour' to defend their unwillingness to let their wives join the labour force.

While many such inhibitions dissolve in the face of necessity, the option of the woman going out to work is often treated as an unpalatable last resort. In such a cultural situation, the intervention policy that seeks to help the families of AIDS victims not by providing unemployment benefits, but by providing alternative forms of employment, needs to be sensitive to the kinds of employment it can offer and the kind of motivational support it can provide.

It is thus obvious that the nuclear family of a relatively young breadwinner (which is what the average AIDS victim is likely to be) can pay a heavy price for the illness in a culture that does not encourage its women to work. This cultural inhibition will be strengthened by the fact that in this kind of household, the woman will not easily be able to join the labour force in the first place, given her heavy and single-handed housekeeping and childcare responsibilities.

Socio-economic Variation in Impact and in Coping Strategies

We now come to the second hypothesis of this section, that the aggregate findings discussed hide much variation, even when the population is as homogeneous and relatively privileged as the sample in this study. We begin with the special vulnerability of households of small means.

The Role of Poverty   The macroeconomic/microeconomic contrast is especially important when one is looking at the economic costs of a potential AIDS epidemic. The aggregate costs to an economy of the disease should be smaller if the poor are more at risk of getting the disease, but the individual or household costs will be greater in such a case. This is because the poor may contribute less to the overall economy, but they are also least able to cope with the costs of the infection.

Tables 6, 7 and 8 present some of the socio-economic variation in the impact of adult ill health and mortality in the study population. The overall finding—that economic status affects the ways in which a household can handle the incapacitation or death of an adult male—is consistent with our expectations. The more revealing factors are the extent of economic variations in such abilities and the variation in different kinds of costs and abilities. For example, there are stark economic differentials in the access to formal insurance systems (Table 5).[9] Table 6 also illustrates how

9. 40 per cent of the highest income group having personal insurance is a low enough figure, but it is high when compared to the level in the lower income categories. Similarly, 42 per cent of respondents who were professionals had their own insurance coverage, compared to 8 per cent of those in manual and unskilled jobs; again, a vast difference.

Table 8: Amount of Time Salaried Staff and Wage Earners can take off from Work without Loss of Income (per cent)

Socio-economic status of male respondents	Not a single day	Up to a week	1 week– 1 month	1 month– 6 months	As much as needed
Total sample	34	12	22	30	2
No. of years of education					
None	78	13	9	0	0
1–7	53	14	0	32	0
8–12	35	13	28	22	1
13+	12	9	28	47	4
Occupation					
Professional	13	11	32	42	1
Manual/unskilled	53	13	13	18	1
Household income per month (Rs)					
0–3,000	55	11	18	15	1
3,001–7,000	24	10	24	40	1
7,001+	11	15	26	43	4

Source: Authors' survey.

much easier it is for the relatively rich to maintain their old standard of living in the event of the breadwinner's incapacitation, and their relatively smaller need to seek other sources of income. As Table 7 shows, their own savings are more often enough to see them through, at least temporarily. Table 8 illustrates vividly how much more quickly the impact of illness starts telling on poor households than on richer households: more than half the respondents belonging to the lowest income categories or in manual and unskilled jobs could not afford to take even a day off from work without loss of income, compared to about 10 per cent of the highest income group or the white-collar group.

The effects of differences in educational level are in the same general direction as those of income, and do not need separate elaboration, except to point out that education is more than a proxy for income. It has a role to play in its own right through the modernization it confers and, more important, through the greater ease with which the more educated can use formal institutions to their benefit.

In addition to the role of income and economic status in determining the household impact of AIDS, one must also consider the converse relationship, that is, the impact on household poverty of an illness such as AIDS. In general, all households affected by AIDS are likely to experience some pauperization as a result of the disease. This is due not only to the direct costs of the illness (medical care, personal care, and so on), which are common to all illnesses (but which in the case of AIDS are likely to be much larger than for other illnesses because of the lengthy duration of the disease and the high cost of the medicines to treat it) but, as demonstrated by Bloom and Glied (1993), is also due to the non-medical costs of AIDS, which can be even more crippling and impoverishing that the medical costs. These arise directly (from the loss of income associated with AIDS victims both during the period of ill health and after their inevitable death, given that, at least at present, a disproportionately large number of AIDS victims are young, productive adults) as well as indirectly (from the opportunity costs of their care-givers' time).

This impact of HIV/AIDS on poverty is also a function of the initial levels of poverty of the affected households and the paucity of state mechanisms to cushion some of the impact. In addition, an affected household tends to become impoverished even if another household member enters the labour force, because he or she can rarely earn enough to make up for the lost income (Feachem and others 1991). Such an interpretation probably explains the finding in a study in Bangladesh (Pryer 1989) that dependency ratios decreased when the head of the household was incapacitated; more than one additional earner was now presumably needed to make up for the income loss. (In reality this loss was rarely made up and overall poverty tended to increase in such households.)

These kinds of coping strategies affect general household welfare in ways that are not all linked to the direct income loss associated with AIDS. For example, if the coping strategy includes a young mother entering the labour force, some adverse impact on her children's health is likely (see for example Basu and Basu 1991). When this happens, households may also withdraw older children from other activities such as school to take over household responsibilities, which may affect the quality of life of these older children as well as of the younger siblings under their care. In addition, there is the income-independent impact on child health and welfare of an ill or missing parent, although this negative impact is greater for motherless than for fatherless children (see for example Koenig and others 1988; Pryer 1989).

All these are possible consequences that any serious AIDS impact intervention strategy must grapple with. In the case of countries like India, which have been affected by the AIDS epidemic relatively late, a wealth of information is available from countries at more advanced stages of the epidemic. Such information should be tapped more effectively to design more targeted strategies.

The Role of the Employment Structure   The kind of employment that individuals are engaged in does have a bearing on their income; so at one level, occupation can be treated as a proxy for economic status. However, the employment structure of a population also has a relationship to behaviour in ways that are not dependent on income and that are difficult to capture in analyses of aggregate data. In the context of a possible AIDS epidemic, our data suggest that the type of occupation individuals are engaged in affects their ability to cope with the kind of physical crisis that HIV infection in a productive household member implies. Table 6 suggests that the main distinction that is not based on income may be that between respondents who are self-employed and those who work for others. The former group is much more easily able to maintain its income levels if the respondent is incapacitated.[10]

10. The self-employed category includes those respondents who are primarily engaged in a trade or business activity that they own. The category of professional and white-collar workers also includes some individuals who are self-employed, mainly as professionals. The group of manual and unskilled workers also has a good proportion of self-employed people. Its main distinction from the other two groups is in its low level of skill compared to the professionals and low levels of income compared to the self-employed businessmen and traders. In other words, self-employment is more an economic category than a clear representation of occupational structure.

In a sense, the self-employed individuals in the professional and unskilled groups in Table 6 contaminate the results and lead to an underestimation of the difference in coping abilities between those who work for themselves and those who work for others. At the same time, this kind of categorization is important, because the self-employed in Table 6 represent a special social category that would become contaminated by including them within the self-employed from the other groups. The reason for this becomes clearer in Table 9, which looks only at the coping mechanisms of the self-employed.

The advantaged position of those in non-petty trade and business is obvious from Table 9. Not only do their have a higher income, which makes it less urgent for them to find other sources of income in the event of ill health (see Table 6), their activities are much more easily taken over by others, dependent as these activities are more on the ownership of productive assets than on skills. It is no surprise, therefore, that only 16 per cent of these respondents feel that they are indispensable to the household economy, compared to 46 per cent of the professionals and 36 per cent of the unskilled self-employed. In addition, a wider range of relations from within and outside the immediate family can substitute for them. Particularly important is the greater ease with which their wives can step into their shoes should the need arise. At the same time there is one mitigating aspect of wage employment that merits mention: the cushioning impact of a regular job in tiding over temporary crises brought about by such events as ill health.[11]

The finding that occupation influences the impact of adult illness and death independently of its relationship to income has important implications for a policy that seeks to target scarce resources in an attempt to ameliorate the impact of HIV/AIDS

11. This advantage only applies to employment in the wage sector, which makes up a small proportion of all wage employment, and also only applies to wage employment in the organized sector when employers take their legal and social responsibility for their workers' welfare seriously, which is not always the case. Moreover, this advantage is less pronounced in the specific case of AIDS-related morbidity and mortality, because the resultant incapacitation is prolonged and eventually final.

Table 9: Percentage of Self-Employed Respondents who have Relations that take over the Business if Respondent is Ill (per cent)

Socio-economic status of male respondents	Person taking over				
	Wife	Father	Brother	Others	No one
Total sample	10	27	23	13	27
Age (years)					
19–24	0	45	23	11	21
25–34	14	20	24	27	29
35+	17	22	9	22	30
Household income per month (Rs)					
0–3,000	15	17	13	19	36
3,001–7,000	5	37	27	13	18
7,001+	8	28	31	15	18
No. of years of education					
None	8	17	4	25	46
1–7	12	12	12	18	46
8–12	12	30	26	10	21
13+	6	34	28	13	19
Occupation					
Professional and white-collar workers	0	9	18	18	46
Self-employed	11	34	27	12	16
Manual/unskilled	11	24	17	12	36
Marital status					
Ever married	14	25	16	9	32
Never married	0	31	38	18	13
Household structure					
Nuclear	10	18	18	15	39
Stem	12	34	17	15	22
Joint	8	46	34	8	4
Others	17	0	25	25	33
Caste and religion					
Hindu upper caste	10	29	18	20	23
Hindu middle caste	13	27	21	10	29
Scheduled caste	21	5	21	11	42
Muslim	5	24	24	14	33
Other religions	0	43	50	0	7
Region of origin					
North India excluding Delhi	12	20	15	16	37
Delhi	7	31	28	14	20
Others states	33	44	11	1	11

Source: Authors' survey.

most efficiently and to pursue development goals that exploit the innate resilience of certain kinds of lifestyles. With regard to the latter consideration, it is significant that current development strategies are pushing more and more workers out of self-employment into wage and salaried employment.

Socio-cultural Factors An important hypothesis of this study that seems to be vindicated is that the cultural context is important. By cultural factors we mean factors that are described by non-economic parameters and that often do not alter in tandem with economic change. Therefore, the lessons that can be learnt about the effects of the spread of HIV/AIDS in India and, more important, the microeconomic impact of this spread, through simple extrapolations from experience elsewhere in the world is limited. The social and cultural contexts are important not only because they distinguish India from other parts of the world, but also because of the tremendous cultural variation within the country.

As our study is limited in size and geographical coverage, it can offer at best only an indication of the socio-cultural diversity of India's population and of the great variation in the potential impact of an AIDS epidemic on households belonging to different socio-cultural groups. Nevertheless, by demonstrating the existence of such socio-cultural variation, this study hopes to underline the need to cast the net further, and to understand the larger picture of socio-cultural differences in the possible household impact of AIDS, instead of inefficiently treating all affected households in the same way.

Within the limited framework of this study, the main socio-cultural determinants of the household impact of AIDS seem to be the type of family, the status of women, the region of origin, and caste and religion, but the last two are not considered separately here.

The Role of the Family

We have already noted the high level of dependence on its own resources that the sample household has to resort to, given the absence of state support or insurance schemes to deal with health- and mortality-related crises. However, the more interesting culturally relevant finding is that by the household we do not mean just the respondent's immediate nuclear family, nor do we include only household members who live together in our conclusion that family support is an important coping mechanism in the event of trouble. The overall finding seems to be that the larger extended family or kin group provides the main cushion for absorbing a crisis, and that this family support is increased by, but not entirely dependent on, household living arrangements.

Looking as Table 6 once more, the joint family is by far the best able to carry on a relatively unchanged lifestyle in the event of a male of productive age falling seriously ill. Fully 60 per cent of respondents living in joint families felt that their households would be able to cope relatively normally with their falling ill. Stem families, by contrast, do more or less the same as nuclear families. Indeed, one would intuitively expect them even to do somewhat worse because they have higher dependency ratios, as the aged now add to the economically inactive group of young children, who are the main dependants in nuclear households.

By the same token, joint families have less need to find other income earners to maintain family standards or to consider leaving the city because they cannot cope with the impoverishment caused by a young man's sudden unproductivity. Table 7 suggests that both joint and stem families also feel less need to get loans to help them at such times. This last finding has two possible explanations, one physical and the other cultural. The first is that the joint or stem family has greater access than nuclear families to other adults who can join the labour force should one earner fall ill (see Table 7). The cultural reason is that movements of funds within the households are characterized as transfers, not as loans.

Table 9 illustrates the role of the larger family even when residential arrangements are independent. In the case of self-employed respondents, even in nuclear families fathers and brothers (who by our definition of the nuclear family do not live with the respondent) are the most important categories of individuals taking over the family enterprise if the respondent is unable to carry on. However, the relatively reduced role of these relatives is also apparent in the last column of Table 9: more nuclear families, even when the respondent is self-employed, have no one to take over his income-earning responsibilities when he is incapacitated. Joint families are rarely handicapped in this way: only 4 per cent of them reported that the family business would have no one available to take over if necessary.

This kind of give and take is the backbone of the household economy in India, and policy interventions to deal with household crises should exploit this interdependence rather than make the state fully responsible for all welfare. In addition, policy designers need to identify the most vulnerable household structures, in this case, those with the least access to help from their relatives. In a broad way, these would be nuclear households living far from their place of origin and with few relatives close by. In addition, these households would face greater costs if their economic hold on their extended families were weaker because they worked in the wage sector.

Finally, those making estimates of the aggregate household costs of an AIDS epidemic should be conscious of the possible rise in such aggregate costs not because the total number of AIDS cases turns out to be greater than expected, but because changing household structures are increasing the proportion of households that is more vulnerable to the impact of the infection.

The Role of the Status of Women

Researchers are now showing some interest in the particular vulnerability of women (all women, not just high-risk groups such as commercial sex workers) to HIV infection, often because of their powerlessness in sexual as well as in medical matters. For example, NACO (1993) estimates that by the year 2000, HIV incidence rates among men and women in India will be the same. Investigators are also increasingly recognizing that women play an important economic role, which increases the household economic costs of AIDS in women. Our case studies of households in which a woman had died underlined the household's weaker economic position after death even when she had not been economically productive herself. Her survivors attributed the main economic loss to the loss of ability to control and manage the household budget.

Some evidence suggests that females become infected with HIV at younger ages than males. In some parts of the world this may by linked to the tendency by men who practice multipartner sex to seek younger and younger women, as well as virgins (see for example Carael and Piot 1992 on the situation in sub-Saharan Africa). This means that the affected women are likely to be in more productive age groups. They are also likely to have young children on whom the impact of their illness and death is greater, and also to bear children after getting the infection, thereby increasing the chances of infecting their children.

The findings are concerned with the impact of women getting AIDS. We look now at another aspect of the 'gender and AIDS' question. Does the role of women have any bearing on the household's ability to meet the economic burden of AIDS in one of its members? Conversely, does AIDS-related morbidity and mortality among men affect the role of women?

When an adult male of productive age acquires a debilitating infection such as AIDS, the impact on and response of the household depends heavily on the presence and position of its women. All over the world, women have traditionally been the care-givers in times of illness, and in a country like India, where households rather than hospitals bear so much of the burden of medical care, women's responsibilities are much greater. The effect of this additional and prolonged care-giving activity by women depends on their position to begin with. One would expect that where women are economically active, their possible withdrawal from the labour force to take care of the ill person will cause some household impoverishment. At the same time, if anyone is likely to leave the labour force to care for the ill, it is women, because they are traditionally believed to be better at care-giving, and also because their contributions to the household's income are usually smaller than those of the men.

In our sample, this kind of impoverishment should not be a major problem because only 16 per cent of the respondents' wives are economically active. However, there are important socio-economic variations in female employment even within this largely conservative population. In particular, respondents from the worst-off groups are mostly likely to have working wives. For example, 25 per cent of the wives of illiterate respondents are employed (compared to 9 per cent of those with eight to twelve years of schooling), and 17 per cent of the wives of respondents in the lowest income group are working (compared to 7 per cent of those earning Rs 3,000 to Rs 7,000 per month).

In such disadvantaged households, women's work provides an essential part of the family's income, in contrast to both the relatively better-off households, in which the women have less need to work, and the most well-off households, where women are again more economically active, but for reasons other than income need. If poor women are now withdrawn from the labour force because their care-giving activities are needed at home, pauperization results, because most of these women are unlikely to be in occupations that allow paid leave, and even if they did, AIDS suffering is so prolonged that any employee benefits that did exist would soon run out.

Even when women do not work outside the home, their care-giving roles can have several adverse effects on the household in general. They are more burdened with overall work (all studies of time allocation by women indicate that they perform additional jobs within or outside the home without a corresponding reduction in their existing domestic responsibilities, but with the primary casualty being their leisure time). Some evidence indicates, however, that an increase in time allocated to health care reduces the time available for other domestic maintenance activities, which could result in adverse effects on general household health and welfare.[12]

At this point we should add that recognition of women's care-giving role is not tantamount to the policy implication that this role must be exploited, and that the state can abdicate its own responsibility for the care of the severely ill. It merely underscores that the family is an important source of such care and must be supported in this activity, given that the availability of non-

---

12. These costs are compounded by the nature of AIDS transmission. The wife of an HIV infected man is quite likely to be infected herself, and thus her physical capacities will also gradually diminish.

domiciliary health care services is unlikely to match the need for them.

When a male dies of AIDS there are other costs to the household that depend on the position of women. One outcome is that the proportion of households headed by women could rise. In the present study, 50 per cent of the married respondents live in nuclear households, and upon their death, such households would either have to move and join the larger family unit, or become female-headed. The literature on the greater poverty and exploitation of female-headed households is large and is not discussed here, but this is an important possible impact of AIDS.

Another consideration is the role of women in income earning when the male breadwinner is dead. Here the hold of culture is strong. Not only do women not go out to work much, they are also less likely to do so in the event of family hardship. Cultural inhibitions were a frequently given reason for women not going out to work. Even in the nuclear family of the self-employed respondent, the wife is much less likely to take over the family business than another male relative (Table 9). This finding has important implications for the status of women, because in such cases one form of authority replaces another.

Regression Estimates

Tables 10 and 11 present some multiple regressions of the determinants of the household's capacity to carry on as before in the event of the respondent being so ill as to be incapacitated for a long time. The findings are consistent with the discussion based on the simpler tables. Both the logit and probit estimates in Table 10 show that household structure, occupation, and marital status are significant factors in explaining the household's ability to cope with the incapacitation of the respondent male. Further analysis in Table 11 (which drops certain variables because of high correlations) finds that age is also negatively related to the respondents' household's ability to carry on as before.

Table 10: Log Likelihood Estimates—Dependent Variable: Ability to Carry on as Before

Variable	Logit coefficient	t	Probit coefficient	t
Constant	−0.4683	−0.24	−0.3565	−0.31
Age	−0.0485	−1.08	−0.0274	−1.04
Education	0.0758	1.32	0.0458	1.36#
Household income	0.00004	1.26#	0.00002	1.35#
Household structure	0.6147	2.75*	0.3718	2.81*
Occupation	−0.8875	−2.33*	−0.5386	−2.36*
Region of origin	−0.5619	−1.55#	−0.3179	−1.47#
Caste and religion	0.0056	0.03	−0.0002	−0.001
Marital status	1.1116	2.49*	0.6798	2.53*

* Significant at 5% level
\# Significant at 10% level
Source: Authors' calculations.

Table 11: Maximum Likelihood Estimates—Dependent Variable: Ability to Carry on as before

Variable	Logit coefficient	t	Probit coefficient	t
Constant	1.2113	0.97	0.7102	0.95
Age	−0.0976	−2.78*	−0.586	−2.84*
Education	0.0357	0.75	0.0238	0.85
Income	0.00004	1.38#	0.00002	1.47#
Household structure	0.5205	2.66*	0.3218	2.71*
Caste and religion	−0.1607	−0.78	−0.1011	−0.80

* Significant at 5% level
\# Significant at 10% level
Note: Futher analysis by dropping certain variables for high correlations shows that age is negatively related to respondents' ability to carry on as before.
Source: Authors' calculations.

The Case Studies

While the survey part of this study looked at the potential impact of male adult morbidity on households, we thought it worthwhile to do a detailed qualitative examination of what happens to a household when it actually experiences an adult death. We therefore did a series of case studies of families that had lost an adult member in the two years preceding the survey and tried to identify the key problems faced and, more important, the key coping mechanisms that came into play.

We did a total of thirty-three case studies, twenty-three in households that had lost an adult male and ten in those that had lost an adult female. The findings from the case studies are, of course, only pointers to the actual situation, but they highlight the great variation in impact that is possible and some determinants of such variation. More elaborate and widespread studies of such households will be necessary (for example, of the kind done by the World Bank in Tanzania) to design the most effective interventions, but the present study should provide a reliable, broad picture and an indication of the direction that future research on this subject should take.

In the twenty-three households that had lost an adult male member, nine received the economic and social support of the joint or extended family. The responsibility of the joint family often remains even when the economic activity of the household is not joint. For example, in one case the deceased had an independent income that made up a significant part of the total household income, so that upon his death there was a perceptible loss of money, but the immediate family of the deceased nevertheless continued to be the economic and social responsibility of the joint family. In such a situation the household must find alternative sources of income, or else suffer a reduction in its living standard. In this case, the adjustment was made by sending the immediate family of the dead man to live with his eldest brother.

Not all the households that received support from extended kin actually lived together. Even families that are predominantly nuclear seem to turn first to, and often automatically receive succour from, the larger family unit. The evidence from the case studies (albeit limited) suggests that substantive help is more likely to be received from the larger family unit at the stage of illness of the male member than for any extended period after his death. At the same time, several of the case studies of nuclear families poignantly illustrate how fragile these possibilities of help from extended kin networks can be when the extended family does not live with the nuclear family. For example, in one nuclear family, three out of four children had to be withdrawn from school when their father died.[13]

At the same time, the life cycle stage at the time of death is also important. A death later in life, when the children in a nuclear family are ready to step in, affects the household much less than one in which very young children are left behind. While in the latter case high fertility is a major impediment to coping strategies, for men who died leaving behind older children, high fertility made bearing the costs of the death much easier.

The role of the family in the absence of support from the state is also conveyed through the unconventional or socially unacceptable strategies that many households had to adopt to keep their heads above water. The employment of women was one such (often unpalatable) strategy. Another unusual mechanism was for the woman's relations or her daughter's family to step in to help when she had lost her husband. This runs counter to the north Indian norm, where the woman is expected to sever her relationship with her own family on her marriage.

Although these case studies refer to death in general and not to deaths from AIDS, and had to be conducted relatively quickly, the results are surprisingly consistent with the findings from the larger survey. In addition, they are consistent with other, more elaborate studies of the household impact of AIDS-related deaths conducted in Africa (e.g. Ainsworth and Over 1994; Anderson 1994) in underlining the great costs of adult death to households; costs that need to be much better understood if we are indeed on the verge of an upsurge in adult mortality.

---

13. The nuclear family with no personal assets or access to state support thus often faces a precarious position upon the death of the principal breadwinner. The community seems to help out at the beginning, extended relations may or may not contribute, and usually the survivors are eventually left to their own resources.

Conclusion

This chapter has tried to highlight the importance of adult health and survival to the health and survival of the household. Most research on morbidity and mortality has concentrated on children and the elderly, because these two groups face higher-than-average risks of illness and death. However, a reconsideration of the costs of ill health and mortality is now necessary because of the possibility that both morbidity and mortality will increase if steps are not taken to combat the growing HIV/AIDS epidemic.

This study has focused on the economic impact of adult illness and death on households, as opposed to the impact on the national economy. We found important differences in the economic impact on households; differences that depended on the household's economic status. This indicates the use of poverty as a major criterion for designing targeted policies in principle, even if not in practice. Indeed, all evidence suggests that not only are the costs of adult illness and death lower for the better off, they are also better at availing themselves of measures provided by the state or their employers to help meet these costs. The poor have to rely primarily on their own resources, and an important and major consequence is their greater impoverishment. It should be noted, however, that for the sample as a whole, the household itself, whether rich or poor, bears the bulk of the costs of crises such as death and ill health.

What was more interesting was the finding that the impact of adult incapacitation on households also depended on other, more socio-cultural factors, the most important of which turned out to be the role of the family: households made up of extended families were the best able to meet the costs of an adult falling ill or dying. The type of employment was also significant: self-employed households were less badly affected by sudden illness or death and were able to cope with these events much better, often by having other household members substitute for the incapacitated individual. Finally, the status of women also determined the impact on households of disease and death.

We have drawn several policy-oriented lessons from this study. Firstly, it demonstrates that using the survey method to obtain information on a whole range of issues related to HIV and AIDS is possible. Secondly, it identifies several areas that a more effective HIV/AIDS prevention strategy must be concerned with. An important role of this strategy that does not seem to have succeeded so far is the dispelling of erroneous notions about the illness. While general awareness levels were high, specifics were poorly understood. Respondents had a poor grasp of transmission routes, leading not only to a lack of appreciation of the need for safe behaviour, but also towards an unsympathetic attitude to possible carriers of the infection.

The information about differences in impact should make it easier for policy makers to estimate the potential impact of an HIV/AIDS epidemic in India. These estimates will have to take into account not only the prevalence of the infection among different socio-economic groups, which experience different impacts, but also changes in the distribution of these socio-economic groups over time. For example, the increasing tendency toward households consisting of nuclear families will increase the aggregate impact of the AIDS epidemic, even if the total number of cases remains unchanged.

In turn, the study indicates that strategies to mitigate the impact of HIV and AIDS will have to move well beyond counselling to take cognizance of some of the large economic costs of the infection to households. Moreover, given that the resources to mitigate these costs will be extremely limited. strategies will have to be targeted at the most vulnerable. These will not necessarily be only the poorest households. A number of social and cultural characteristics of the households affected will contribute to the costs they face and to the mechanisms available to them to meet these costs in the event of an adult member acquiring HIV. The state will need different strategies to supplement these coping mechanisms in different kinds of households.

Finally, we need to remember that this was an exploratory study. Given the limited time available, it had to be conducted on a relatively small scale and was unable to take many of the complexities of the Indian context into account. In particular, it was unable to explore the existence of large regional differences in attributes that affect both risk and impact. For example, NACO (1993) has found great geographic variation in the spread of the

152   *The Economics of HIV and AIDS*

disease, with the largest number of cases so far being in the states of Maharashtra, Manipur, and Tamil Nadu.

The primary aim of this study, however, was not to quantify differences in any definitive manner. It was to demonstrate that such differences exist, to identify high-risk situations, and to develop a methodology for collecting data on a larger scale and in a more ongoing manner. Such an ongoing process of data collection could conceivably be piggy-backed onto one of the several large-scale surveys being carried out around the country. Obvious candidates are the National Sample Survey (NSS) and the Sample Registration Scheme. Specialized surveys by various other government departments could also be tapped for this purpose, as could the larger studies by survey agencies such as the Operations Research Group (ORG) and the Marketing and Research Group (MARG). This kind of continuous monitoring of the field situation would permit better tracking of the epidemic's progress and of any accompanying rise in adult mortality as it occurs. In addition, it would allow the development of more effective and targeted intervention strategies to deal with the specific problem of the household impact of HIV and AIDS.

However, an important contribution of this study is also to demonstrate that not all questions related to HIV/AIDS awareness and impact are amenable to large-scale survey investigation. Questions about high-risk sexual behaviour are particularly difficult to ask in a one-shot quick survey, but information on these matters is relatively stable, and perhaps does not require the kind of continuous monitoring necessary to track the progress of the disease. It is probably better collected through more intensive methods of the kind anthropologists use. It is more relevant to capture differences across space, with changes over time being recorded at relatively long intervals.

References

Ainsworth, M. and A.M. Over. 1994. 'The Economic Impact of AIDS on Africa.' In M. Essex and others, eds., *AIDS in Africa*. New York: Raven Press.
Anderson, D. 1994. *Towards a More Effective Policy Response to AIDS*. Liege, Belgium: International Union for the Scientific Study of Population.

Basu, A.M. 1992. *Culture, the Status of Women and Demographic Behaviour.* Oxford, U.K.: Clarendon Press.

Basu, A.M. and K. Basu. 1991. 'Women's Economic Roles and Child Survival: Illustrated with the Case of India.' *Health Transition Review* 1(1):83–103.

Basu, A.M., D.B. Gupta, and G. Krishna. 1994. *The Household Impact of Adult Morbidity and Mortality.* New Delhi: Institute of Economic Growth.

Berman, P. 1991. *Health Economics, Health Financing and the Health Needs of Poor Women and Children.* New Delhi: The Ford Foundation.

Bloom, D. and S. Glied. 1993. 'Who is Bearing the Cost of the AIDS Epidemic in Asia?' In D.E. Bloom and J.V. Lyons, eds., *Economic Implications of AIDS in Asia.* New Delhi: United Nations Development Programme.

Bloom, David E. and Joyce V. Lyons. 1993. *Economic Implications of AIDS in Asia.* New Delhi: United Nations Development Programme.

Carael, M. and P. Piot. 1992. 'The Aids Epidemic in Sub-Saharan Africa.' In E. van de Walle, G. Pison, and M. Sala-Diakanda, eds., *Mortality and Society in Sub-Saharan Africa.* Oxford, U.K.: Clarendon Press.

Duggal, R. and S. Amin. 1989. *Cost of Health Care: Survey of an Indian District.* Bombay: Foundation for Research in Community Health.

Feachen, G.A. and others. 1991. *The Health of Adults in the Developing World.* Washington, D.C.: World Bank, Population and Human Resources Department.

Gilks, C.F. 1993. 'The Clinical Challenge of the HIV Epidemic in the Developing World.' *The Lancet,* 342:107–9.

Head, J. 1992. 'Behavioural Assumptions about the Spread of HIV Infection in South Africa: Myth of Reality?' *AIDS Bulletin,* 1(2):16–19.

Koenig, M.A. and others. 1988. 'Maternal Mortality in Matlab, Bangladesh.' *Studies in Family Planning* 19(2):69–80.

Nandraj, S. 1994. 'Beyond the Law and the Lord: Quality of Private Health Care.' *Economic and Political Weekly* 29(27):1680–5.

National AIDS Control Organization, India. 1993. *Country Scenario: An Update.* New Delhi: National AIDS Control Organization.

Pryer, J. 1989. 'When Breadwinners Fall Ill: Preliminary Findings from a Case Study in Bangladesh.' *IDS Bulletin* 20(2):49–57.

Ramasubban, R. 1991. 'Sexual Behaviour and Conditions of Health Care: Potential Risks for HIV Transmission in India.' In T. Dyson, ed., *Sexual Behaviour and Networking: Anthropological and Sociocultural Studies on the Transmission of HIV.* Liege, Belgium: International Union for the Scientific Study of Population.

154   *The Economics of HIV and AIDS*

Reddy, K.N. 1994. 'Many Problems of Medicare.' *Business Standard* (New Delhi). July 20.

UNDP (United Nations Development Programme). 1993. *The Economic Impact of Fatal Adult Illness in Sub-Saharan Africa.* Report of a workshop on this subject held in Bukoba, Kagera Region, Tanzania, September 1992.

Wyatt, H.V. 1994. 'The Popularity of Injections in the Third World: Origins and Consequences for Poliomyelitis.' *Social Science and Medicine* 19(9):911–5.

5

Socio-economic Dimensions of the HIV/AIDS Epidemic in Sri Lanka*

David E. Bloom, Ajay Mahal, Lene Christiansen, Amala de Silva, Soma de Sylva, Malsiri Dias, Saroj Jayasinghe, Swarna Jayaweera, Soma Mahawewa, Thana Sanmugam, Gunatillake Tantrigama

Introduction

This study has three main objectives. Firstly, it seeks to develop a better understanding of the socio-economic dimensions of the

* We would like to thank the following: Mr. J.K. Robert England, formerly the Resident Representative of the UNDP in Sri Lanka, Mr. Arve Ofstad, the Resident Representative of the UNDP in Sri Lanka, the UNDP's Regional Project for HIV/AIDS in New Delhi; Peter Godwin, Chief Technical Adviser of the Regional Project; his predecessor, Dr. Joyce Lyons, who helped initiate the project; Hariet Solheim; Dr. Pat Alailima, Mr. Joe Fernando, Mr. George Fernando; Dr. Gamini Jayakuru; S.B. Abeykoon, Daya Abeywickrema, Iyanthi Abeywickrema, T. Arulanantham, A.M.L. Beligaswatte, Lucian Jayasuriya, W.D. Lakshman, Nalaka Mendis, Karen Merrey, Aung Myint, E.A. Padmasiri, W. Ransi, Nandasena Ratnapala, Rajiv Sethi, A.V.K.V. de Silva, Harsha de Silva, Sam Stembo, P. Wedisinghe, Malathi Weerasooriya, Dr. Wickremasuriya and Nandrani de Zoysa; the research support staff at CENWOR, especially Chintha Parera, Shama Herath, Anula Madduma Bandara, Chandra Muddugama, W.A.L. Weerasinghe, and G.G. Sarath Wickremasinghe; Geraldine Ratnasingham and Niloufer Hassan; the Harvard Institute for International Development; Alice Dowsett and Sarah Newberry; CTC Eagle Insurance, Ceylinco Insurance Ltd., Department of Census and Statistics (Colombo), Family Planning Association of Sri Lanka, Access to Voluntary and Safe Contraception of Sri Lanka (SLAVSC), Insurance Corporation of Sri Lanka, the Ministry of Policy Planning and Implementation, the Ministry of Health and Women's Affairs, National Insurance Company, National STD/AIDS Project, Union Assurance Ltd., UNDP, the United Nations Fund for Population Activities (UNFPA), WHO and the University of Colombo.

HIV/AIDS epidemic in Sri Lanka. It does so by evaluating the epidemic's economic and development consequences, and by analysing its social and economic roots in Sri Lanka.

Secondly, it seeks to contribute to a better appreciation of the epidemic's socio-economic dimensions in Asia in particular, and in both developing and developed countries in general. To this end, we pose a set of general research questions with regard to the AIDS epidemic and rigorously examine them in the context of Sri Lanka, thereby demonstrating the feasibility of such research.

Thirdly, results from this study will, we hope, bear upon key research and policy questions with regard to HIV/AIDS. By analysing, for example, the link between HIV and poverty, the net benefits of blood testing, and the cost-effectiveness of adopting universal precautions in the medical care system, the study is intended to inform the design of policies and programmes directed at HIV prevention and control.

Background

The World Health Organization (WHO) estimates that, by May 1995, 19.5 million people world-wide had been infected with HIV, with a cumulative total of 4.5 million cases of full-blown AIDS (WHO 1995). WHO also estimates that a majority of the world's HIV and AIDS cases are in sub-Saharan Africa (WHO 1995). By contrast, Asia's share of HIV and AIDS cases has been small, primarily because the virus did not establish itself in the region until the late 1980s, much later than in Africa and North America. Currently, Asia accounts for fewer than 17 per cent of those infected with HIV, even though 55 per cent of the world's population lives in the region (Bloom and Mahal 1995a). WHO projects, however, that HIV will spread significantly in the future, infecting a global total of some 30 to 40 million people by the year 2000 (Kallings 1992), with the bulk of new infections occurring in Asia. Projections indicate that by 1997, Asia will account for more new HIV infections that Africa, and by 2000 will account for more than half of the world's new HIV infections (Kallings 1992). Clearly, the centre of gravity of the global HIV and AIDS epidemic is moving rapidly towards Asia.

The alarmingly rapid spread of HIV is already apparent in several Asian countries (Table 1). As of late 1994, estimates indicated that India, Myanmar, and Thailand had approximately 1.5 million, 400,000, and 830,000 cumulative HIV infections, respectively (personal communication with Dr James Chin; Brown, Gullaprawit, and others 1994). These estimated figures are equivalent to 0.28 per cent, 1.53 per cent , and 2.20 per cent respectively, of the population aged fifteen to sixty-four in these countries. By 2000, the cumulative number of HIV infections is expected to grow to between 1.25 and 1.80 million in Thailand, and to between 2.10 and 6.70 million in India (personal communication with Dr James Chin; Brown, Gullaprawit and others 1994). Indeed, India, is expected to become the AIDS capital of the world.

HIV arrived in Sri Lanka somewhat later than in other Asian countries. The first HIV/AIDS case in Sri Lanka was recorded in 1987 (Jayakuru 1992), well after HIV cases had been reported in Hong Kong, Japan, the Philippines, and Thailand (WHO 1994). Thus one would expect HIV prevalence to be lower in Sri Lanka than in the latter group of countries. So far, only about 139 HIV cases (of which fifty-five are AIDS cases) have been officially reported among Sri Lankan nationals by the National AIDS Programme (NAP). By contrast, the number of reported AIDS cases in Thailand is nearly 9,000 (see Table 1).

However, experts believe that in most countries the reported number of HIV/AIDS cases does not accurately reflect the actual number of cases (Chin 1995; Peterson and Sarda 1995). They often estimate the true number of HIV and AIDS cases to be thirty to a hundred times the number of reported cases.[1] The number of HIV cases in Sri Lanka is currently estimated to be around 6,800 (*Daily News* 1994), which translates into a prevalence rate of about 0.06 among those aged fifteen to sixty-four, well below the prevalence levels in India, Myanmar, and Thailand. This low rate does not, however, imply that Sri Lanka has any special immunity to the HIV/AIDS epidemic.

1. Epidemiologists use of the results of sero-surveillance studies among various at-risk groups along with estimates of the sizes of these groups to construct national estimates of HIV prevalence (see for example Brown, Gullaprawit, and others 1994; Chin, Dunlop, and Pyne 1994a).

Is Sri Lanka Vulnerable to HIV/AIDS?

Sri Lanka's experience with the epidemic is unlikely to be any different from that of other Asian countries. The low rate of HIV prevalence in Sri Lanka simply reflects the early stage of the epidemic in Asia. As Table 1 shows, even though the adult HIV prevalence level is markedly lower in Sri Lanka than in the most severely affected Asian countries, it is higher than in several others. In addition, in terms of its age and gender incidence, the AIDS epidemic in Sri Lanka is proceeding along lines similar to other countries in the region (Table 2). Of the total number of HIV cases reported in Sri Lanka so far, 30 per cent are among women, compared to 35 per cent in Asia as a whole. Furthermore, almost 79 per cent of the reported HIV cases in Sri Lanka are among those aged twenty to forty-four, which in comparable to the figure for Asia as a whole, where nearly 73 per cent of HIV cases have occurred among those aged twenty to thirty-nine. In other words, just as elsewhere in the world, in Sri Lanka the HIV/AIDS epidemic will affect those people who are most productive economically.

Even though the AIDS epidemic in Sri Lanka appears statistically similar (certainly in terms of age and sex distribution) to the epidemic in other Asian countries, a number of factors suggest that Sri Lanka could be especially vulnerable to the spread of HIV.

Firstly, Sri Lanka is close to India, a country with a large number of HIV cases. This proximity is associated with significant cross-border movements of people, and the attendant risk of HIV transmission. In 1991 Indian nationals accounted for nearly 6.4 per cent of all tourists arriving in Sri Lanka (Department of Census and Statistics 1993a). In addition, the struggle for a separate state in the north and north-east of Sri Lanka has resulted in significant movements of refugees to and from the Indian state of Tamil Nadu (Sivaratnam 1992; UNICEF 1991), which has one of the highest rates of HIV prevalence in India (Jain, John, and Keusch 1994a, b).

Secondly, many of the factors associated with an increased risk of HIV transmission in other countries are also present in Sri Lanka. For example, mobile populations are particularly prone to

Table 1: Cumulative Numbers of HIV-Infected Individuals and AIDS Cases in Selected Economies in Asia and the Pacific and by Region (thousands)

Country/ Region	Reported Cases		Recent Estimates		Estimates for 2000		Seroprevalence Rate (per 100,000)
	HIV	AIDS	HIV	AIDS	HIV	AIDS	
Thailand	n.a.	8.63	830	90	1,170	460	1,875
Myanmar	7.2	0.26	150–400	10	805	160	1,100
India	50.1	0.89	1500	80	3,900	820	275
Singapore	0.2	0.08	2	0.10	6	1	100
Nepal	0.2	0.03	10	0.30	53	9	90
Hong Kong	0.4	0.12	3	0.25	10	2	70
Sri Lanka	0.1	0.04	7	0.10	25	3	60
Philippines	0.5	0.13	5–30	0.40	51	10	45
Bangladesh	0.02	0.003	20	0.03	295	33	30
Indonesia	0.23	0.06	34	1.26	100	20	30
Korea, Republic of	0.3	0.02	2–3	0.09	7	1	8
China	1.2	0.04	5–11	0.30	24	5	1
Africa	n.a.	347.7	>11,100	>3,150	15,000	>6,400	2,360
Asia	64	17.1	>3,050	<270	10,300	>2,200	165
Europe	n.a.	127.9	>550	180	1,000	n.a.	170
Latin America	n.a.	94.4	2,000	>450	2,400	1,300	700
North America	n.a.	432.3	>1,000	>450	1,600	n.a.	530
Oceania	18	5.7	>25	>5	n.a.	n.a.	140
Would	n.a.	1,025	18,000	4,500	30,000–40,000	12,000–18,000	520

Note: n.a.: Not available.

Sources:

Thailand: reported cases, WHO, Southeast Asia Regional Office; estimated cases and projections, Brown, Gullaprawit, and others (1994).

Myanmar: reported cases, Htoon and others (1994) (HIV), and WHO, Southeast Asia Regional Office (AIDS); estimated cases and projections, Daniel Tarantola, and authors' calculations.

India: reported cases, WHO, Southeast Asia Regional Office, personal communication; estimated cases and projections, Dr. James Chin (personal communication).

Singapore: reported cases, WHO, Regional Office for the Western Pacific; estimated cases, Dr. James Chin (personal communication) (HIV), authors' calculations (AIDS); projections, authors' calculations.

Nepal: Chin, Dunlop, and Pyne (1994a).

Hong Kong: reported cases, WHO, Regional Office for the Western Pacific (HIV), Chin (1994) (AIDS); estimated cases and projections, Chin (1994).

Sri Lanka: reported and estimated cases, National AIDS Programme data, Colombo; projections, authors' calculations.

Philippines: reported cases, Tan and Dayrit (1994); estimated cases, Dr. James Chin (personal communication), Shenon (1992a); projections, authors' calculations.

Bangladesh: Chin, Dunlop, and Pyne (1994b).

Indonesia: reported cases and estimates (HIV), WHO, Southeast Asia Regional Office; estimates (AIDS) and projections, authors' calculations.

Korea: reported cases, WHO, Regional Office of the Western Pacific; estimates, Dr. James Chin (personal communication) (HIV); projections, authors' calculations.

China: reported cases, Xinhua, Junhua, and Qili (1994); estimated cases, Jianhua and Yanlin (1993); projections, authors' calculations.

Regions: reported and estimated cases, WHO (1995); projections, Chin (1992).

Table 2: Distribution of HIV Cases by Gender, Age, and Transmission Category for Selected Asian Economies and by Region

Country and Region	Percentage in age group 20–39	Percentage female	Percentage in Transmission Category			
			HS	HBM	IVDU	BTBP/Other
Thailand	81	29	81	13	7	0
Myanmar	88	11	n.a.	n.a.	n.a.	n.a.
India	67	34	59	0	21	20
Singapore	88	7	49	42	3	6
Hong Kong	59	5	31	41	2	26
Philippines	70	48	52	18	1	30
Nepal	n.a.	50	n.a.	n.a.	n.a.	n.a.
Japan	n.a.	21	19	6	0	74
Indonesia	73	20	45	24	2	29
Sri Lanka	>67	27	67	19	0	14
Korea, Rep. of	78	10	69	20	0	11
China	80	9	7	0	82	11
Africa	n.a.	55	83	1	<1	15
Asia	73	35	67	8	14	11
Europe	n.a.	15	14	48	32	7
Latin America & Caribbean	n.a.	20	35	42	10	13
North America	65	15	9	56	27	8
Oceania	n.a.	15	6	87	3	4
World	n.a.	40	66	14	7	14

Notes: 1. n.a.: not available
2. Except for Thailand, where estimated numbers have been used, the data are based on reported cases
Sources:
Distribution by age: Myanmar: Htoon and others (1994); India: NACO data; Indonesia: Abednego (1993); Sri Lanka: NAP (1994); China: Jianhua and Yanlin (1993); Thailand: Brown and Sittitrai (1993); Philippines: Solon and Barozzo (1993); Korea: Yang (1993); Singapore: Chan (1992); Hong Kong UNDP (1992).
Percentage of female cases: Singapore, Hong Kong, and the Republic of Korea: WHO Regional Office for the Western Pacific data; Japan:

(Contd)

Notes to Table 2 continued from previous page

Kitamura (1994); India: NACO data; Philippines: Solon and Barozzo (1993); Shi Lanka: NAP (1994); Nepal: Gurubacharya and Suvedi (1992); Indonesia: Jalal and others (1994); China: Xinhua, Junhua, and Qili (1994); regions: WHO (1993).

Transmission patterns: Singapore, Hong Kong, and the Republic of Korea: WHO Regional Office for the Western Pacific data; Japan: Kitamura (1994); India: NACO Data; Philippines: Solon and Barozzo (1993); Sri Lanka: NAP (1994); Indonesia: Jalal and others (1994); China: Xinhua, Junhua, and Qili (1994); regions: Mann, Tarantola, and Netter (1992).

activities that place them at high risk of HIV infection (Bloom and Mahal 1995a,b; Panos Institute 1992; Ratnapala 1994; Sivaratnam 1992). Such mobile populations in Sri Lanka consist of displaced people and other intracountry migrants, including those moving from rural to urban areas; international migrants, including those moving from rural to urban areas; international migrant workers; and tourists. A number of authors have suggested that some of the migrant groups, such as female workers in the free trade zones (FTZs), may be at particularly high risk of HIV infection, primarily because of the economic and social conditions under which they work and live (Hettiarachchi 1994; Ratnapala 1994).

Sri Lankan workers employed overseas constitute another group of migrant workers considered to be at relatively high risk of HIV infection. A recent study published by the International Labour Office (Stalker 1994) estimates that in 1990 nearly 288,000 Sri Lankan nationals were employed abroad, which amounts to almost 2.7 per cent of Sri Lanka's population aged between fifteen and sixty-four in that year. This is a much higher percentage than in most other countries in the region, and the number is increasing steadily (Mahawewa 1993; Stalker 1994; World Bank 1993). A particularly worrying trend is the increasing number of female Sri Lankan workers employed in the Middle East who, it is suspected, are vulnerable to sexual exploitation by their employers (Mahawewa 1993; Stalker 1994).

Foreign tourists, especially those who engage in high-risk sexual activities, are considered a potential source of HIV transmission (Gallwey and Judson 1991; Ratnapala 1994; Richardson 1992; Srisang and others 1991; Waningasundara 1991). Although Sri Lanka's share of tourism in Asia is comparatively small, amounting roughly to 0.85 per cent of all arrivals in Asia, the number of tourists per capita is considerably greater in Sri Lanka than in several of its neighbours. In 1992, for example, Sri Lanka's approximately 394,000 visitors (Ceylon Tourist Board 1993) translated into 23 per 1,000 Sri Lankans, compared to 2 per 1,000 population for India and about 1 per 1,000 for Bangladesh (World Bank 1994a; WTO 1992).[2] Moreover, the number of tourists visiting Sri Lanka has been increasing sharply, by about 10 per cent per year since 1986 (Ceylon Tourist Board 1993).

A number of studies point to two other mobile population groups that could emerge as significant vectors in HIV transmission: the nation's armed forces, which grew steadily through the 1980s and currently employ more than 100,000 people (Gallwey and Judson 1991; Ratnapala 1994; Sivaratnam 1992), and people displaced by the civil strife in Sri Lanka (Ratnapala 1994; UNICEF 1991). Although this report does not focus on these groups, Ratnapala's recent work in that area, and continued hostilities in the north-east, strongly suggest that these groups are likely to remain at high risk for HIV infection and transmission in the near future.

In addition, two other population groups may serve as core groups for HIV infection, namely the country's approximately 13,000 male and female commercial sex workers, for whom risky sexual activities are reportedly common (Ratnapala 1994), and Sri Lanka's large gender-segregated prison population, which consisted of nearly 70,000 people in 1990[3].

Finally, the health care sector itself can serve as a source of HIV infection for both health workers and patients. HIV transmis-

2. But much smaller than in Thailand, where the number of tourist arrivals was 88 per 1,000 population in 1991 (WTO 1992).
3. Evidence on whether HIV transmission is facilitated in prison settings is not well documented, although a few studies in other countries note high levels of risky behaviour in prisons, primarily through the sharing of drug injecting equipment (Carvell and Hart 1990; Richardson, Ancelle-Park, and Papaevangelou 1993). Moreover, one might suspect a significant level of homosexual activity in prisons, given the practice of gender segregation among the (predominantly male) prison population.

sion can occur through the transfusion of blood contaminated with HIV, or through injuries involving contaminated medical instruments. As a number of highly-publicized cases in the United States and Europe indicate, the risk of HIV infection through the health care system may not be trivial, even in the most economically advanced societies (Island 1993; Simons 1992). A 1993 study on the transmission of hepatitis B among nurses in Gampaha district concluded that they were at substantially higher risk of being infected with hepatitis B than was the general population (Eswaraaratchige 1993). These risks are not confined to medical personnel. Another study concluded that diabetics receiving insulin injections at the General Hospital, Colombo, were at considerably higher risk of being infected with hepatitis B than were those receiving oral doses (Fernando and others 1992). There is great concern that existing practices of needle and syringe use (together with the absence of other precautions, such as the use of gloves) in hospital settings in Sri Lanka are inadequate to eliminate the possibility of HIV transmission during the provision of medical care (Jayasinghe 1994a; Wijetunge 1992).

Potential Health Implications of HIV/AIDS in Sri Lanka

Given the circumstances described, it is not surprising that experts project that the cumulative number of HIV cases in Sri Lanka will increase to nearly 22,000 in the next five years, representing about 0.15 per cent of adults aged 15 to 64 (NAP 1994). If this rate of increase were of continue over the long term, Sri Lanka could well have more than 80,000 cumulative cases of HIV by the year 2005 and an HIV prevalence level of 0.54 per cent among the adult population.

Other health concerns are also pertinent in the context of increased HIV/AIDS. The association of HIV/AIDS with the rise of tuberculosis in Africa, Europe, and North America and the fact that many people in South Asia are carriers of the tuberculosis bacillus suggest that if left unchecked the HIV epidemic may also promote a future tuberculosis epidemic (Murray, Styblo, and Rouillon 1993). Thus, the HIV epidemic has the potential of triggering other public health problems in Sri Lanka in the future years.

The HIV/AIDS Epidemic as an Econimic Issue

Although biomedical and public health issues continue to dominate the collective agenda of AIDS researchers around the world, in recent years people have come to realize that the epidemic is more that just a health problem. It is also a problem with deep economic roots and potentially serious economic consequences.

Several influential policy makers and economists have warned that the AIDS epidemic could have significant negative consequences for economic growth and development (Cohen 1993; Merson 1992); Panyarachun 1995; World Bank 1993).[4] Others have emphasized microlevel effects on specific populations and subgroups (for example, those living with HIV/AIDS and thier families), and on particular sectors of the economy, such as agriculture, tourism, transport, and health care (Barnett 1995; Barnett Blaikie 1992; also see the papers in Bloom and Lyons 1993).

A growing literature has also documented relatively high rates of infection among sex workers, injecting drug users, long-haul truck drivers, commercial blood donors, migrant workers, sailors, and fishermen, thereby providing strong evidence of the role played by economic factors in the transmission of HIV (Bloom and Mahal 1995a; Orubuloye, Caldwell, and Caldwell 1993; Panos Institute 1992; U.S. Bureau of the Census 1993; World Bank 1992). Indeed, research on the economic implications of AIDS is increasingly being guided by models built around the observation that HIV is transmitted as a direct by-product of purposeful behaviour, and much less randomly than in the case of some other infectious disease (Bloom, Mahal, and O'Flaherty 1995; Kremer 1995; Philipson and Posner 1993).

An economic analysis of the AIDS epidemic is not limited to quantifying its impact or to exploring the underlying causes of the spread of HIV infection. Investigators are also increasingly noting the usefulness of the economic tools of cost–benefit and cost–effectiveness analysis to guide policy making in the area of HIV/AIDS (Bloom and Mahal 1995b). This is indicated by the emerging literature on the economic evaluation of HIV/AIDS

---

4. For a somewhat different claim about the effects of HIV/AIDS on economic growth, see Bloom and Mahal (1996).

prevention and care strategies (for useful surveys see Holtgrave, Valdiserri, and West forthcoming; Sisk 1995).

So far, economic research along these lines has been relatively limited in the Asia and Pacific region. For example, with the notable exception of Bloom and Lyons (1993), which focused on Asia, most work on the economic impact of HIV/AIDS has either been conducted in the setting of a developed country or has consisted of simulations carried out for some countries in Africa (e.g. Bloom and Carliner 1988; Bloom and Glied 1993; Cuddington 1993a, b; Cuddington and Hancock 1994; Hellinger 1993; Kambou, Devarajan and Over 1992). The paucity of research on the economic impact of HIV/AIDS at the sectoral level is particularly disturbing, since it is here that the impacts of AIDS are most likely to be felt initially. Indeed, prior to this there have been few systematic attempts to examine the impact of AIDS at the micro-level of households and sectors in Asia (for an exception, see Giraud 1993).[5] Impacts on key sectors such as tourism, which have been the focus of much attention from the media and from policy makers, have simply not been researched. Other areas in crucial need of research input are the impacts of HIV/AIDS on poverty and income distribution.[6]

The general lack of rigorously founded research in the Asia and Pacific region is also apparent in the literature on the economic roots of the epidemic. For example, additional research on the relationships between the risk of HIV and labour mobility, poverty, tourist inflows, and commercial sex work, is urgently needed.[7]

The paucity of research on the economic roots and impacts of the HIV/AIDS epidemic in Asia has hampered policy making with

5. For examples of such research in Africa, see Barnett and Blaikie (1992), and Ainsworth and Ovev (1994).
6. Recent work by Bloom and Mahal suggests that the impact of HIV/AIDS on economic growth is likely to be very small (Bloom and Mahal 1996). It is, however, possible that HIV/AIDS has implications for other indicators of economic well-being, such as poverty, income inequality, and life expectancy. See Bloom and others (1996) for some analysis along these lines.
7. Existing research has relied primarily on anecdotal evidence (Bloom, and Mahal 1996).

regard to the epidemic. In particular, with little information on the epidemic's economic determinants or consequences, it has proved extremely difficult to carry out economic evaluations of HIV/AIDS prevention and care programmes, and hence to make a case for government intervention in HIV prevention and care activities. Lacking this information, but facing other immediate and more visible problems (such as high rates of child and infant mortality, malaria, and tuberculosis) governments are, not surprisingly, unwilling to devote substantial resources to HIV prevention or the care of people living with HIV/AIDS. This unwillingness is compounded by the fact that HIV, at least in its early stages, is an invisible problem because of its long latency period. Moreover, even if countries were willing to invest in activities to prevent HIV and to care for those already infected, hardly any high-quality cost–benefit or cost–effectiveness studies are available to help policy makers choose among alternative policy instruments to address the HIV epidemic (for one such study see Over and Piot (1993)). This, in turn, means that they might misallocate scarce resources by choosing strategies that are not socially optimal.

Aggregate Consequences of the AIDS Epidemic in Sri Lanka

This section estimates the economic magnitude of the AIDS epidemic in Sri Lanka. It also examines the consequences of the epidemic for a variety of aggregate indicators of economic performance, including the pace of economic growth and human development, and the levels of poverty and economic inequality. The implications of the epidemic for two large sectors of the economy—tourism and health care—are also explored.

Economic Magnitude of the Epidemic

Three methods can be used to estimate the magnitude of the AIDS epidemic in economic terms. The first and most popular involves applying the standard cost-of-illness (COI) method to measure the cost of AIDS (Rice 1966). The second method, developed by Mishan (1971), estimates the economic cost of the epidemic to be the sum of individuals' willingness to pay (WTP) to avoid the burden of

AIDS. The third method focuses on the impact of the AIDS epidemic on broad measures of economic growth and development, such as growth of income per capita, and of quality of life indicators like the human development index (HDI) (e.g. Bloom and Mahal 1996; Bloom and others 1996; Cuddington 1993a,b; Over 1992).

The Cost-of-Illness (COI) Method

Under the COI method, the aggregate cost of the AIDS epidemic is expressed as the sum of direct costs, indirect costs, and psychological costs. Direct costs consist of out-of-pocket expenses that represent a diversion of scarce resources from other uses. They include personal medical care costs resulting from an illness, such as the cost of diagnosis, treatment, and care, as well as nonpersonal expenditures on education, research, blood screening, and other preventive activities. Indirect costs are the earnings foregone by AIDS patients and those caring for them, including the value of household production activities that they might otherwise have undertaken. Psychological or non-pecuniary costs refer to the pain and suffering caused by HIV and AIDS, to those living with HIV, and their families and friends. No COI studies exist that measure the monetary value of such psychological discomfort. We do not attempt to measure this value either, although the WTP approach discussed later typically does arrive at some approximation of the cost.

Direct Costs Per AIDS Case   One can estimate the lifetime personal medical care costs per person living with AIDS in three ways. The first method uses data on actual medical costs and charges, including the cost of drugs, for AIDS patients from the moment of diagnosis until death (as in Viravaidya, Obremskey, and Myers 1993). This approach requires detailed financial records for clinical hospital-based care. The second method simulates the cost based on information about a typical distribution of opportunistic infections associated with AIDS; expert assessment of the duration of each illness and hospital stay; the treatment protocol; and associated treatment, care, and drug costs (e.g. Bloom and Glied 1993). The third method estimates the relationship between per capita income and per case medical care expenditures on AIDS using cross-country data for countries in which one of the foregoing two methods were applied (see Bloom and Mahal 1993; Over 1993). The estimated relationship is used to predict the medical care costs for a country using information of its per capita income.[8]

Using the second and third of these methods, we estimate that personal medical care costs per AIDS case in Sri Lanka range from $US 290 to $US 1,150. We derived a first set of estimates by simulating the cost of WHO treatment protocols in combination with the clinical profiles of twenty AIDS patients in Sri Lanka, the cost of hospital stays, and the cost of outpatient visits (Tables 3 and 4). The lower estimate is the cost of inpatient treatment and care under the most basic treatment options, similar to level A of WHO guidelines (WHO 1991). The upper estimate is the cost of inpatient treatment and care under a more sophisticated protocol, i.e. level C of the WHO guidelines (WHO 1991). We assumed that the typical length of hospital stay for AIDS patients was thirty days, and we multiplied this duration by the daily cost of such stays (the costs per day are based on Attanayake and de Silva 1987, on direct quotations of prices by a number of private hospitals, and on personal communication with Drs Harsha de Silva and Lucian Jayasuriya). We calculated outpatient costs on the assumption of one visit per month during the symptomatic period. Costs per outpatient visit were based on consultation rates quoted by five general practitioners in Colombo, and on personal communication with Dr Harsha de Silva. Table 4 presents our estimates of personal medical care costs per AIDS patient in Sri Lanka.

We obtained a second set of lifetime personal medical care cost estimates in Sri Lanka by interpolation based on the results of a cross-country regression of medical care costs per case of AIDS on per capita income. In particular, we obtained our estimates using the following equation from Bloom and Mahal (1993):

$$\ln MCE = 1.038 + 0.955 * \ln PCY$$

$$(0.698) \ (0.086)$$

$$R^2 = 0.88; \ N = 20$$

---

8. Other factors can be introduced into the model as well.

Table 3: Expected Cost of Diagnosis and Treatment per Case of AIDS, Sri Lanka

Condition	Proportion of AIDS patients with disease/illness	Costs of treatment and/or investigation of conditions ($US)	Expected treatment costs ($US)
Tuberculosis	0.30	26.80–68.87	8.04–20.66
Herpes zoster	0.20	200.20	40.04
Candida of mouth	0.65	1.16–1.72	0.75–1.12
Candida of oesophagus	0.30	9.50–31.25	2.85–9.38
Bacterial pneumonia	0.20	0.70–24.96	0.14–5.00
Pneumocystic carinii	0.30	18.35–175.70	5.51–52.70
Taenia cruris	0.10	0.90–2.03	0.09–0.21
Scabies	0.15	0.00–3.13	0.00–0.47
Cryptococcal meningitis	0.25	58.12–1,328.40	14.53–332.10
Herpes simplex	0.05	71.50–1,115.40	3.58–55.77
Perianal abscesses	0.15	2.70–68.40	0.41–10.26
Continued fever	0.75	1.80–174.04	1.35–130.53
Wasting	0.60	2.51–43.70	1.51–26.21
Diarrhoea	0.50	0.75–68.94	0.38–34.47
Chronic cough	0.50	1.80–119.70	0.90–59.85
Lymphadenopathy	0.20	0.90–64.68	0.18–12.94
HIV test	1.00	37.25	37.25

Total expected costs: $US 117.51 to $US 828.96   117.51–828.96

Note: An exchange rate of $US 1 = SLRs. 48 was used. The two ranges for the cost of treatment correspond to the WHO treatment protocols A and C (WHO 1991). The lower bound are the costs if treatment protocol A were adopted, and the upper bound corresponds to treatment protocol C of the WHO guidelines; Dr. Soma de Sylva's data was used to estimate the proportion of patients diagnosed with each condition; we assumed that the full cost (costs of personnel, equipment, test kit, etc.) of testing a single sample of blood using the ELISA kit is $US 7.25, and $US 30 using the Western Blot. The former estimate is based on the price in Sri Lanka for getting AIDS-free certificates for overseas workers, and the latter estimate is from Bloom and Glied (1993).

Source: Dr Soma de Sylva's data; WHO (1991)

Table 4: Personal Medical Care Costs per Case of AIDS, Sri Lanka

Category	Amount ($US)	
	low scenario	*high scenario*
Diagnosis and treatment	117.51	828.96
Hospitalization	156.25	192.19
Outpatient visits[a]	13.74	37.50
Total $US	287.50	1,058.65

a. We estimated the cost of outpatient visits based on the following formula:

cost = duration of AIDS × visits per unit time × cost per visit (excluding the costs of drugs and investigations)

We assumed that a typical AIDS patient will live for twelve months and that he or she will make one visit per month on an average. A range of estimates of consultation costs per outpatient visit was considered. The lower-bound estimate for cost per visit was SLRs. 50 (based on a survey of five general practitioners in suburban areas). The upper-bound estimate was SLRs. 150 (based on data from five different health institutions in Colombo).
Note: An exchange rate of $US 1 = SLRs. 48 was used.
Sources: Dr. Soma de Syalva's data; information from hospitals and general practioners.

where *MCE* refers to estimates of average lifetime AIDS medical care expenditures (circa 1992), *PCY* is 1992 per capita income, and countries are the unit of observation. The numbers in parentheses are the standard errors of the coefficient estimates. Using an estimated per capita income level for Sri Lanka of $US 540 (World Bank 1994a) yields an estimate of personal medical care costs of $US 1,150 (For more details about cross-country data on the cost of treatment and care for AIDS patients see Bloom and Mahal 1993).

Indirect Costs Per AIDS Case Indirect costs per case are measured by the discounted value of earnings foregone by individuals who die prematurely because of AIDS.[9]. Measured in

9.   Although actual or imputed income foregone by family members or friends who care for people with AIDS can also be estimated and included in the overall calculation, it is not included here.

this manner, the indirect costs are a more accurate measure of private rather than social earnings losses, although if suitably adjusted (see for example, Bloom and Mahal 1993; Rice 1966) they can be used to provide a first approximation of reductions in the gross domestic product (GDP) or per capita income resulting from the AIDS epidemic.

Table 5 presents our estimates of indirect costs resulting from a single case of death caused by AIDS under alternative assumptions about the discount rate, retirement age, gender, and rural or urban location. It is immediately apparent from this table that foregone earnings (or indirect costs) per AIDS case are significantly higher than the costs of personal medical care associated with AIDS (which themselves are high in relation to Sri Lanka's per capita income; they range from approximately one-half to twice the annual per capita income depending on the treatment protocol). Furthermore, differences in gender and location affect the estimates of foregone earnings significantly. For example, if future income is discounted at 3 per cent, the death of an urban man from AIDS will result in foregone earnings ranging from $US 15,110 to about $US 17,870, whereas for a rural woman the loss will be considerably smaller, ranging from $US 4,460 to $US 5,310.

Adding the estimates of the direct and indirect costs yields an estimate of the cost of illness per AIDS case that ranges from $US 5,600 to $US 19,020 (presuming a discount rate of 3 per cent, and retirement at age sixty—see Table 5).

Note, however, that these estimates are merely lower bounds of the actual COI measures, because they do not include psychological costs and nonpersonal direct costs. Table 6 provides estimates of nonpersonal direct costs for the economy as a whole. The total of approximately $US 4 million is a lower-bound estimate of all HIV prevention related expenditures in Sri Lanka during 1993. At this rate, nonpersonal direct costs will account for nearly one-fifth of the total cost of illness due to AIDS in Sri Lanka during the next decade.

The Willingness-To-Pay (WTP) Method
Personal medical care costs and nonpersonal costs constitute only a portion of the total cost of AIDS, primarily because they fail to

Table 5: The per Case Direct and Indirect Costs of AIDS ($US thousands)

	Medical care costs per case	Lost earnings per case[a]		Cost of illness per case	
		low scenario	high scenario	low scenario	high scenario
Discount rate of 3 per cent					
Urban Areas					
Male	1.15	15.11	17.87	16.26	19.02
Female	1.15	7.87	9.39	9.02	10.54
Rural Areas					
Male	0.29	9.28	10.97	9.57	11.26
Female	0.29	4.46	5.31	4.75	5.60
Discount rate of 5 per cent					
Urban Areas					
Male	1.15	12.01	13.62	13.16	14.77
Female	1.15	6.26	7.12	7.41	8.27
Rural Areas					
Male	0.29	7.38	8.37	7.67	8.66
Female	0.29	3.55	4.05	3.84	4.34

a. Lost earnings were calculated on the basis of the following assumptions: under the low scenario, individuals are assumed to retire at fifty-five years of age, and under the high scenario at sixty. In both cases, they are assumed to die from AIDS at age thirty (NAP 1994). Furthermore, both case scenarios assume an average annual growth rate of labour income of 3.6 per cent (Central Bank of Sri Lanka 1994).

Note: An exchange rate of $US 1 = SLRs. 48 was used.

Source: Sex-specific survival rates, Department of Census and Statistics (1991); unemployment rates by location and sex, Department of Census and Statistics (1993b).

Table 6: Nonpersonal Direct Costs of AIDS, Sri Lanka, 1993

Source of funding	Activities funded	Cost ($US thousands)
Local		
Non-governmental organizations	Education, counselling, research, education of health workers	>3.90
Government of Sri Lanka	Education, HIV testing, precautions for health workers, National AIDS Programme	>233.00
International		
United States Agency for International Development	Education, condom distribution, counselling, HIV testing, drug use education, employment alternatives for youth	494.00
United Nations Development Programme	National AIDS Programme, blood screening, research	525.47
United Nations Fund for Population Activities	Education, research	>30.00
Norwegian Agency for Development Cooperation	Education, counselling National AIDS Programme	140.23
World Health Organization (WHO)	Education, blood screening HIV testing, condom distribution	2,000–2,500
Other international donors	Education, counselling, condom distribution, HIV testing	>263.00
Total		3,685–4,185

Source: Karen Merrey (personal communication); NAP data.

take into account the cost of pain and suffering. Such costs are likely to be especially significant in the context of AIDS-related illness and death, particularly considering the stigma associated with AIDS in many societies. In addition, several authors have argued that the COI method is methodologically inappropriate for measuring the economic burden imposed by illness or premature death (Mishan 1971; Schelling 1987). For example, the work of Mishan and that of Schelling suggests that indirect costs are not a fully satisfactory measure of the economic burden that results from a premature death caused by AIDS. Schelling has argued against using earnings or losses in national output as indicators of social cost, because it is not obvious 'to whom this loss accrues' (Schelling 1987: 794). Mishan argues against equating the estimates produced by the COI method with the value of lives lost, because this leads to such morally repugnant conclusions as assigning a zero value, or even a positive value, to the death of retirees who have no earnings (Mishan 1971: 690–1)

The WTP method, which Mishan (1971) suggests as an alternative to the COI method, can be used to measure the economic losses resulting from AIDS by evaluating the amounts that individuals would be willing to pay to reduce AIDS-related mortality risks. That is, if an individual facing a 1 per cent mortality risk is willing to pay $US 10,000 to avert that risk, then we could say that the value of a 'statistical' AIDS case to that individual is $US 1 million (see for example Schelling 1987). To this we add the amounts others—family members, friends, and so on—are willing to pay to avert the risk of death to those at risk. Thus, the WTP method may capture both medical care costs as well as psychological and other costs associated with illness and death.[10]

---

10. The conceptual basis for using the WTP method is that our calculations are the relevant ones for gains from HIV prevention programmes (see for example Broome 1978; Jones-Lee 1974). An alternative valuation scheme focuses on the amounts individuals would accept as compensation to forego risk reduction (that is, the willingness to accept [WTA] method). It can be shown that the WTA method can lead to substantially different (and higher) estimates of the value of a statistical life (Hanemann 1991; Shogren and others 1994). See our results on the survey of medical personnel below.

From a practical point of view, however, the accuracy of the WTP method depends on individuals' perception of risk and on the precision with which they can evaluate small changes in risk.[11] Thus, the estimates of the value of a statistical life produced by the WTP approach are likely to vary considerably depending on the perceived reduction in risk of infection and consequent mortality form AIDS. In particular, estimates based on willingness to pay for small reductions in risk typically exceed the monetary value of a life that results from WTP values for large reductions in risk, since the rupee value of risk reduction is greater at the margin (Jones-Lee 1974; Moore and Viscusi 1988a).[12]

Our WTP estimates of the value of statistical lives lost because of AIDS are based on surveys of students in the Department of Economics at the University of Colombo and members of the general population of Colombo. We constructed these estimates as follows. Firstly, we collected survey data on the amount individuals would be willing to pay to avoid becoming infected with HIV. Secondly, because HIV infections lead to death from AIDS only after a period of time (which we assumed to be eleven years), we interpreted the amount that individuals were willing to pay to avoid HIV infection as the present discounted value of avoiding an AIDS death eleven years in the future.

We derived estimates of the value of avoiding the risk of infection among economics students and the general population in two ways: (a) by evaluating their willingness to pay for disposable syringes; and (b) by evaluating their willingness to pay for HIV testing of blood hypothetically intended for transfusion to them.

Our surveys revealed that, on an average, individuals were willing to pay more than of forty cents per set of disposable needle and syringe (See Table 7).[13] Next we estimated the risk of HIV

---

11.   A vast literature deals with the evaluation of risk by individuals. See, for example, Kahneman and Tversky (1979); Lichtenstein and others (1978); Viscusi and Magat (1987); and Viscusi, Magat, and Huber (1987). In general, small risks tend to be overestimated.

12.   Simply put, the individual would be willing to put up less and less money for additional reductions in risk as that would necessitate taking away resources from other uses.

13.   Indeed, the WTP estimates for disposable equipment for respondents in the general population and in the undergraduate economics class at the University of Colombo are remarkably similar.

infection for an individual who, needing an injection, opts for a reusable needle and syringe in a hospital setting in Sri Lanka. Ideally, this should be the risk as perceived by such an individual, as that would be likely to be the key determinant of an individual's willingness to pay for safety. Our survey question did not, however, include a question that directly estimated the perceived probability of infection. This we do indirectly as follows. We take the relevant risk as given by p_i where p_i is assumed to depend on the chance that either the needle or the syringe is contaminated with HIV, and the probability of transmission of HIV from a contaminated syringe/needle to the person being injected. Studies on HIV transmission from needle-prick injuries in health settings suggest that the latter probability is about 1/250 (see for example Kaplan and O'Keefe 1993). The chance that the injecting equipment is contaminated with HIV will depend on whether it is adequately sterilized, and on whether or not it was previously used to inject people who might have been HIV positive. Individuals' perceptions of the frequency of sterilization were obtained from a survey of fifty doctors and nurses at Colombo's General Hospital carried out by the authors. According to the survey, nearly 66 per cent of the respondents believed the syringes to be adequately sterilized, whereas 50 per cent of the respondents believed the needles to be adequately sterilized. Assuming that needles and syringes are matched randomly, the perceived probability of drawing a set of inadequately-sterilized injecting equipment for a single injection is 0.67. At this rate of sterilization and assuming that the chance of a randomly-drawn injectee being HIV-positive is 0.038 per cent (the HIV prevalence rate in Sri Lanka), there is a 0.077 per cent chance that a reusable set of injecting equipment is contaminated with HIV.[14]

---

14. We assume that reusable equipment lasts on an average for sixty uses (personal communication with W. Ransi at General Hospital). Thus the average injectee can expect equipment to have been used about thirty times previously. With previous injectees having an HIV-prevalence rate of 0.038 per cent, and the sterilization failure rate perceived to be about 67 per cent, the chance of injecting equipment being contaminated with HIV is approximately 0.077 per cent. In our calculations, we used the following formula:

$$p_1 = [p_0 s + (1 - s p_0) q]$$

Table 7: The Willingness-to-Pay to avoid HIV infection, Selected Groups, Sri Lanka

Population group	Probability of infection (%)	Willingness to pay to avoid risk ($US)	Value of avoided HIV infection ($US thousands)
Students			
Non-disposable injecting equipment	0.000308	0.43	139.44
Untested blood	0.013950	58.54	419.64
Health Care Workers			
Injuries	0.004700	51.70–437.50	1,100–9,410
General population			
Non-disposable syringes and needles	0.000308	0.38	123.23
Untested blood	0.013950	56.00	401.43

Note: WTP estimates for students and the general population for avoiding the risk of infection were the arithmetic means for each group (obtained from surveys carried out for this study). For doctors and nurses, the required compensation was taken to be the arithmetic mean of the amounts reported.
Source: Authors' calculations.

Table 7 reports the two groups' willingness to pay to avoid the risk of HIV infection by using disposable instead of reusable needles and syringes. For economics students the value of avoiding certain HIV infection is estimated to be $US 139,000, whereas for the general population sample, the value of avoiding an HIV infection is estimated to be $US 123,000. To estimate the value of avoiding death from AIDS, we assume that the value of an

---

Where p_0s is the probability that injecting equipment is contaminated with HIV prior to an injection, whereas p_i ($i = 0, 1$) is the post-injection probability of contamination, q is the probability that a randomly selected injectee is HIV-positive (0.038 per cent), and s is the sterilization failure rate (0.67).

averted HIV infection is equivalent to the present discounted value of an individual's willingness to pay to avoid a future death from AIDS. Assuming that it takes eleven years from the date of HIV infection to AIDS-related death, we estimate that the loss caused by death from AIDS ranges from $US 171,000 to $US 193,000 (discount rate of 3 per cent).[15] In both cases, the WTP to avoid death from AIDS is much greater than the estimates produced by the COI method.[16]

Next, we evaluated individuals' willingness to pay for HIV testing of blood intended for transfusion to them. Our surveys of economics students and members of the general population suggest that these groups are willing to pay more than $US 55 for such testing (See Table 7). As our surveys did not include a question on the probability of HIV infection perceived by people about to receive blood, we calculated the risk of HIV infection as follows. It was assumed that each potential transfusee receives three units of blood after prescreening.[17] The chance that a randomly drawn unit of blood would be HIV positive is assessed to be 0.005 per cent, the same as the HIV prevalence rate in blood drawn at the National Blood Bank (de Zoysa 1995). Moreover, the probability of transmission of HIV when transfused with HIV-contaminated blood is 95 per cent (Kallings 1992). Under these assumptions, we estimated the risk of HIV transmission from a blood transfusion to be 0.014 per cent. This yields a value of averting an HIV infection ranging from $US 401,000 to $US 419,000. The corresponding values for averted AIDS deaths are $US 555,000 and $US 580,000 respectively.

Although large in relation to the COI estimates, the estimated value of a 'statistical' life in Sri Lanka is reasonably close to

15. If Val_H denotes the value of averting an HIV infection, and Val_A the value of averting an AIDS death, we have

$$Val_H = Val_A/(1 + i)^{11}$$

where i is the rate of discount.

16. The similarities in the WTP estimates for the general population and the undergraduate economics students are not surprising, because education levels and AIDS awareness are closely comparable among the samples of the two groups that we included in our survey.

17. Based on requests received by the National Blood Bank on a typical day.

estimates reported for the United States (Moore and Viscusi 1988), which range from $US 2.58 million to $US 8.25 million (in 1993 dollars). Indeed, as a check on the reasonableness of our estimates for Sri Lanka, we deflated the average of the value of life estimates in the United States by the ratio of the per capita incomes in the two countries expressed in purchasing power parity adjusted terms (UNDP 1994). This exercise yields an estimate of $US 650,000 for Sri Lanka, which exceeds the estimates we obtained.

Finally, we estimated the value to health care workers at the General Hospital, Colombo of avoiding HIV infection. We inquired about the monetary compensation they would require (the willingness to accept (WTA) method) if asked to work in hospitals where the HIV prevalence rate among patients was higher than the current national level. Our calculations are based on workers' responses about the compensation they would need to move from the General Hospital to another hospital where the HIV infection rate was 0.2 per cent. Our estimates of the risk of HIV infection that medical personnel face are based on their survey responses to questions on needle-prick injuries, and their perceptions about the use of sterilized injecting equipment in hospital settings. Assuming a rate of HIV transmission of 1/250 if injured by a contaminated needle, we estimate that the additional risk of HIV infection as perceived by medical personnel is approximately 0.0047 per cent. The average compensation desired by the fifty-five doctors and nurses included in our sample ranged from $US 51.70 to $US 437.50 depending on whether we included a single outlying observation. Thus, our estimates of the value of averting an HIV infection under the WTA approach range from $US 1.11 million to $US 9.41 million. Needless to add, the value of avoiding a current AIDS death is even higher.

Although our estimates of the value of life under the WTA approach are considerably greater than those produced by either the WTP or COI method, the results should not come as a surprise. Several experimental studies over the last decade have reached much the same conclusion (see for example Shogren and other 1994). Indeed, as Hanemann's (1991) work suggests, WTA estimates of the value of life are likely to exceed WTP estimates by a considerable margin, because safety cannot be easily substituted by another good (in this case, monetary compensation).

Aggregate Impacts of the Epidemic

Aggregate Costs of Illness We examine the aggregate impacts of the AIDS epidemic from three methodological perspectives. The first set of analyses relies on the COI method to construct an estimate of the aggregate costs of AIDS. This involves using the estimates of the direct and indirect costs per AIDS case and multiplying them by the cumulative number of AIDS cases that have occurred or are projected to occur over a defined period of time. Table 8 provides estimates of the aggregate personal medical care and indirect costs of the AIDS epidemic in Sri Lanka from 1994 to 2005 under different assumptions about the impact of the epidemic. Thus, with the sum of personal medical care and indirect costs amounting to between $US 16,260 and $US 19,020 for urban men per AIDS case, and between $US 9,020 and $US 10,540 for urban women, the aggregate cost of illness of an HIV/AIDS epidemic concentrated in urban areas could range from $US 200 million to $US 230 million by the year 2005, using a discount rate of 3 per cent. If we assume that nonpersonal costs would amount to an average of $US 4 million annually, the aggregate direct and indirect costs of the epidemic would be 15 to 20 per cent higher (see Table 6). [18] Multiplying projected cases by the per case cost is, of course, only an approximation of the true medical care costs of AIDS, since this procedure abstracts from coping strategies that might lower long run per case costs, or economies of scale that might arise in treatment of AIDS patients.

Aggregate Costs Under The WTP Approach This method constructs an aggregate measure of the costs of AIDS by multiplying WTP estimates of the value of life by number of AIDS cases. Using Mishan's approach, the aggregate costs of AIDS from 1994 to 2005 could range from $US 2.34 billion to $US 7.96 billion, using a discount rate of 3 per cent. Our calculations do not allow for the possibility that the

---

18. These calculations include only the costs of AIDS cases during 1994 to 2005. If we were to include the costs resulting from all new HIV infections that occurred during this period (not just the AIDS cases), the aggregate impacts measured in COI terms would be considerably larger.

Table 8: The Aggregate Costs of AIDS during 1994–2005: Estimates from the COI and WTP Approaches

Category	Number of AIDS cases[a]	Costs per case[b] ($US thousands)	Aggregate costs ($US millions)
Discount rate of 3 per cent			
COI[c]			
Urban epidemic			
Urban males	10,300	16.26–19.02	167–196
Urban females	3,430	9.02–10.54	31–36
Rural Epidemic			
Rural males	10,300	9.57–11.26	99–116
Rural females	3,430	4.75–5.60	16–19
WTP[d]	13,730	171–580	2,348–7,963
Discount rate of 5 per cent			
COI[c]			
Urban epidemic			
Urban males	10,300	13.16–14.77	136–152
Urban females	3,430	7.41–8.27	25–28
Rural Epidemic			
Rural males	10,300	7.67–8.66	79–89
Rural females	3,430	3.84–4.34	13–15
WTP[d]	13,730	211–717	2,897–9,844

Note:

a. The assumptions made were that the rate of growth of HIV prevalence forecast for 1994–9 (NAP 1994) will continue through 2005 (forecasts were made using EPIMODEL [Chin and Lwanga 1991]), and (b) that the proportions of rural and urban AIDS cases by sex will continue as at present.

b. The range of costs represents different assumptions about the retirement age.

c. Does not include nonpersonal direct costs. When calculating aggregate costs using the COI method, we assume two separate epidemics, one urban and one rural.

d. We calculated the value of life under the WTP method by converting the cost of avoiding an HIV infection into a cost per AIDS case by interpreting the former as a present discounted value of the latter. The range of estimates per case is based on estimates of the value of avoiding HIV infections reported in Table 7.

Source: Authors' calculations.

value of avoiding certain HIV infection will be likely to increase in the future with the rate of HIV seroprevalence.[19]

Note that estimates of aggregate cost obtained by the WTP method are much higher than those obtained by the COI method—ten to thirty-five times as high. This suggests that, in addition to the relatively young average age at which individuals die from AIDS, psychological costs and the risk-averse nature of individuals may be key factors inflicting significant welfare losses on the public.

Impacts on Economic Growth and Human Development

A third strand of the literature on the aggregate impacts of AIDS looks at its effects on the growth of real income per capita and other measures of development. Among the key contributors to the literature in this area are Cuddington (1993a,b); Cuddington and Hancock (1994); Kambou, Devarajan, and Over (1992); and Over (1992). In the context of a detailed macroeconomic model of Cameroon, Kambou, Devarajan, and Over find that AIDS could have had significant impacts on the rate of growth of GDP in that country. In other simulation exercises, Cuddington (1993a,b) and Cuddington and Hancock (1994) estimate that the AIDS epidemic will depress the annual growth rate of per capita GDP in Tanzania and Malawi by about one-fourth of one per cent through the year 2010. For more details, see Chapter 2 in this volume.

Given that the AIDS epidemic in Sri Lanka is much less severe than in Malawi or Tanzania (and is likely to remain so in the foreseeable future), models such as Cuddington's are unlikely to support the hypothesis that AIDS will have significant adverse effects on Sri Lanka's economic growth. Indeed, there are a number of reasons to suppose that the AIDS epidemic poses even less of a threat. These include (a) the presence in Sri Lanka of considerable surplus labour that could replace workers who die from AIDS, thereby mitigating output losses that might otherwise result from AIDS mortality; (b) the positive link that seems to be emerging between HIV infection, poverty and low schooling (Bloom and Glied 1993), which is probably due to more educated people being more aware of HIV and its routes of transmission and more

---

19. On the other hand, our estimates would be reasonable if people systematically overestimate risks.

willing to take suitable precautions; and (c) the likelihood that HIV and AIDS case projections will overestimate actual numbers of cases by relatively large amounts in Sri Lanka, a country to which HIV came relatively late, because individuals perceive and respond to the disincentives associated with the forms of behaviour that put them at high risk of contracting HIV (Bloom and Glied 1992; Philipson and Posner 1993; Kremer 1995).

To explore these issues, Bloom and Mahal (1996) use socioeconomic and AIDS data from fifty-one countries to examine empirically the question of whether the AIDS epidemic has had a significant effect on economic growth during the past decade. According to their results, the AIDS epidemic has a negative but statistically insignificant effect on the rate of growth of real income per capita. Specifically, they find that an annual average increase in cumulative AIDS prevalence of 1 per 1,000 adults will reduce the annual rate of growth of real income per capita by a statistically insignificant 0.04 percentage points. Using cumulative AIDS case projections, we can use this result to evaluate the impact of the AIDS epidemic on economic growth in Sri Lanka. If we assume that future HIV prevalence in Sri Lanka will follow the NAP's forecasts, then cumulative AIDS prevalence will increase from its 1994 level of 0.016 per 1,000 adults to about 1.064 per 1,000 adults by 2005, which amounts to an average annual increase in cumulative AIDS prevalence of about 0.095 per 1,000 adults.[20] Thus, we estimate that from 1994 to 2005 the AIDS epidemic will reduce the rate of growth of real income per capita by 0.0038 percentage points below its trend rate, further confirmation that the epidemic's macroeconomic impact in Sri Lanka will be tiny in the foreseeable future.

In a recent study, Bloom and others (1996) examine the impact of the AIDS epidemic on the UNDP's human development index (HDI), a broader measure of economic well-being than income per capita. They demonstrate that even though the AIDS epidemic will not affect per capita income significantly, it may nonetheless

---

20.   We calculated the cumulative prevalence of AIDS using projections from EPIMODEL (Chin and Lwanga 1991), and obtained data on population size and forecasted rates of population growth from Would Bank (1994) and on the proportion of adults aged fifteen to sixty-four from World Bank (1993).

adversely affect the HDI, primarily through its negative effects on life expectancy. In particular, they find that the HDI is reduced by nearly 0.002 for every increase in cumulative AIDS prevalence of 1 per 1,000 adults. Their results suggest that the AIDS epidemic will reduce Sri Lanka's HDI in 2005 to 0.0019 below its projected level of 0.765 in the year 2005.[21] Because Sri Lanka's HDI is projected to increase at an annual rate of 0.0077 from 1994 to 2005, the AIDS epidemic will cost Sri Lanka just three months of progress in human development during this eleven-year period, another indication that the epidemic does not threaten Sri Lanka with a major crisis in national development.

Distributional and Sectoral Impacts

Effects on Poverty and Economic Inequality

The impact of the HIV/AIDS epidemic on poverty and income distribution is examined at two levels. Firstly we explore the link between income and educational status and the risk of HIV infection. In the absence of mechanisms to redistribute the economic burden that individuals with HIV/AIDS (and the families of such persons) face, the link between income status and the risk of HIV infection is crucial in evaluating the epidemic's impact on poverty and income distribution. For example, if individuals with higher incomes face a greater risk of HIV infection, the epidemic might well promote a decline in income and wealth inequality. According to some researchers, this pattern describes the situation in Africa, at least among men (see for example Over and Piot 1993).[22] However, according to some investigators, the situation in Asia appears to be different. Although no conclusive studies are available, anecdotal evidence from a number of countries suggests that the relatively poorer segments of the population in Asia, whether male or female, face a disproportionately high risk of HIV infection (Basu 1995; Bloom and Mahal 1995a; Thant 1993).

21. The projection is based on an estimated non-linear relationship between the HDI for 1992 and its lagged value in the year 1980 using cross-country data (for details, see Bloom and others 1996). The HDI data used are from the *1994 Human Development Report* (UNDP 1994).
22. They argue that the risk of HIV infection is greater among men with higher incomes because of their greater access to and demand for foreign travel and commercial sex.

Thus, the HIV/AIDS epidemic would worsen the plight of the poor and increase inequality, even though it might not increase the number of households below the poverty line. Alternatively, the relationship between HIV infection and socio-economic status could be U-shaped, but no studies appear to have pursued this line of enquiry.

Secondly we examine the extent to which the economic burden imposed by AIDS is distributed across different agents in the economy. Even if the epidemic adversely affects the poor, to the extent that these costs are distributed over a large number of agents—via, for example, social or private health and life insurance—the final outcome in terms of the epidemic's poverty and income distribution effects will not be significant.

Income and Educational Status and the Risk of HIV Infection

We examined the link between income and educational status by carrying our several small surveys among households directly affected by HIV/AIDS, commercial sex workers, prisoners, workers in the FTZs, Sri Lankans who had worked abroad, and health care workers.

Previous studies in Sri Lanka suggest a positive correlation between income and educational status and knowledge about HIV. In a national-level knowledge and attitudes survey among the general population, Dharmasene and Karunaratne (1992) found that respondents in the estate sector had relatively poor knowledge about AIDS.[23] Moreover, this group had lower levels of education than other respondents in both rural and urban areas. Similarly, anecdotal evidence suggests that patients with sexually transmitted diseases (STDs) at the Central Venereal Disease Clinic in Colombo are disproportionately from the lower socio-economic groups (communication with the STD/AIDS Programme). However, there is always the possibility that many cases from higher socio-economic groups go unrecorded because the patients seek treatment for STDs in the private sector.

To examine the associations between income and educational status and knowledge about HIV/AIDS and risky behaviour, we

---

23. Their sample of nearly 3,400 individuals in the age group eighteen to sixty-four covered all of the districts in Sri Lanka excepting those in the Northern and Eastern provinces.

conducted two sets of surveys. We carried out rapid assessment surveys among members of the general population and among economics students at the University of Colombo, and we carried out more detailed survey of knowledge, attitudes, behaviour, and practices among migrant workers, health care workers, FTZ workers, commercial sex workers, and prisoners. In all, about 450 individuals were surveyed, with the number of respondents being close to a hundred each in the surveys of health care workers, members of the general population, and commercial sex workers, and fifty each for the remaining groups. Larger sample sizes for each group were precluded by financial and time constraints.

Although the small sample size for each group appears to limit the generalizability of responses to our surveys, there are a number of mitigating factors. First, our surveys were designed and carried out by a highly experienced team. Moreover, survey respondents were chosen with care. In the survey of health care workers at Colombo's General Hospital, for example, an appropriate stratified random sampling procedure was followed in choosing respondents from among various categories of medical personnel. There remains, of course, the possibility that survey responses of personnel from the General Hospital, one of the best hospitals in Sri Lanka, may not be fully representative of personnel in other areas of Sri Lanka. However, it appears likely that responses relevant to several of the questions that we are interested in, such as the impact of income and educational status on risk of HIV infection, may not be too susceptible to this source of bias.[24] Similarly, in our survey of the general population, considerable care was taken to include respondents from different locations in urban, rural, and suburban areas (in Colombo and Anuradhapura districts), and from among different socio-economic, age and gender categories.[25] Al-

24. As an illustration, our survey responses suggest that the relationship between income and educational status and the risk of HIV infection is quite similar across the different groups surveyed. This seems to indicate that, in this area at least, medical personnel at General Hospital are unlikely to be radically different from personnel at other health institutions.

25. Our sample did, however, have an average level of schooling of 9.1 years, higher than the 7.2 years for Sri Lanka as a whole. Moreover, nearly two-thirds of the respondents were women, which is higher than their share in the total population of 50 per cent.

though our survey of commercial sex workers is limited by the fact that all the respondents are from Colombo and neighbouring areas, it is balanced in its inclusion of members of both genders, sex workers by differing class of service, and workers belonging to different age-groups. Moreover, the sample size consists of nearly 1 per cent of the total population of sex workers in Sri Lanka (Ratnapala 1994).

Although the sample sizes are relatively small and include only women, our surveys among overseas returnees and among workers in FTZs are, in fact, quite representative of the overall population in each category. Our focus on women returnees is justified by the fact that the proportion of women amongst individuals taking up employment overseas has increased dramatically in recent years. Moreover, our survey includes respondents from a number of rural, urban, and suburban locations, and members of different socio-economic groups. Similarly, the survey among women workers in FTZs simply reflects the fact that most of the workers in FTZs are women (Hettiarachchi 1994). In addition, survey participants include workers in both the Katunayake and Biyagama FTZs which together account for 97 per cent of the total employment in FTZs in Sri Lanka.

We conducted two types of analyses on the survey data. First, we examined the extent to which inter-group differences in education and income status could explain differences in knowledge about HIV/AIDS across these groups. Table 9 presents some of our survey results. It is immediately apparent that an overwhelming majority of the Sri Lankan public (96 per cent of those surveyed) has heard of AIDS, and is generally well-informed about the major means of HIV transmission, such as unprotected sexual intercourse and the use of contaminated injecting equipment. However, there are several groups in which most respondents had not heard of HIV, and a significant proportion thought that HIV could be transmitted by mosquito bites. Furthermore, the correlation between the proportion of individuals within each group who had heard of HIV and their average years of schooling turned out to be large and positive. By contrast, average years of schooling turned out not to be highly correlated with the perception that mosquito bites could transmit HIV. A similar conclusion holds

Table 9: Income and Educational Status and Knowledge about HIV/AIDS, Sri Lanka

Group	Sample size	Average annual income ($US)	Education (years of schooling)	Knowledge about HIV/AIDS[a]		Knowledge about HIV transmission[b]			
				HIV	AIDS	Mosquito bite	sex	needles	swimming pool
General population	100	950	9.1	53	96	5	98	92	2
Economics students	50	n.a.	12.0	94	100	6	96	92	4
FTZ Workers	50	670	10.3	34	100	36	100	100	24
Overseas workers	50	n.a.	7.8	8	98	52	94	88	16
Commercial sex workers	100	2,286	6.6	35	100	14	100	96	9
Men	30	876	5.9	53	100	27	100	90	3
Women	70	2,890	6.9	27	100	9	100	99	11
Prisoners	50	low	6.2	26	100	42	100	94	20
Health care workers	100	1,550	13.4	100	100	9	98	98	15

Note:
a. Knowledge about HIV and AIDS is the percentage of respondents in each group who reply in the affirmative to questions about whether they have heard of HIV and AIDS.
b. Knowledge about means of transmission is the percentage of 'yes' responses in each group to inquiries about whether respondents believed that mosquito bites, swimming pools, unprotected sex, and the use of unsterilized needles were possible sources of HIV transmission.
n.a.: Not available.
Source: Authors' research.

for the relationship between average years of schooling and the proportion of people who thought that HIV could be caught in a swimming-pool. These results suggest that, if anything, the survey respondents were likely to err on the side of caution; that is, to overestimate the risk of HIV infection.

In addition to conducting aggregate cross-group analyses, one can also examine the extent to which knowledge about the HIV epidemic and risky practices is correlated with income and educational status within each group. Consider, for example, the general population survey. As noted, overall awareness of HIV/AIDS was high, with 96 per cent of the sample having heard of AIDS. Only 5 per cent thought that it was currently curable. Within the sample, an individual's education and income levels were positively correlated with knowledge about the HIV/AIDS epidemic. For example, all individuals with twelve or more years of schooling had heard of either HIV or AIDS (80 per cent had heard of both), whereas 92 per cent of those with less than twelve years of schooling had heard of one of the terms (only 27 per cent had heard of both). Similarly, 24 per cent of those with incomes of $US 625 or less annually had heard of both HIV and AIDS (8 per cent had heard of neither), whereas among those with annual earnings in excess of $US 625, 82 per cent had heard of both HIV and AIDS with all individuals having heard at least of one of the two. Moreover, there appears to a positive correlation between the level of schooling and the accuracy of perception of the different modes of HIV transmission.

Similar patterns are noticeable in the responses to surveys among other groups. For example, all fifty FTZ workers surveyed had heard of AIDS. Again, this is a group that is relatively highly educated (84 per cent had ten or more years of schooling), with an average annual income of $US 670, both of which are above-average, so this result is perhaps not surprising. However, only 34 per cent had heard of both HIV and AIDS, which parallels the results for the general population survey when one notes that all the respondents in the FTZ sample had twelve or fewer years of schooling. Among those with ten or less years of education, nearly 56 per cent thought that HIV could be transmitted by mosquito bites, whereas only about 10 per cent of those with more than ten years of schooling thought so.[26] Similarly, 26 per cent in the lower education category thought that HIV could be transmitted in the swimming-pool, compared to 10 per cent in the higher education category. There is, however, little evidence of a statistical association between income levels and knowledge about HIV/AIDS in the in the FTZ sample. Our survey results also indicate that safer sexual practices among FTZ workers are positively correlated with income and educational status.[27]

The results from the survey of prisoners also support the hypothesis that knowledge about HIV and AIDS is positively correlated with education. As only one prisoner had twelve or more years of schooling, we compared prisoners with seven or fewer years of schooling with those with more than seven years of schooling. Although the percentage of correct responses to the survey questions for the two categories was about the same for some questions, for others the more educated group demonstrated better knowledge. For example, nearly 39 per cent in the less educated group either agreed with or were unsure whether HIV could be transmitted merely by touching, compared to 22 per cent in the more educated group. Similarly, 48 per cent of the less educated group thought that HIV could be transmitted by sharing meals, whereas the figure was 26 per cent for the more educated group. This pattern was repeated when we focused on sexual practices among prisoners: of those with eight or more years of schooling, 40 per cent used condoms during sex with regular partners, compared to 20 per cent for those with less than eight years of schooling. The differences persist when we consider sex with casual partners.

Results from our survey of female commercial sex workers also support the hypothesis that the risk of HIV infection is negatively associated with income and educational status. For example, while all the commercial sex workers had heard of AIDS, 50 per cent of 'high-class' brothel workers (those with the highest earnings and educational levels) had also heard of the term HIV, com-

26. Unfortunately our results are confounded by the fact that 39 respondents of the sample of 50 had ten or fewer years of schooling.
27. Only 24 per cent of our sample reported having sexual partners (none had casual partners).

pared to only 28 per cent of 'low-class' brothel workers and 8 per cent of streetwalkers (with the least earnings and education).[28] Whereas none of the high-class brothel workers thought that HIV could be transmitted by touch, 8 per cent of the low-class workers and 32 per cent of the streetwalkers thought it could be. Of some concern was the finding that 16 per cent of the streetwalkers were unsure whether sharing needles with people with HIV/AIDS could result in HIV transmission, compared to none of the high-class brothel workers. The degree to which the women engaged in risky practices was less clearly matched to class. Streetwalkers, the lowest stratum of commercial sex workers, reported the lowest condom-usage rate: 44 per cent always used them, compared to 87 per cent of high-class brothel workers. The suggests a greater degree of risky sexual activity at lower levels of income and education. However, high-class brothel workers reported twice as many clients per month as streetwalkers, negating at least in part some of the risk-reducing effects of condom usage.[29]

The positive relationship between education and knowledge about HIV/AIDS holds even in the health care sector. A survey of a hundred medical personnel in Colombo General Hospital clearly demonstrated that doctors are better informed about HIV and AIDS than are nurses and lab technicians, who in turn are better informed than labourers and other attendants (the least trained medical personnel). All the medical personnel interviewed had heard of AIDS. Moreover, none of the doctors in our sample identified mosquito bites or the use of public toilets as risk factors in HIV transmission. However, 8 per cent of the nurses and laboratory technicians and 20 per cent of the labourers and attendants thought that mosquito bites were a risk factor. Similarly, 10 percent of the last two groups thought that public toilets could be a source of HIV transmission.

---

28. Female commercial sex workers in high-class brothels earn about $US 4,710 annually, compared to $US 2,390 for low-class brothel workers and $US 1,930 for streetwalkers. High-class brothel workers were also the most educated, with 80 per cent having eight or more years of education, compared to figures of 60 per cent for low-class commercial sex workers and 12 per cent for streetwalkers.

29. In our survey, high-class commercial sex workers averaged about 42 clients in the previous month compared to about 22 for sex workers in the lower categories.

In contrast to the pattern noted in the foregoing paragraphs, the survey of overseas returnee workers reveals little connection between income and education and knowledge about HIV and AIDS. However, there is some evidence that individuals with lower income and education levels are less likely to use condoms when engaging in sexual activity with casual partners.

Quite apart from the risks faced by people in different income and educational categories within a single occupational category, poverty and HIV risk could be correlated if poverty leads individuals to enter into more risky professions, such as commercial sex work. Indeed, it has been argued that poverty, in addition to influencing individuals' choices of risky employment, also affects their choice of work location. For example, it can encourage labour mobility, whether local or international (Over and Piot 1993). In turn, this may affect the frequency with which poorer people engage in kinds of behaviour that put them at higher risk for HIV infection (Bloom and Mahal 1995a).

To explore the impact of poverty on the choice of profession in the context of a simple example, consider an individual with an option of working outside the commercial sex industry at a wage w_0 (the reservation wage). Let the prevailing wage inside the sex industry be w_s, where w_s exceed w_0. Everything else being the same, standard economic theory suggests that the individual will choose to work as a sex worker as long as the difference between w_s and w_0 exceeds the expected cost of working in the sex industry, including the cost of HIV infection. However, if survival is valued for its own sake, and if w_0 is not enough to sustain life, then the relevant differential for the purposes of decision making is the larger $w_s + v - w_0$ (where v is the added benefit from survival resulting from choosing a career as a sex worker). In other words, for a given wage differential, individuals who expect to face survival problems elsewhere would be willing to accept a greater expected cost to work in the sex industry than those who do not face such problems. These individuals would tend to crowd out those willing to accept less risk of HIV infection, excepting those segments of the sex market where the supply elasticity of workers can be expected to be small, as among high-class sex workers. Moreover, with other things unchanged, one might expect the reservation wage w_0 to be lower for individuals with lower levels of education or for those from inferior economic backgrounds. Thus, we should expect a disproportionately large representation of individuals from economically disadvantaged households in the sex industry.[30]

In the survey of commercial sex workers, all except the high-class brothel workers reported survival as the most common reason for joining the sex trade, This reason appears even more compelling given Sri Lanka's high rates of unemployment, especially among women. During 1992, for example, the national unemployment rate was around 15 per cent, whereas the unemployment rate among women was 22 per cent (Department of Census and Statistics 1993a). Nearly 60 per cent of the street-walkers (the lowest among the classes of female sex workers we surveyed) admitted that at the time of joining the sex trade they had no other job options. This concern with survival as an explanation for entering the commercial sex trade is also particularly apt in the case of child prostitution. Although we did not survey child sex workers, Ratnapala (1994) has noted that most children involved in prostitution come from very poor families or from broken homes. In some case, where the children were sold into prostitution by their parents (Ratnapala 1994: 12), the decision to enter the sex industry was not made by the sex worker. As it is the survival of parents rather than children that gets primacy here, the consequences may be especially troubling because the ownership of sex services lies with the brothel owner who presumably has less of an incentive to care about the health of the sex worker, compared to a scenario in which these services are provided voluntarily.[31]

Not all entrants into commercial sex work, however, enter the profession to survive. Some probably view it as an economic opportunity. This was obvious from some of the sex workers'

30. Again, it is possible that a sex worker's level of education could affect her income, especially in the upscale sex market. However, the impact of educational differences on differential between w_s and w_0 is less clear.
31.   Readers may note that, apart from the issue of equity, there is an 'efficiency' problem as well in this case, since the brothel owner is less likely to include the harm to the health of the sex worker in his or her calculation of the net gain from providing sexual services (see Bloom and Mahal 1995a for examples from other countries).

responses to survey questions. More than half of all commercial sex workers (male and female) admitted having other job options at the time of entry into the sex trade. However, there is some evidence that this opportunity varied by educational ·status. For example, in comparison to other classes of female sex workers, a greater proportion (nearly 60 per cent) of those (also better educated) sex workers belonging to high-class brothels had other job options at the time of joining the sex trade.[32] Moreover, it would appear that among those who had outside job options, the better educated had better options. When asked how much they could currently expect to earn annually if they were not sex workers, the reported amounts varied from $US 250 per year for streetwalkers to between $US 750 and $US 2,050 per year for high-class sex workers. Given that the average annual income for a streetwalker or a sex worker from a low-class brothel was around $US 2,000, this would indicate that the more educated have less of an incentive to enter the lower quality, and presumably more risky, segment of the sex market.

Who Will Bear the Cost of the AIDS Epidemic in Sri Lanka?

The foregoing analyses suggest the AIDS epidemic will have at least a modest impact on Sri Lanka's economic well-being. But who will bear the burden of these losses? A central issue here is the distribution of the costs of the AIDS epidemic among different possible payers: individuals who develop AIDS and their families and friends, employers of individuals with AIDS, health and life insurance companies, health care providers, users of the health care system who do not have AIDS, taxpayers, and international agencies and charitable organizations (Bloom and Glied 1993).

Based on the earlier discussion, we can break down the welfare losses of the AIDS epidemic into direct costs, indirect costs, and psychological costs. Psychological costs, which include the costs of pain and stigmatization, are likely to comprise a major portion of the welfare cost of the AIDS epidemic. Direct costs refer to the full cost of medical care of people with AIDS and expenses on prevention programmes. Indirect costs are earnings lost because

---

32. The average years of schooling among high-class brothel workers was about 8.3 years, higher than the 5.1 years for streetwalkers.

of increased morbidity, premature AIDS-related death, and the diversion of other family members from productive activity. A focus on the distribution of direct and indirect costs can provide a basis for further inferences about the impact of the AIDS epidemic on income and earnings inequality.

We can obtain information on the sharing of the costs of pain and suffering due to AIDS from two sources. Firstly, we can examine the experiences of those living with HIV/AIDS and of their families. A number of news articles have documented the stigmatization faced by people with HIV/AIDS (e.g. Abeynayake 1993; Berenger 1992; Jayasinghe 1994b). In addition, based on our survey of thirty-four households, we conclude that individuals living with HIV/AIDS and their families, including in some cases their extended families, are likely to bear the brunt of significant psychological costs. In several of the cases we studied, families maintained strict secrecy to hide the nature of the disease from outsiders. This even included private, hastily organized funerals. In some case in which neighbours found out about an HIV-infected person living in the household, instances of social ostracism and protests did occur. Only in a few cases, however, was the HIV-infected person left to fend for himself or herself without any support from the extended family. In no case was community support to families living with AIDS sought (or probably offered) in contrast to the situation involving other serious diseases. Thus, in the early stages of the epidemic, social coping mechanisms appear to be dysfunctional.

Secondly, one can infer the likely sharing of psychological costs from knowledge, attitude, and behaviour surveys. For example, in a recent nationwide survey in Sri Lanka (Dharmasene and Karunaratne 1992), nearly 50 per cent of those interviewed agreed with the statement that 'AIDS is a punishment given by God', and some 47 per cent agreed that 'AIDS patients ought to be disgraced' and that one should not associate with them. This suggests both that families with AIDS patients are likely to suffer significant costs from social ostracism and stigmatization, and that AIDS patients and their families will bear these psychological costs alone.

As Table 9 shows, although the population is generally well-informed about modes of HIV transmission, a significant portion of individuals, especially those at the lower end of the income and education scale, think that HIV can be transmitted by touch, by sharing meals, or in a swimming-pool. This type of misinformations appears to promote ostracism. Conversely, ongoing IEC activities may be compacted to promote more compassionate and more efficient ways of coping socially with AIDS.

A particularly worrying result is that many health care workers in Sri Lanka's leading hospital, primarily nurses, labouers, and attendants, have misconceptions about HIV/AIDS transmission. Even more worrying is that nearly 36 per cent, if informed that a patient was HIV-positive, would notify other people without seeking permission from the patient. This raises an important concern about the privacy of those infected with HIV. In addition, most health workers support a policy of isolating AIDS patients in separate wards: 75 per cent of the medical personnel surveyed either agreed or agreed strongly with the statement that 'AIDS patients are very infectious, and should therefore be isolated in separate wards to reduce the risk of infecting medical personnel and other patients'.

As for the personal medical care costs of AIDS patients, available evidence for Sri Lanka indicates that taxpayers and HIV-negative users of the health care system will bear a significant portion of this burden. This is due, in large part, to two features of Sri Lanka's health care infrastructure: public-sector health facilities provide the bulk of health care—for example, the private sector accounts for only about 10 per cent of beds in impatient facilities (Griffin 1990); and services in the publicly-owned health facilities are provided free of charge and are typically as good as or better than those provided in private-sector facilities (Griffin, Levine, and Eakin 1994). However, the use of outpatient facilities is somewhat more evenly distributed between the public and private sectors. This suggests that private-sector health facilities will be more widely used in the early stages of HIV infection, with public-sector facilities used more often during the advanced stages of the disease, when expensive and high-quality care is needed.

The tendency to use public-sector facilities is likely to be particularly high in the case of HIV/AIDS patients. A knowledge and attitudes survey (Dharmasene and Arunaratne 1992) suggests that people perceive public-sector facilities as being better able to treat AIDS patients. Similarly, our survey of thirty-four households that either had a person living with HIV/AIDS or had experienced a death from AIDS provides evidence that publicly-provided health services will bear a significant share of the epidemic's medical care burden. Of the sixteen households in our sample where members had sought treatment for AIDS-related illnesses, most (more than 60 per cent) had relied heavily on public-sector health facilities.

Another feature of health care provision in Sri Lanka is the lack of widespread formal private health insurance. Indeed, the overwhelming presence of the public sector in the provision of health facilities leaves little incentive to participate in privately provided insurance. In 1992 private health insurance claims accounted to less than 0.5 per cent of public-sector health care expenditures (Department of Census and Statistics 1993a; Ernst and Young Company 1994: 30), compared to 65.4 per cent for the United States (Health Insurance Association of America 1995). Moreover, anecdotal evidence suggests that most buyers of health insurance in Sri Lanka are the relatively better-off, and hence health insurance in its present state is unlikely to serve as a mechanism for redistributing the costs of an epidemic that may well be concentrated among the poor (Ceylinco Insurance Company 1992; Ernst and Young Company 1994). In addition, the existence of exclusion clauses that rule out payments to people with HIV/AIDS further limits the provision of health insurance to people living with AIDS. However, as the exclusion clause is triggered only by a doctor's report identifying a person as HIV-positive, not necessarily by the insurance company's doctors (communications with the Insurance Corporation of Sri Lanka, Ceylinco Insurance, National Insurance Company, CTC Eagle Insurance, and Union Assurance, which together account for 98 percent of the health insurance business in Sri Lanka [Ernst and Young Company 1994]), health insurance payments might be made in the absence of an accurate diagnosis of HIV or failure on the part of the doctor to disclose the presence of HIV infection. Failure to diagnose HIV is quite often a possibility because many illnesses common in Sri Lanka are similar to AIDS-related afflictions. This disincentive to report AIDS diagnoses also suggests that reported AIDS cases will underestimate the true number.

Informally provided health insurance is another mechanism for sharing the medical care costs of AIDS. Two sources document the existence of this practice in Sri Lanka. Firstly, according to the consumer finance surveys of 1981–2 and 1986–7, income pooling and zero-interest loans are relatively common among members of extended families and among friends (Central Bank of Ceylon 1984; Central Bank of Sri Lanka 1990). Secondly, our household survey provides some evidence that people with HIV/AIDS receive financial help from their extended families: fourteen of the sixteen people in our sample who died from AIDS had received some form of family support and care. Thus, limited informal health insurance may well be available in the from of help from extended family networks, just as in Africa (Panos Institute 1992). Indeed, data from the consumer finance survey suggest that transfers to income pools amount to about 7 to 11 per cent of a household's monthly income (Central Bank of Sri Lanka 1990: 723). It is unlikely that private insurance will ameliorate the distributional impacts of AIDS. Ethical issues surrounding HIV testing and the very private nature of information on high risk activities suggest that AIDS will continue to remain off-limits for insurance companies.

Because AIDS patients will tend to rely on medical care provided by the public sector, some of the burden of the AIDS epidemic may also fall upon other users of the health care system, in the form of longer queues, increased waiting times, and so on. The size of this burden will depend on the speed with which public-sector health delivery systems can expand capacity to meet the needs of AIDS patients—in other words, it depends on the elasticity of supply for health services (in the form of bed capacity, number of medical personnel, and so on). As noted below in the discussion of the impact of AIDS on the health sector, this elasticity might be quite low. In that case, some of the burden may well be borne by other users of the health care system, instead of being passed on to taxpayers at large.

The financial burden of the nonpersonal direct costs of AIDS is likely to be distributed among taxpayers and international donor agencies. Foreign donors currently pay for nearly 90 per cent of Sri Lanka's expenditures on prevention (see Table 6). If this pattern continues, the burden of these costs will fall on foreign countries. While a full list of donors is unavailable, they include the Asian Development Bank (ADB), the U.S. Agency for International Development (USAID), the UNDP, WHO, the United Nations Fund for Population Activities (UNFPA), and the Norwegian Agency for Development (NORAD).

Unlike direct costs, the burden of earnings losses (or the indirect costs) will fall mostly on HIV-infected individuals and their families, as life insurance and social welfare insurance are not common in Sri Lanka. In 1990, only about one in thirty-three Sri Lankans held life insurance policies with private-sector insurance firms (Department of Census and Statistics 1993a). Furthermore, as in the case of health insurance, most life insurance policies carry exclusion clauses that rule our payments in the case of AIDS-related death, although in some cases minimum amounts are paid to the indiviual's family, provided premium requirements have been fulfilled (communication with Insurance Corporation of Sri Lanka, Ceylinco Insurance, National Insurance Company, CTC Eagle Insurance, and Union Assurance). There are entry restrictions as well. In some cases in which the policy applied for exceeds a certain amount, coverage is not granted until the results of an HIV test are provided. As with health insurance, life insurance policies tend to be held by upper income groups (Central Bank of Sri Lanka 1990), which suggests that these groups are the ones using insurance to manage the risk of AIDS-related earnings losses.

Another way to insure against income losses would be for extended families and groups of friends to pool resources. As noted earlier, the survey data on thirty-four households affected by HIV/AIDS provide some support for the hypothesis that financial support may be forthcoming from other family members in the case of the breadwinner's death. Evidence from the consumer finance survey of 1986–7 also supports the existence of income pooling as an insurance device in Sri Lanka. However, such transfers can account for only a portion of lost earnings caused by premature death from AIDS. Also, Sri Lanka does not have a system of social welfare insurance in place that could provide support to families that have experienced an AIDS death.

It is also possible that provident funds for public- and private-sector employees would help check the survivors' slide down the income scale. Currently, more than a quarter of Sri Lanka's population is protected under these schemes. However, the drawing down of provident funds to replace lost earnings merely results in the displacement of future consumption, even in the absence of a penalty for early withdrawal. For this reason, and because only a small proportion of the total population is covered, these funds, while serving as temporary financial support, do little to insure against the large earnings losses associated with the AIDS epidemic.

Sectoral Impacts of the HIV/AIDS Epidemic
A key feature of the AIDS epidemic is that its economic effects will be felt unevenly across sectors. This section explores the effects of the epidemic on the tourism and health care sectors.

Tourism   The tourism sector is an important contributor to Sri Lanka's economy. In 1990, it accounted for 1.76 per cent of the total value added in the economy (UNDP and World Tourism Organization [WTO] 1993), and provided employment to nearly 55,000 people, or about 1.1 per cent of the total labour force.[33] Apart from its direct contribution to national output and employment, the links between the tourism sector and the rest of the Sri Lankan economy imply that expenditures in this sector contribute to increased output and employment in other sectors in the economy by increasing the demand for their products. Of special significance are the so-called backward linkages of the tourism sector, represented by its purchase of inputs from other sectors (see for example Tantrigama 1994). According to one study, the 'tourism-multiplier' (the change in national output caused by a $US 1 change in the demand for tourist-sector output) is about 1.82, one of the highest multipliers for any sector in Sri Lanka's economy. Tourism is also an important source of foreign exchange (UNDP and WTO 1993). It has been increasing its share of foreign exchange earnings steadily after record lows in 1987, when tourism accounted for just 5.9 per cent of Sri Lanka's foreign

---

33. We calculated the size of the labour force by using population data on those aged fifteen to sixty-four (Department of Census and Statistics 1993a) and multiplying it by the labour force participation rate of about 50 per cent (Department of Census and Statistics 1992a).

exchange earnings (Tantrigama 1994). By 1992, tourism earnings accounted for 7.9 per cent of all foreign exchange earnings in Sri Lanka. The tourism sector compares favourably with other traditionally important sources of foreign exchange earnings: tea, rubber, and coconut exports, whose combined share in foreign exchange earnings was 47.4 per in 1982, but only 19.6 per cent in 1992; and the gem industry, whose share has remained stable at roughly 7 per cent since 1982 (Tantrigama 1994).

Since the mid-1960s, Sri Lanka's tourism industry has experienced three distinct phases. From 1966 to 1982, it expanded rapidly, with the number of tourists increasing at an average annual rate of 20 per cent (UNDP and WTO 1993). When conflict broke out in the north-east, the number of tourists fell dramatically. In 1987, only 182,000 tourists visited Sri Lanka, less than half the corresponding number in 1982. Since 1987, the tourism industry has revived, with an average annual growth rate in the number of tourists of about 17 per cent.

The rapid growth of tourism in recent years has been accompanied by plans for even more rapid development of this sector in the near future. Sri Lanka's *Tourism Master Plan*, jointly sponsored by the UNDP and WTO, envisages an ambitious tourism development strategy for Sri Lanka that will increase the number of tourists to 874,000 annually, and increase foreign exchange earnings by 300 per cent between 1987 and 2001 (UNDP and WTO 1993: 85–6).

In this context we examine the likely impact of an AIDS epidemic on Sri Lanka's tourism industry. The motivation for our analysis is the concern (mostly anecdotal) that prospective tourists will be frightened away if they think that HIV prevalence rates in the host country are high (Moreau 1992). This concern may also have led policy makers in some countries to downplay the importance of HIV, and to make smaller investments in information and education programmes related to AIDS (*Economist* 1989; Shenon 1992a). Alternatively, public opinion towards foreign tourists may suffer if Sri Lankans perceive tourists to be an important source of HIV infection (Milhuisen 1992; Shenon 1992a; *U.S. News and World Report* 1992).

In general, little consensus exists on whether the AIDS epidemic will adversely affect the tourism sector in Sri Lanka. For example, it has been suggested that AIDS will not affect tourism adversely, except for those visiting the country specifically to engage in unprotected sex (Economic and Social Council for Asia and Pacific 1991). A survey of 122 foreign tourists at Hikkaduwa carried out by the Natural Resources and Environmental Policy Project indicated that only about 7 per cent of foreign tourists visited Sri Lanka for sex (Tantrigama and White 1994; see also UNDP and WTO 1993: 188). This survey would tend to support the hypothesis that tourism to Sri Lanka will not be adversely affected. Other authors, however, suggest that a higher proportion of tourists visit Sri Lanka at least partly for sex (Aloysius 1993; Seneviratne and Peiris 1991; Waningasundara 1991). Available evidence has little to say on whether HIV prevalence in a country will have an adverse impact on inflows of other tourists (i.e. those who do not visit the country for sex). In this context it is interesting to consider the results of a small survey we conducted of Sri Lankan professionals and others connected with the tourist industry, about 50 per cent of whom thought tourist arrivals would be adversely affected by HIV/AIDS.[34]

The following is the first rigorous effort that we are aware of to examine the impact of the HIV/AIDS epidemic on tourist flows into a country. In the analysis that follows, we report the results of a cross-country study of the impact of HIV/AIDS prevalence on tourist flows during 1980 to 1991 in a sample of thirty-one countries.

We obtained the HIV and AIDS data used for this analysis using methods described more fully in Bloom and Mahal (1996). We obtained data on tourist flows from the WTO and data on population from *World Tables 1993* (World Bank 1994a).

We estimated the parameters of the following equation

$$TOUR_i = \beta_0 + X_i\beta_1 + \beta_2 AIDS_i + e_i$$

where *TOUR* is a measure of tourist flows (we used the natural logarithm of tourist arrivals in 1991 per 1,000 population as well

---

34. However, only twelve people out of our target sample of sixty responded to the questionnaire on tourism, a response rate of 20 per cent.

as each country's share of world tourist arrivals); *AIDS* is a measure of the severity of the HIV/AIDS epidemic in each country (we used both the annual average increase in cumulative AIDS cases per 100 adults and the annual average increase in the cumulative number of HIV infections per 100 adults); X is a vector of other variables that might also influence tourism; e_i are i.i.d. errors with zero mean; β_0, β_1, and β_2, are coefficients to be estimated; and 'i' is the country index.

The vector of control variables X might naturally include exchange rates, price trends, hotel capacity, cost of travel, quality of life, and so on from 1980 to 1991. Unfortunately, data on many of these variables are not readily available. Thus, we regressed a measure of tourism flows in the year 1991 on HIV/AIDS and a lagged measure of tourist flows (the logarithm of tourists per 1,000 population in 1980 and the country's share in world tourist flows in 1980, respectively). Presumably, the inclusion of the lagged dependent variable acts as a proxy for the other explanatory variables. Indeed. when we used quality-of-life indicators (for example, the HDI) in a regression that also included the lagged dependent variable, the coefficient of the quality-of-life variable was positive, but statistically insignificant.

Table 10 reports the results of the econometric analysis. Although the small size of our sample and the fact that, owing to data limitations, we were able to include only two sub-Saharan African countries (Kenya and Zimbabwe) limit the generality of our analysis, our results suggest that the AIDS epidemic has had a negative, but statistically insignificant, effect on tourist arrivals and countries' share in world tourism. Indeed, we were unable to reject, at the 5 per cent level of significance, the null hypothesis that the HIV/AIDS epidemic has not affected tourism in any of the econometric specifications reported in Table 10. Moreover, if we control for the fact that the AIDS epidemic in Asia is of comparatively recent origin by including a dummy variable for Asia, the coefficient of the HIV/AIDS variable becomes even less well determined. The magnitudes of the coefficients remain unchanged even when we include an additional explanatory variable to take account of changes in the exchange rate, although we do not report the results in Table 10. Nonetheless, the sign of the coefficient of

Table 10: The Impact of the HIV/AIDS Epidemic on Tourist Flows: A Cross-country Study[a]

	Regressors							
	Number of tourists per 1000 population, 1991[b]				Country's share in world tourist arrivals, 1991			
Constant	0.90 (0.25)	0.61 (0.33)	0.89 (0.25)	0.57 (0.32)	0.01 (0.05)	0.01 (0.04)	0.01 (0.03)	0.01 (0.06)
Average annual change in cumulative AIDS cases per 100 adults, 1980–91	-5.18 (2.73)	-2.51 (3.41)			-0.07 (0.06)	-0.11 (1.76)		
Average annual change in cumulative HIV infections per 100 adults, 1980–91			-0.42 (0.37)	-0.13 (0.36)			-0.01 (0.01)	-0.01 (0.01)
Number of tourists per 1000 population in 1980	0.93 (0.04)	0.97 (0.05)	0.93 (0.04)	0.97 (0.05)				
Countrys' share of world tourist arrivals, 1980					0.97 (0.15)	0.95 (0.15)	0.97 (0.15)	0.95 (0.15)
Asia dummy		0.28 (0.21)		0.31 (0.20)		-0.004 (0.005)		-0.004 (0.005)
R^2	0.96	0.96	0.96	0.96	0.81	0.81	0.81	0.81
Sample size	31	31	31	31	31	31	31	31

Notes: Heteroskedasticity consistent standard errors are reported in parentheses below the coefficient estimates.

a. Our sample includes thirty-one countries: in Africa: Kenya, Zimbabwe; in Asia: China, Hong Kong, India, Indonesia, Japan, Republic of Korea, Nepal, Singapore, Sri Lanka, Thailand; in Latin America: Brazil; in Europe: Austria, Bulgaria, Czechoslovakia, France, Germany, Greece, Hungary, Iceland, Ireland, Israel, Italy, Portugal, Spain, Switzerland, United Kingdom; in North America: Canada, United States; in Oceania: Australia.

b. Expressed in natural logarithms.

Source: Authors' calculations.

the HIV or AIDS variable is negative in all specifications (see Table 10), suggesting that countries with more severe epidemics may have experienced slower growth or a decline in numbers of tourists and shares of world tourist flows.

In analyses not reported in Table 10, we estimated the above equation by using two-stage least squares methods (TSLS). We instrumented the HIV and AIDS variables by the logarithm of the tourism variable in 1980; 1989 percentages of the population that were Christian and Muslim; the adult literacy rate in 1985; the growth rate of the urban population from 1970 to 1980; doctors per 1,000 population in 1990; and the year in which the HIV epidemic was estimated to have established itself in the sample countries (see Bloom and Mahal 1996 for further details). In principle, TSLS procedures account for the possible reciprocal influence of income growth on HIV transmission and AIDS. However, accounting for possible simultaneity had little effect on the coefficient estimates.

In addition to being statistically insignificant, the magnitude of the coefficient of the AIDS variable suggests small negative effects of AIDS on tourism in Sri Lanka even in a worst case scenario, as demonstrated by the following calculation. If the HIV and AIDS forecasts by the National AIDS Programme (NAP 1994) are correct, the annual average increase in cumulative AIDS prevalence per 100 adults will be of the order of 0.00396 during the years 1991 to 2001. From the estimates under the first specification in Table 10, it follows that the number of tourist arrivals will decrease by approximately 0.92 per 1,000 below their expected levels of 45 per 1,000 in the year 2001 (UNDP and WTO 1993), that is, a shortfall of nearly 17,700 tourists, or 2 per cent below the anticipated levels for that year.[35] However, if we use our preferred specification (the second in Table 10), the shortfall

---

35. The change in tourist prevalence for the year 2001 can be calculated by using the formula

$$d(TOUR) = 5.18 \times 0.00396$$

where *TOUR* is the natural logarithm of tourist arrivals per 1,000 population in 2001.

is considerably less, about 8,600 tourists, or less than 1 per cent
of the 874,000 tourist arrivals expected for that year.

The Health Care Industry The impacts of the AIDS epidemic
on the health sector are likely to be felt at several levels, although
not all of them can be quantified at this stage. For convenience
we categorize them into effects that work on the demand side and
those that are supply-oriented.

Demand-side factors will take the form of an increased demand
for health care services. The demand will be for both curative and
preventive services. We project that from 1994 to 2005 Sri Lanka
will have nearly 13,700 AIDS patients, with about 2,000 new
AIDS patients every year from 2000 to 2005. If all these patients
seek health care, they will account for an estimated 410,000 inpatient days of health care from 1994 to 2005, and for nearly
60,000 inpatient days annually from 2001 to 2005. On the average,
this amounts to an increase in total demand for inpatient days of
only one-third of one percentage point annually, although if one
assumes that this increased demand will be directed toward larger
and better equipped hospitals (such as base, provincial, and teaching hospitals), the demand for inpatient services in these hospitals
will increase by about three-fifths of one percentage point.[36] The
demand for outpatient services will also increase, although this
increase will be somewhat smaller, amounting to no more than
0.12 percentage points on an annual basis for the better equipped
hospitals (on the assumption that each AIDS patient would make
twelve outpatient visits).[37]

The demand for certain preventive services may also rise as
consumers of health services increasingly seek to obtain safer
blood supplies and to see better safety measures practiced in health
care settings, including the use of disposable injecting equipment
and the adoption of universal precautions. This is indicated in

36. Taken annually, 410,000 inpatient days over eleven years is approximately
37,000 days per year. In Sri Lanka, inpatient days amounted to nearly 11 million in
1991 (Ministry of Health and Women's Affairs 1992; 6 million for larger
hospitals).
37. During 1991, outpatient attendance in Sri Lanka was approximately 28.6
million for all health institutions (11.3 million for the better equipped hospitals
[Ministry of Health and Women's Affairs 1992]).

surveys conducted among economics students at the University of Colombo and members of the general population, who revealed a high willingness to pay for safety in a health care setting. Among economics students, for example, 94 per cent of those surveyed indicated that they were 'ready to pay for disposable injecting equipment', with 66 per cent ready to pay $US 0.50 or more for a single disposable needle/syringe. Moreover, 98 per cent of the students were willing to pay for the testing of blood for transfusion purposes, with nearly 40 per cent ready to pay up to $US 100. We obtained similar results in the survey of members of the general population: 90 per cent of those surveyed said they were willing to pay for the testing of blood, with nearly 50 per cent of the group willing to pay $US 100 or more; 83 per cent said they were willing to pay for disposable injecting equipment, with 35 per cent of the sample willing to pay $US 0.50 or more for a set of disposable injection equipment.

Most of the increases in demand for medical services will be for modern rather than indigenous medicine. According to the 1986–7 consumer finance survey (Central Bank of Sri Lanka 1990), nearly 80 per cent of Sri Lankans sought Western medical treatment, with another study (Department of Census and Statistics 1992b) reporting usage rates in excess of 85 per cent. Furthermore, public-sector services are likely to bear the brunt of the increases in demand, for two reasons. Firstly, as noted earlier, health care services in the public sector are provided free of charge, or at least at less cost than in the private sector (Ernst and Young Company 1994); and secondly, the quality of services provided by the public sector is typically at least as good as that provided in the private (Griffin 1990; Griffin, Levine, and Eakin 1994). 91 per cent of individuals receiving inpatient care receive it in the public sector, while a smaller fraction choose the public sector for outpatient treatment: in urban areas 53 per cent of those choosing outpatient treatment opted for the public sector, for Sri Lanka as a whole 64 per cent did so (Department of Census and Statistics 1992). While it might be argued that the public sector's dominance in the provision of inpatient services results simply from the private sector not having enough capacity to meet demand (Griffin 1990), this by itself is unlikely to be a satisfactory explanation.

Indeed, as Griffin, Levine, and Eakin (1994) note, capacity utilization rates are higher in public-sector hospitals than in hospitals in the private sector, supporting our earlier point that the lower relative cost of treatment in the public sector is probably significant (Ernst and Young 1994).

Although the increased demand for medical care because of AIDS is small in relation to overall capacity in the health care sector, the supply side of the sector is rather tight. Table 11 provides information on health sector capacity in Sri Lanka and a selected set of Asian countries. While the data suggest that Sri Lanka's health facilities compare favourably with Asian countries in terms of bed capacity, Sri Lanka is relatively short of medical personnel, especially qualified doctors. In addition, closer examination reveals that Sri Lanka will face a shortage of both doctors and bed capacity in the future.

Inpatient bed capacity in Sri Lanka has increased slowly during the last thirty years, at an annual average growth rate of 0.65 per cent. If bed capacity in the future continued to increase at this rate, given the projected trends in AIDS cases in Sri Lanka, AIDS patients would account for more than 30 per cent of the annual increase in bed capacity during 1994 to 2005 and nearly 50 per cent during 2001 to 2005. The supply shortage is likely to be compounded by the fact that the facilities most likely to face this increased demand are already operating at close to full capacity; capacity utilization in the better equipped, larger hospitals is 98 per cent (Ministry of Health and Women's Affairs 1992).

The problem of inadequate supply of heath services may be particularly acute in the case of health care personnel. Our survey of health care workers at Colombo General Hospital suggests that an increase in HIV prevalence among the overall population of patients, to 1 per 500, up from its current level of 0.19 per 500 (if one assumes that the prevalence rate among hospital patients is the same as the national seroprevalence rate), would lead 24 per cent of the medical personnel (31 per cent of doctors and nurses) to demand higher salaries. For the sample as a whole, the average monthly increase that would be demanded is estimated to be approximately $US 30 per month, a substantial amount when compared to the average salary of $US 129 each month for our

Table 11: Comparison of Health Facilities, Selected Countries and Groups of Countries, 1990

Country or Country Group	Facilities and personnel (per thousand population)			Health expenditures as proportion of GDP (%)			Health insurance spending (% of total health expenditures)
	Beds	Doctors	Nurses	Private	Public	Total	
Sri Lanka	2.8	0.14	0.71	1.9	1.8	3.7	<0.3
Bangladesh	0.3	0.15	0.12	1.8	1.4	3.2	0.0
India	0.7	0.41	0.45	4.7	1.3	6.0	2.0
Thailand	1.6	0.20	1.10	3.9	1.1	5.0	0.6
Asia	1.8	0.78	0.68	2.7	1.8	4.5	n.a.
Sub-Saharan Africa	1.4	0.12	0.61	2.0	2.5	4.5	n.a.
Industrialized countries	9.3	3.09	6.49	3.4	5.4	8.7	n.a.
World	3.6	1.34	1.88	3.2	4.9	8.0	n.a.

Note: n.a.: not available
Source: Ernst and Young Company (1994); Griffin (1990); World Bank (1993).

survey respondents.[38] If HIV prevalence rates increased still further, the medical personnel surveyed would ask for even larger raises. This is not surprising given that, in our survey, a significant majority (57 per cent) of medical personnel believe that caring for HIV/AIDS patients poses a risk. This belief might also mean that the supply of doctors and nurses will not keep pace with increased requirements in the absence of appropriate precautions in health care settings. Thus, the AIDS epidemic may promote medical care cost inflation in Sri Lanka or weaken the country's ability to satisfy its manpower requirements in this sector.

We conclude our discussion on the health sector impacts of AIDS by focusing on its likely consequences for public-sector health care expenditures in Sri Lanka. With an estimated 13,700 AIDS cases projected from 1994 to 2005, the aggregate personal medical care costs of AIDS are projected to range from $US 3.98 million to $US 15.79 million during this period. Given that the bulk of these cases (nearly 10,000) are projected for 2001 to 2005, and given that public-sector health care expenditures were estimated to be $US 174 million in 1994,[39] the impact on health care budgets will be quite small up to the year 2000. However, from 2001 to 2005, the average annual medical care expenses on AIDS could range from $US 0.59 million to $US 2.34 million, or about 7 to 22 per cent of the annual increase in public-sector health care expenditures, assuming that all care for AIDS patients in the public sector is provided free.

Economic Roots of the Epidemic

Our study of the economic roots of the epidemic focuses on two questions: (a) to what extent is the prevalence of forms of behaviour that increase the risk of HIV infection linked to a person's income or educational status; and (b) do certain occupations, ac-

38. In our calculations, we chose to omit a single outlying observation where the average increase demanded was seven times the rest of the group combined. If we included that observation, our estimate of the increases in monthly salary demanded to compensate for increased risk would be $US 238.
39. We estimated public sector health sector expenditures in 1994 by assuming that these were 1.8 per cent of GDP in 1994, the same percentage as in 1990 (World Bank 1993).

tivities, or situations have characteristics that increase the risk of HIV infection?

The previous section addressed the first question. There we concluded that, just as in other countries in Asia, the less educated and lower income groups in Sri Lanka face a greater risk of HIV infection because they are less well-informed about HIV and less likely to take adequate precautions. This section takes up the second question, and looks specifically at risks among FTZ workers, overseas workers, commercial sex workers, and prisoners. In this section, we also analyse the impact of foreign tourism on HIV transmission in Sri Lanka.

Workers in the Free Trade Zones (FTZs)

Sri Lanka currently has three FTZs that employ a total of nearly 75,000 workers. The three FTZs are located at Katunayake, Biyagama, and Koggala, and were set up in 1978, 1984 and 1991 respectively. We carried out our survey in Katunayake and Biyagama, which together account for 97 per cent of all FTZ workers.

Members of the general public (Milhuisen 1992) as well as researchers (Hettiarachchi 1994; Ratnapala 1994) tend to think that FTZs are places where workers face a high risk of HIV infection and that policy action is urgently required. They cite three main reasons to support their view. Firstly, most workers in FTZs are migrants from other areas who have little contact with their families, and hence are relatively free of the social controls on high-risk behaviour. Secondly, it is thought that the workers, who are typically young women from poor families with little access to other well-paying jobs, are sexually exploited by their employers (Hettiarachchi 1994). Thirdly, the high concentration of women in FTZs 'disturbs' the gender balance of the surrounding community, leading to substantial indulgence in risky behaviour, including multiple sexual partnering (Hettiarachchi 1994; Ratnapala 1994).

We conducted a survey of fifty female FTZ workers to evaluate the nature of risky behaviour in the FTZs. 70 per cent of the workers in the sample were twenty to twenty-four years old, and most (92 per cent) were migrants from rural or semi-urban areas.

Many of those interviewed were attracted to the FTZs by the stable and reasonably high incomes offered, which averaged about $US 670 annually. With two exceptions, respondents either had no other job options (70 per cent of the sample), or had much lower-paying alternatives (an average of $US 235 per year) at the time of joining the FTZ.[40] Moreover, an overwhelming majority of the unmarried respondents lived within the FTZs and had little day-to-day contact with their families. However, they were not totally cut off from their relatives, as nearly 85 per cent of the respondents provided financial assistance to their families, which on an average amounted to one-third of their incomes. The working conditions were typically harsh, with little time available for recreational activities, socializing, or visits home.

The distance form home, the harsh work environment, and the large number of women workers does not seem to be leading to large-scale, high-risk sexual activity in the FTZs. The workers did not cite sexual harassment as a major problem, although loneliness was. One respondent noted that a shortage of men could increase the likelihood of the women choosing a sexual partner of the same sex; however, researchers have noted the dramatically lower risk of HIV transmission in lesbian relationships than in male homosexual relationships (*The Island* 1994). We found no evidence of multiple sexual partners among workers in FTZs. Only 18 per cent of the unmarried respondents had prior sexual experience, which in most cases had had occurred before they started work at the FTZ.

Finally, results from the survey suggest that women working in the FTZs are reasonably well educated and well informed about AIDS and HIV transmission. There is some cause for concern, however, regarding their level of knowledge about other sexually transmitted diseases (STDs): 48 per cent had heard of 'social diseases', but fewer than 15 per cent had heard of herpes, syphilis, and gonorrhoea. A mitigating factor is that condom awareness is quite high. Eleven out of the twelve sexually active women in the sample had used condoms, and all recognized condoms as a method of preventing pregnancy and transmission of STDs.

40. The exceptions were two women who had been working as housemaids in the Middle East at salaries in excess of $US 1,500 per year. Their choice of FTZ jobs reflected their desire to return to Sri Lanka.

Overall, we find little evidence to support the view that FTZ workers are a high-risk group. This conclusion is consistent with their self-reported perception, as 90 per cent of our sample responded that they did not view themselves to be at a high risk of becoming infected with HIV.

Tourists

As noted earlier, following a decline in foreign tourism during the mid-1980s, Sri Lanka had experienced rapid growth both in the number of tourists and in earnings from tourism. Indeed, tourist arrivals are expected to increase by nearly 300 per cent during the period 1991 to 2001 (UNDP and WTO 1993). One possible concomitant of increased tourism, however, is an increase in HIV infections in Sri Lanka. For example, several authors and policy makers have suggested a link between tourism and HIV transmission in Sri Lanka, operating primarily through foreigners' demand for risky sexual activity (Aloysius 1993; Gallwey and Judson 1991; Ratnapala 1994; Sivaratnam 1992; UNDP and WTO 1993; Wijesinghe 1993; Waningasundara 1991). In a small survey conducted for this study among people involved with the tourist industry, nearly 40 per cent of the respondents agreed with this view.

We evaluate the impact of tourist flows on the spread of HIV in Sri Lanka by addressing the following question: What is the expected contribution of tourism to the number of new HIV cases in Sri Lanka in any recent year, and how does this result compare to the total number of new HIV cases per year?

Out estimates suggest that the HIV prevalence rate among adult tourists visiting Sri Lanka in 1992 was approximately 198 per 100,000.[41] On the assumption that 92 per cent of the visitors were adults (communication with the Ceylon Tourist Board), approximately 362,500 adult tourists would have visited Sri Lanka

41. For each country for which data on HIV were available (twenty-seven countries, which accounted for 89 per cent of the tourist flows to Sri Lanka), we calculated the adult HIV prevalence rate using unpublished data cited in Bloom and Mahal (1996). Next we multiplied this by the number of tourists from that country to Sri Lanka, and thereby estimated the number of seropositve tourists from that country. Summing up of all the countries yielded an estimate of the total number of seeropositive ·tourists, allowing us to estimate the HIV prevalence rate among tourists.

in 1992. From these figures we estimated the number of HIV-positive tourists visiting Sri Lanka in 1992 to be about 720.[42]

Whether any of the estimated 720 HIV-positive tourists transmitted HIV to the local population would depend on how many engaged in high-risk activities. A survey conducted in Hikkaduwa found that about 7 per cent of the tourists visiting Sri Lanka did so for sexual pleasure (Tantrigama and White 1994). On the assumption that the likelihood of seeking sex is the same for HIV-positive and HIV-negative individuals, about fifty of the HIV-positive people would be seeking sex. Given an average length of stay of some ten days (UNDP and WTO 1993), and assuming one unprotected sex act a day with a seronegative commercial sex worker, we estimate at most five new HIV infections among the population of sex workers each year, assuming a transmission rate of 1 per cent (Kallings 1992). Thus, the direct contribution of foreign tourists to HIV transmission in Sri Lanka in 1992 was less than one-half of 1 per cent.[43]

The previous computations do not allow for the possibility that a single HIV infection today will contribute to additional infections in the future. If, as suggested by projections in Sri Lanka, we assume that a single person infected with HIV infects another person once every four years, then Bloom and Mahal (1993) show that a single HIV infection today translated into 6.5 extra infections over the next decade. Including these downstream infections leads to the conclusion that over the course of the next decade, the total number of HIV infections caused by tourism in 1992 would be 3.1 per cent of all new infections in 1992. Seemingly large, it must be noted that this number (of downstream infections resulting from tourism) will be a very small proportion of *total* downstream infections resulting from the 1,267 new HIV infections of 1992.

Another possibility, especially in view of Sri Lanka's supposed reputation as a haven for paedophiles and others seeking commercial sex, is that tourists visiting Sri Lanka are self-selected, with

42. This method of estimation assumes either that tourists to Sri Lanka do not make more that one visit per year or that multiple visits are uncorrelated with HIV status.
43. We used EPIMODEL to estimate the number of new HIV infections (1,267) that would have occurred in that year.

seropositve individuals being more likely to visit. However, even if one were to assume that the HIV infection rate among tourists were 1 per 100, or 5 times our estimate, that would still result in only about 25 HIV infections, or less than 2 per cent of the new HIV infections in 1992. This last assumption is, however, rather extreme, because nearly one-third of the foreign visitors are women who, presumably, have a lower usage rate of commercial sex. In addition, a non-trivial and possibly sizeable share of sex acts undoubtedly involves the use of condoms (for levels of condom use by tourists see Kleiber and Wilke 1993; Vorakitphokatorn and Cash 1992). In our survey of commercial sex workers in Sri Lanka, all classes of female sex workers other than streetwalkers reported high rates of condom use.[44] More than 85 per cent of the female sex workers in brothels reported always using condoms. Condom-usage rates were, however, lower for male sex workers, only 47 per cent of whom reported using condoms 'very often'.

Thus foreign tourists do not appear to present a major HIV threat to Sri Lankans, and two additional factors suggest that tourism will be even less of a threat in the future. First, HIV prevalence rates in European countries, which provide the bulk of the tourist flows to Sri Lanka, have stabilized (Kallings 1992); and second, if HIV prevalence rates in Sri Lanka rise, especially among commercial sex workers, the associated rise in the probability of being infected from a local source means that the chances of a Sri Lankan getting infected form unprotected foreign sexual contacts will decline further.

Overseas Workers

In 1990, nearly 288,000 Sri Lankan nationals, or about 5.2 per cent of the domestic labour force (calculated based on a participation rate of about 50 per cent of the population aged fifteen to sixty-four [Department of Census and Statistics 1992a]), were employed in foreign countries (Stalker 1994). This percentage is significantly higher than among Sri Lanka's neighbours (Stalker 1994) and an important component of Sri Lanka's economy. Overseas workers are an important source of foreign exchange

---

44. In comparison, only 52 per cent of the streetwalkers reported using condoms always.

earnings. Net workers' remittances (of nearly $US 632 million in 1993) amounted to nearly 37.5 per cent of Sri Lanka's foreign exchange reserves at the end of 1993 (World Bank 1995). In recent years, however, concerns about overseas workers have arisen in connection with their being a potentially important vector for the "immigration" of HIV.

A number of authors consider overseas workers to be at high risk for HIV infection (Gallwey and Judson 1991; Ratnapala 1994; Sivaratnam 1992). They cite three main reasons for this view. Firstly, they argue that working abroad increases loneliness, a phenomenon that is usually accompanied by a breakdown of social and other constraints on promiscuous behaviour because of the distance from home (Bloom and Mahal 1995a; Ratnapala 1994). The problem could be especially acute for Sri Lankans employed in the Middle East, as they typically do not bring their families with them and generally find travelling home difficult (Stalker 1994: 244). Secondly, there is anecdotal evidence that female workers in the Middle East are sometimes sexually exploited by their employers or by the middlemen involved in arranging their travel and employment (Ratnapala 1994; Stalker 1994). Thirdly, a large proportion of overseas workers are employed in unskilled occupations, including domestic work, and these jobs are likely to attract relatively less educated people, who may also have relatively limited knowledge of HIV or of the various means of protection from HIV infection.

To explore these issues, we carried out a survey of fifty women who had worked abroad, mostly in the Middle East, but who had returned to Sri Lanka by the time of the survey.[45] This focus on women and returnees rather than on current overseas workers limits the generalizability of our conclusions; however, nearly 60 per cent of the respondents indicated that they intended to return overseas, and will thus be overseas workers in the future. In addition, the proportion of female workers among overseas workers is large and increasing (Mahawewa 1993). For example, airport

45. The interviews were conducted among returned workers at one urban location (Slave Island), one suburban location (Madiwela), and three villages in Kegalle district.

survey records for 1994 indicate that the share of migrant workers who are women was well above 80 per cent.

The general picture that emerges is one of young women (the average age at the time of first going abroad was 28.5), with moderate education (the average level of schooling in our sample was 7.8 years compared to the national average of 7.2 years (UNDP 1994)), and with few good job prospects at home. The average annual earnings of those working at the time of migration was around $US 355, with a significant proportion having no job at all. Such women are attracted to overseas work by salaries that are around four times what they could earn in Sri Lanka (the average annual earnings of this group while overseas was $US 1,390). For those who were married, their husbands were generally employed in low-paying occupations. Thus, in general, these women belonged to economically disadvantaged groups, undoubtedly an important factor drawing them overseas. Once abroad, most of the women were employed as domestic workers: more than 84 per cent of the sample reported working as housekeepers or baby-sitters.

In response to a query about difficulties faced while abroad, 56 per cent listed loneliness as a problem (the most common response) while 20 per cent listed sexual harassment either at work or while travelling. Feelings of loneliness do seem to have translated into sexually promiscuous behaviour in several cases. Nearly a quarter of the respondents reported having sex with casual partners or with someone other than their spouses, with half of them reporting sexual experiences with one or more casual partners while abroad.[46] In addition, nearly 32 per cent of the workers felt sexually 'uncomfortable' at their place of work, and 58 per cent either knew or had heard of other workers who felt the same way.

If a woman works in an environment where she is totally under her employer's control, she can often do little to avoid exposure to sexual harassment and any associated risk of HIV infection, even if she is knowledgeable about HIV/AIDS and methods of HIV prevention. This is especially true of domestic workers, who

46. The differences arise because of our survey distinction between casual and regular partners (see Sittitrai and others 1992).

have few opportunities to move out of their employers' residences. Nonetheless, examining the level of knowledge of female overseas workers about the HIV/AIDS epidemic is instructive for two reasons. Firstly, we can evaluate the extent to which female overseas workers are making informed choices when deciding whether to work abroad, that is, whether they take the risk of contracting HIV into account. Second, as roughly 12 per cent of the sample reported multiple casual sexual partnerships, a survey of knowledge, attitudes, and behaviour among overseas workers can yield insights into the risk of HIV transmission in such relationships.

In general, workers returning from overseas are knowledgeable about the HIV epidemic and the major means of HIV transmission: more than 90 per cent of the respondents had heard of AIDS, 92 per cent agreed that AIDS could be transmitted by unprotected sexual intercourse, and more than 80 per cent agreed that it could be transmitted via needle-sharing. However, there is some scope for improvement. For example, 92 per cent of the respondents had not heard of HIV, and most had little knowledge of the symptoms of AIDS. They were also relatively poorly informed about the different modes of mother-to-child transmission (awareness levels were about 55 per cent), and significant proportions thought that HIV could be transmitted by mosquito bites, donating blood, or using public toilets.

Overseas workers also lacked specific information about STDs other than AIDS. It may well be that STDs are broadly understood in the general population as 'social diseases', without reference to specific types. Nonetheless, only 14 per cent of the survey respondents were familiar with syphilis, and 24 per cent with gonorrhea, whereas these two diseases have been identified by Gallwey and Judson (1991) as the most commonly occurring STDs in Sri Lanka.

Overseas returnees also exhibit poor awareness of condom use as a method of protecting themselves against HIV/AIDS. For example, survey responses indicate that the practice of condom use during sex with regular partners was no different from that during sex with casual partners. In addition, among those who claimed they knew how to protect themselves from STDs, only 16 per cent mentioned condoms. However, most respondents knew about condoms, knew where they could be purchased, and did not consider them expensive.

Thus our survey results provide some support for the proposition that overseas workers face risks of HIV infection that are directly related to the nature of their work, whether in the farm of sexual abuse in the workplace or through the formation of casual sexual partnerships. The riskiness of their situation is compounded by the fact that a large proportion of overseas workers are unaware of condom use as a way of protecting themselves from STDs, including HIV/AIDS.

Commercial Sex Workers

Workers in the commercial sex industry, both male and female, are among the groups considered extremely vulnerable to HIV infection and a core group for HIV transmission. Indeed, a vast literature documents the high risk of HIV infection that workers in this industry face throughout the world (Bloom and Mahal 1995a and references cited therein; Brown, Sittitrai and others 1994; Kaldor and others 1994; Mann, Tarantola, and Netter 1992; Tan and Dayrit 1994; U.S. Bureau of the Census 1993). The importance of sex workers as a factor in HIV transmission can be gauged from a calculation reported in Bloom and Mahal (1995a) which suggests that in the absence of condom use, commercial sex practices in Bangkok, Bombay, and Chiang Mai could result in 900,000 new HIV infections annually. Not surprisingly, the sex industry has come under great scrutiny in Sri Lanka (Aloysius 1993; Gallwey and Judson 1991; *Island* 1994; Srisang and others 1991; UNDP and WTO 1993; UNICEF 1991). It has also been a focus of attention for researchers (Ratnapala 1994; Sivaratnam 1992).

Sex workers are considered to be at high risk for several reasons. The first is the very nature of their work. Secondly, investigators agree that sex workers are relatively unaware of the risks of unprotected sex both because they have relatively low levels of education (Ratnapala 1994; Sivaratnam 1992) and because commercial sex work is illegal and it is difficult, therefore, to identify and inform sex workers about the risks they face (Ratnapala 1994: 19). Finally, even if they are fully aware of the risks, sex workers may be unable to protect themselves from HIV infection because of their low bargaining power in commercial sex transactions. Investigators have attributed this lack of bargaining strength either to the fact that the sex worker is controlled by the brothel owner, who may have bought the worker for a financial consideration, especially in the case of children (see Ratnapala 1994), or to the highly competitive nature of the sex market with a high elasticity of supply of sex workers (in conjunction with a clientele that prefers not to use condoms) (Bloom and Mahal 1995a). Results from a 1993 sentinel surveillance survey, in which 0.24 per cent of a sample of sex workers tested positive for HIV (the highest rate of any group included in the surveillance study), further highlight the importance of focusing on this group (NAP 1994).

Our survey of commercial sex workers had three key objectives: (a) to ascertain commercial sex workers' level of knowledge about the risks of contracting HIV/AIDS; (b) to document the extent of risky practices among Sri Lankan commercial sex workers; and (c) to explore the bargaining power theory of condom use in the commercial sex market.

Our study goes beyond Sivaratnam's (1992) in that it analyses the knowledge, attitudes, and behaviour of sex workers and the functioning of the commercial sex market in significantly more detail. Also, as the work has been carried out more recently than either Ratnapala's or Sivaratnam's studies, it provides information about knowledge and behaviour changes among workers in this market during the last few years.

Knowledge, Attitudes, and Practices Among Commercial Sex Workers   Table 12 reports some of the results of the knowledge, attitudes, and practices portion of our survey of one hundred commercial sex workers and some of the results Sivaratnam (1992) obtained. As the table shows, the sex workers we interviewed were quite well-infromed about the HIV/AIDS epidemic and various modes of HIV transmission, as all of them had heard of AIDS and knew that it could be transmitted by unprotected sexual intercourse. This level of knowledge carries over to other means of HIV transmission; for example, 96 per cent knew that HIV could be transmitted through the use of non-sterile injecting equipment. These are significantly higher numbers than those reported in

222 The Economics of HIV and AIDS

Sivaratnam's study, where 78 per cent had heard of AIDS and only 51 per cent were aware that HIV could be spread by sexual intercourse (Sivaratnam 1992: 49). Thus, not only are the HIV awareness levels among commercial sex workers high, they seem to have increased over time.

Unfortunately, as Table 12 also reveals, this high level of knowledge about HIV/AIDS risks does not carry over to other sexually transmitted diseases or to the practice of safe sex. While most respondents knew about syphilis, only 22 per cent knew about herpes. In addition, Table 12 reveals that only about 50 per cent of the commercial sex workers in our sample reported using condoms during sex (69 per cent reported that condoms were 'no fun').

Although high levels of risky behaviour still prevail in the commercial sex industry, Table 12 provides striking evidence of behaviour change in the commercial sex industry since Sivaratnam's study. Putting aside the various conceptual issues involved in making comparisons between the two studies, reported condom-usage rates increased by 27 percentage points from 1992 to 1994, while the percentage of sex workers holding the view that 'condoms reduce the fun' fell by 14 percentage points. These results also provide evidence of a positive relationship between knowledge of HIV/AIDS and the adoption of safe sexual practices among those at risk. However, most of the reported behaviour change has occurred among female sex workers. Most female commercial sex workers reported that they had increased their use of condoms after learning about AIDS, sometimes through outright refusal to engage in sexual activities with clients who would not use condoms. Only 3 per cent of the male commercial sex workers reported a change in their behaviour (one out of thirty). Indeed, the data reported in Table 12 show that the proportion of males who reported that 'condoms are no fun' remained stable at around 90 per cent during the period 1992–4, helping to confirm the validity of our survey results.

Condom-usage rates differ considerably by gender. Table 12 reveals that even though the general information levels in the two groups are similar (with male commercial sex workers being, if anything, somewhat better informed), female sex workers report

Table 12: Knowledge, Attitudes and Practices among Commercial Sex Workers, Sri Lanka, 1992 and 1994

Survey group	Sample size	Knowledge about HIV/AIDS and its transmission (per cent)		Knowledge about other STDs (per cent)		Attitudes and practices relating to condoms (per cent)		
		Heard of AIDS	Sexual transmission	Syphilis	Herpes	Usage rate	No fun	Inexpensive to obtain
Our survey (1994)								
All sex workers	100	100	100	88	22	50	69	74
Male	30	100	100	80	37	0	90	60
Female	70	100	100	91	16	71	60	80
High class	45	100	100	100	22	87	62	80
Low class	25	100	100	100	4	44	56	80
Sivaratnam (1992)								
All sex workers	160	78	51	n.a.	n.a.	23	83	n.a.
Male	58	93	71	n.a.	n.a.	9	89	n.a.
Female	102	70	39	n.a.	n.a.	31	79	n.a.

Note: n.a.: not available.
Source: Sivaratnam (1992); Authors' research.

significantly higher condom-usage rates than male sex workers. This is borne out in the attitudes of female sex workers towards condoms: a relatively higher proportion of them view condoms as inexpensive (compared to male sex workers), and a relatively lower proportion view condoms as spoiling the fun. In responses not reported in Table 12, 70 per cent of the female sex workers in our survey indicated that they would require their clients to use condoms even if the clients did not want to, whereas only 40 per cent of the male sex workers said they would do the same. In addition, in comparison to male sex workers, a greater proportion of female sex workers reported that they had been tested for HIV (50 per cent compared to 17 per cent).[47] Some of these differentials in behavior could be accounted for by the fact that the male sex workers in our sample had spent twice as many years (five years, on the average) in the profession as the female sex workers. As a consequence, they may have less of an incentive to take precautions during sexual acts if they perceive themselves to be already infected with HIV. It could also be that female sex workers use condoms to avoid the additional risk of getting pregnant, although there is little evidence to support this.[48]

However, the fact that female sex workers take more precautions than male sex workers does not necessarily mean that their risk of contracting HIV infection is small.

Our survey reveals that on an average, female commercial sex workers meet with two clients per day, often engaging in risky vaginal and anal sex.[49] This implies a non-trivial probability of infection, because as Table 12 indicates, condom usage among female sex workers is still far from universal (i.e. around 70 per

47. Further evidence for the gender differences in risk behaviour comes from sex worker reponses to queries about their STD history. 19 per cent of the female sex workers in our survey had STDs during the previous year, compared to 50 per cent for the male sex workers.
48. In a national survey of married women in the age group fifteen to thirty-four carried out by the Family Health Bureau (personal communication), fewer than 3 per cent of those who reported using some method of contraception also reported the use of condoms.
49. Although male sex workers report an average of just one client a day, they also report a greater frequency of sex than female sex workers, contributing to a high overall risk of infection.

cent). In addition, female sex workers' knowledge of STDs is relatively poor, a major concern given that many STDs are co-factors in HIV transmission. Thus it is no wonder that our survey reveals that fully 50 per cent of the female commercial sex workers viewed themselves to be at moderate to high risk of HIV infection.

Our survey also explored the extent of drug use among sex workers. Nearly 44 per cent of the sample of female respondents reported having used drugs at some stage in their lives, although they did not inject. By contrast, 73 per cent of the male sex workers in our sample reported ever having used drugs, and of them nearly one-third injected. Moreover, 20 per cent of the male sex workers had used drugs within the last six months. Of special concern was the fact that most of the drug injectors had also shared needles.

Market Power of Commercial Sex Workers In general, commercial sex workers appear to have below-average levels of education: the average level of schooling in our sample of one hundred was 6.5 years (with negligible gender differences), somewhat lower than the Sri Lankan average of 7.2 years. However, this hides considerable differences by class in educational levels among sex workers. The average years of schooling for high-class brothel workers in our sample was nearly 8.3 years, much higher than the 5.1 years for streetwalkers. Furthermore, about 80 per cent of our sample reported that other people were financially dependent on them. Nearly 37 per cent of the female commercial sex workers (48 per cent in the case of streetwalkers) described survival considerations as important factors in their decision to become sex workers. Of the female sex workers, 46 per cent reported that they did not have an option of another job at the time that they joined the sector (60 per cent in the case of streetwalkers). Although most of the male sex workers reported the possibility of other jobs, they too cited economic survival as an important factor in their decision to join the industry. Thus, economic necessity appears to play a crucial role in promoting entry into the commercial sex industry, particularly in the case of those at the lower end of the commercial sex hierarchy (streetwalkers). However, male sex workers seem to have more options:

83 per cent of male commercial sex workers had a secondary occupation, compared to 15 to 25 per cent of the female commercial sex workers.

We also find some evidence to support the claim that sex workers are constrained in condom use by demand and supply conditions prevailing in the commercial sex market. In particular, our survey results indicate that high-class commercial sex workers perceive the demand curve for their services to be more inelastic in response to changes in price, than among other classes of female sex workers.[50] Inquiries about the effect of price increases on the demand for their services revealed that high-class sex workers expected little short-run reduction in demand for increases that were less than 20 per cent of the original price charged. Moreover, for increases that amounted to a little more than 50 per cent of the original price, they expected the short-run demand for their services to fall by around 12.5 per cent. In other words, the perceived short-run elasticity of demand for a price increase appeared to range from 0 to 0.22 for this group of sex workers. Conducting similar exercises for other categories of sex workers, we estimate the perceived elasticity of demand for low-class brothel workers to range from 0.11 to 0.36, and for streetwalkers from 0.27 to 0.43.

Standard economic theory suggests that a high responsiveness of quantity demanded to changes in price may indicate competitive conditions in a market. Thus, it appears that the lower-quality market among sex workers is characterized by a greater level of competition. One explanation for the competitive nature of this market could be that services of lower classes of sex workers are more easily substitutable for each other. This suggests, in turn, that there is less scope for these sex workers to demand condom use of their clients. Competitive conditions also exist in the market for male sex workers. Here the elasticity of the perceived demand curve exceeded 0.5. Not surprisingly, condom-usage rates among the male sex workers are also low.

---

50. By elasticity of a demand curve, we refer specifically to the ratio of percentage changes in the quantity demanded of a good or a service to percentage changes in the price of that good or service.

Prisoners

Little information is available about prisoners in the context of the literature on HIV/AIDS. Yet the approximately 71,000 prisoners in Sri Lanka (of whom only 5.3 per cent are women [Department of Census and Statistics 1993a]) may be highly vulnerable to HIV infection for several reasons. Firstly, anecdotal evidence suggests that prisons in South Asia are poorly managed, and are typically populated by relatively large numbers of drug users who often contrive to consume drugs in prison (Rahman 1995). Secondly, the existence of a large pool of adults living in close proximity under conditions of extreme segregation by gender suggests the possibility of considerable homosexual activity. Sexual interaction in such circumstances will probably be unprotected, because condoms are not easily obtainable in prison stettings and because prisoners typically have relatively low levels of education and perhaps low awareness of the risks of HIV infection as well.

We report here the results of a survey carried out among 50 prisoners in Sri Lanka, 30 men and 20 women. The average length of schooling in the sample was 6.2 years. An overwhelming majority of this group had been employed in low-level occupations prior to being in prison, with 14 per cent being commercial sex workers and 16 per cent being drug dealers (42 per cent of the sample were in prison for drug possession).[51] The average length of prison stay in the group at the time of the survey was 1.75 years. Conditions in jails are bleak: they have poor sanitary conditions, are extremely crowded (more than 50 per cent of our sample was housed in cells with twelve or more inmates, with the average space per prisoner estimated at approximately 8 square feet), and there is considerable fighting among inmates.

Our prisoner survey yields evidence of high-risk behaviour in Sri Lanka's prisons. Nearly 22 per cent of our sample (27 per

51. The current estimate for the drug-using population in Sri Lanka is around 50,000 (communication with Ravi Kandiah of the National Dangerous Drugs Control Board). Heroin, opium, and cannabis are the most commonly used drugs. There are no reliable estimates for the drug-injecting population, although in one study of 371 drug users, 13 per cent were found to be drug injectors (communication with Ravi Kandiah).

cent of the men and 15 per cent of the women), reported sexual experiences while in prison, all of which were with members of the same sex. Furthermore, half of the sexual activities among men were compensated, providing evidence of commercial sex activity within prisons.

Most of the prisoners in our sample reported sexually promiscuous behavior prior to being imprisoned; an additional reason for concern about HIV transmission. Almost all the unmarried prisoners had experienced sexual intercourse in the past, and among 'ever married' prisoners, nearly 80 per cent had sex with someone other than their spouse. Nearly 28 per cent of the prisoners had engaged the services of commercial sex workers in the past (45 per cent for male prisoners and 5 per cent for females). Although prisoners reported a relatively high condom-usage rate (67 per cent reported 'ever' having used condoms), there is still cause for concern in view of their sexual history, the possibility of high-risk homosexual activity within prisons, and the near impossibility of obtaining condoms in prisons. Indeed, nearly 34 per cent of the prisoners viewed themselves as being at high risk for HIV infection.

These concerns are magnified by the prisoners' rather uneven knowledge of the various means of transmission of HIV: 42 per cent thought that HIV could be transmitted by sharing meals with an HIV-infected person. Prisoners' knowledge of other STDs is also a cause for concern. Only 56 per cent had heard of syphilis, and 28 per cent of gonorrhoea. Also disturbing were prisoners' attitudes towards condom use: 44 per cent of the survey participants reported that 'condoms make sex no fun', and nearly 20 per cent thought that condoms were expensive.

Policy Issues

The headline of a 1994 article in the *Sunday Times* was 'Injecting Infections'. (Jayasinghe 1994a). The article described the risks patients faced because of the reuse of improperly sterilized needles and syringes in health care settings. This was not the first time that Sri Lanka's health care sector had come under scrutiny. A 1992 article in the *Island* (Wijetunge 1992) had addressed the same issue. The concern with reusable needles has also been noted in connection with risks faced by medical personnel (Fernando and others 1992; Kuruppuarachchi and Jayasinghe 1992a, b, 1993; Rahulla and Jayasinghe 1993).

Cost is a major barrier to safeguarding Sri Lanka's blood supply from HIV infection and to reducing the risk of infection through injection and other practices. Whether funds should be allocated to these activities depends on the returns afforded by such 'investments'. Cost-benefit analysis is one method economists use to measure and compare the costs and benefits of such investments. This section reports economic evaluations of three often-discussed policies and programmes for addressing the HIV/AIDS epidemic in Sri Lanka: (a) screening the supply of blood used for transfusion, (b) making the use of disposable injection equipment mandatory by law, and (c) adopting universal precautions in health care settings.

Screening Sri Lanka's Blood Supply

This section describes our cost-benefit analysis of Sri Lanka's current policy towards screening blood donated for transfusion and estimates the net economic gain from this policy, which involves testing all donated blood for HIV. This can establish whether it is economically beneficial to carry out HIV tests of donated blood, given the currently low seroprevalence rate in Sri Lanka. Our analysis will also enable policy makers to make economically rational decisions about investing in blood testing versus using funds for other activities.

The screening strategy currently followed by Sri Lanka's National Blood Transfusion Service (NBTS), a public-sector organization with a central blood bank in Colombo and 47 regional blood banks that collect blood from about 100,000 donors each year (de Zoysa 1995) is a multistage process consisting of (a) pre-test screening, (b) confidential blood unit exclusion, and (c) the testing of all donated blood for HIV.

Pre-test screening refers to efforts by the NBTS to minimize the prevalence of HIV and other infectious conditions, such as malaria and hepatitis B, among the pool of blood donors (de Zoysa 1995). For example, blood donations are accepted only from voluntary, non-remunerated donors.[52] Moreover, potential donors are given leaflets, which discuss the risk of HIV infection from blood donation and include appeals for self-exclusion if the donor belongs to a high-risk group. Finally, the donor is asked to sign a form indicating that he or she is free of a variety of potentially infectious conditions (including HIV infection). Apart from these safeguards, the blood collection staff is trained to look for evidence of such conditions among potential donors.[53] Following pre-screening, all donated blood is tested for HIV and other infectious conditions. Confidential unit exclusion refers to the procedure whereby the blood of perceived high-risk donors is eventually discarded without the donors' knowledge even if it tests negative for HIV. If a sample tests positive, it is subjected to repeat testing as well as to the confirmatory Western Blot (WB) test.[54] If at any stage a donor's sample tests positive, it is discarded, even if it later tests negative.

To evaluate the benefits of testing donated blood for HIV we must first estimate the number of HIV infections that it would help to avert and then place a monetary value on these averted infections. The value of each HIV infection averted can be monetized either as the discounted sum of personal medical care costs and indirect costs per person, or as the average willingness to pay to avert a certain HIV infection.

To estimate the number of HIV infections averted by HIV testing, we have to make an assumption about the type of screening mechanism that would exist in the absence of HIV testing. We believe it reasonable to assume that in the absence of explicit HIV testing of blood, the standard protocol would include pre-test screening of donors along with confidential unit exclusion, but without any testing of their blood for HIV. This strategy does not, however, preclude testing blood for hepatitis B, malaria, and so

52. It is well known that blood collected form 'commercial' donors has a greater chance of being contaminated with STDs (including hepatitis B). See, for example, Titmuss (1971).
53. For example, they may look for injection marks, skin lesions indicating Kaposi's sarcoma, and so on (de Zoysa 1995).
54. The standard approach is first to test blood for HIV by the ELISA, SERODIA, or HIVSPOT tests, followed by a confirmatory test only if the sample tests positive (de Zoysa 1995).

on. Indeed, testing for these conditions preceded HIV testing of donated blood in Sri Lanka (communication with Nandrani de Zoysa).

To estimate the number of HIV infections averted under the NBTS screening strategy, we consider two cases: a low scenario and a high scenario. Under the low scenario, we assume that the HIV prevalence rate in the prospective donor pool is 0.08 per cent; under the high scenario, we assume it is 0.7 per cent (our projection of the seroprevalence rate among blood donors in the year 2005 if the epidemic proceeds unabated). HIV projections for the donor population are made using EPIMODEL (Chin and Lwanga 1991) and assume that men account for 70 per cent of these infections. The basis for this assumption is that during the early stages of the HIV epidemic, men typically account for a greater proportion of the infections (see Table 2).[55]

Even if there were no HIV testing of blood, the existence of pre-screening implies that HIV prevalence in donated blood is likely to be substantially less than the HIV prevalence rate among the pool of prospective donors. Indeed, in 1993, the seroprevalence rate in donated blood was only about 0.005 per cent (de Zoysa 1995), compared to an estimated donor seroprevalence rate of 0.034 per cent, amounting to a nearly 85 per cent reduction in risk of HIV infection. On the assumption that a similar rate of risk reduction occurs for higher levels of seroprevalence among blood donors, we estimate that the HIV infection rate in blood donated after pre-screening would be 0.011 per cent and 0.1 under the low and the high scenarios, respectively.

To estimate the number of HIV cases averted by pre-screening, we begin by estimating the number of units of blood and blood products that would be contaminated with HIV. On the assumption that 80,000 units of whole blood were collected from 100,000 donors (de Zoysa 1995), we estimate that during 1994, a total of 125,000 units of blood and blood products would have

55. We assume that the proportion of men in total HIV infections continues to be the same in the year 2005. We also assume that 80 per cent of the donors are men (de Zoysa 1985; Titmuss 1971).

been transfused.[56] The chance that each of these units of blood is contaminated with HIV in the absence of any screening will be 0.08 per cent under the low scenario and 0.7 per cent under the high scenario, if we assume that blood donors are selected randomly from the donor age-group, after taking account of gender differences in the propensity to donate blood.

Data on requests for blood from the central blood bank reveal that, on an average, about 2.24 units of blood are needed for each donee (communication with Nandrani de Zoysa). Thus we estimate the number of transfuses in 1994 to be approximately 55,800. If there were no screening, and if the probability of infection from transfusion of HIV-infected blood is taken to be 0.95 (Gelles 1993), between 95 and 831 new cases of HIV would occur annually from blood transfusions, depending upon the seroprevalence scenario. This analysis assumes no further 'downstream' infections caused by the initial infection via seropositive blood. If, however, we allow for downstream infections, then the number of new infections that would result because of the absence of blood screening would be substantially greater. For example, using formulae developed in Bloom and Mahal (1993) and assuming that on an average an HIV-positive individual infects another every four years (based on projected trends in Sri Lanka during 1994–2005) implies that a single HIV infection today would lead to 6.5 new infections over the next ten years. If so, not screening for blood in any one year alone could result in 708 to 6,193 new HIV infections over the next decade.

Next, we estimated the number of infections that would be expected to occur with pre-screening only. The difference between the number of infections that would occur in the presence and in the absence of pre-screening is the expected number of HIV cases averted under this strategy. Under our assumptions, after pre-screening is the seroprevalence in donated blood falls to 0.011

56.   Each unit of whole blood can be processed into roughly two units of transfusable components such as washed red cells, fresh frozen plasma, cryoprecipitate, packed red cells, and platelet concentrates (Gelles 1993; Sandler and AuBuchon 1987). In 1993, nearly 90,000 units of blood components were produced in Sri Lanka, which accounted for 45,000 units of whole blood. The remaining 35,000 units of whole blood plus the 90,000 units of components constitute the 125,000 units of whole blood and blood components that were available for transfusion.

per cent under the low scenario, and 0.1 per cent under the high scenario. Thus, in a single year, pre- test screening averts 82 new HIV infections under the low scenario, and 713 HIV infections under the high scenario (Table 13). Allowing for the possibility of downstream infections, this translates over the next decade into 610 and 5,308 averted cases of HIV under the low and the high scenarios, respectively.

With testing of blood following pre-screening in any given year, an additional thirteen to 117 new HIV infections can be averted (or 96 to 872 new cases of HIV can be averted over the next decade, including downstream infections). This is a direct consequence of the fact that the sensitivity of tests used to check for the presence of HIV in blood is typically high, of the order of 98 to 99 per cent (Eisenstaedt and Getzen 1988; Spielberg and others 1989).[57]

To monetize the benefits of each screening protocol, we multiply the number of averted HIV infections by the total savings in the form of personal medical care expenses and indirect costs avoided (after appropriate discounting) or by the averted costs of HIV infection as measured by the WTP approach. For our calculations under the COI method, we used the mid-point of the range of estimates of the cost per avoided infection for urban men, as reported in Table 5. For calculations under the WTP method, we used the mid-point of the range of estimates reported for the general population in Table 7. Table 13 indicates that even if we exclude downstream infections, the marginal benefits of HIV testing in the form of avoided medical care and personal income losses range from $US 227,000 under the low scenario to $US 2.1 million under the high scenario (we have assumed that the epidemic is concentrated among urban men). Although not reported in Table 13, if future benefits are discounted at 5 per cent, the gains in terms of avoided medical care and indirect costs would be somewhat smaller, ranging from $US 180,000 to $US 1.6 million.[58] When evaluated in terms of the WTP criterion, how-

57. By sensitivity we mean the probability that the test will register a positive result, conditional on the event that the sample of blood is contaminated with HIV.
58. For our calculations, we use the mid-point of the range of estimates for urban men (see Table 5).

Table 13: Evaluating the Benefits and Costs of Blood Screening in Sri Lanka (HIV infections assumed to occur among urban men, discount rate of 3 per cent)

Benefits and Costs	Downstream infections excluded		Downstream infections included	
	Low scenario	High scenario	Low scenario	High scenario
Expected number of infections averted				
Pre-screening only	81.94	712.50	610.45	5,308.13
Pre-screening plus HIV testing	94.80	829.47	706.26	6,179.55
Marginal benefits from HIV testing[a] ($US thousands)				
Cost of illness method	226.85	2,063.35	1,690.09	15,371.85
Willingness to pay method	3,373.56	30,684.74	25,133.84	228,599.60
Costs of HIV testing ($US thousands)				
Cost of test kits/personnel	748.30	752.16	748.30	752.16
Cost of blood disposal[b]	6.94	7.24	6.94	7.24
Cost of replacing destroyed blood[c]	24.98	26.07	24.98	26.07
Total costs	780.22	785.47	780.22	785.47
Net Benefits ($US thousands)				
Cost of illness method	553.37	1,277.88	909.87	14,586.38
Willingness to pay method	2,593.34	29,899.27	24,353.62	227,814.13

a. The monetary measure of aggregate benefits from averting HIV infections per case under the COI method is the product of the expected number of HIV cases averted and the sum of the personal medical care costs and indirect costs per HIV infection for urban males (see Table 5). We assume this to be $US 17,640 (the mid-point of the range of estimates for a 3 per cent discount rate). The WTP measure of the benefits per case of HIV infection averted in the process of blood transfusion is the mid-

(Contd)

point of the estimates obtained from the survey of members of the general
population $US 262, 330 thousand)—(see Table 7).

b. The full cost of blood disposal is derived by first estimating the total
volume of blood destroyed. We estimate the full marginal costs of disposing of a single donation to be $US 3.

c. Refers to the costs in the presence of a blood supply shortage (see
text). The cost of replacing blood includes the cost of HIV testing.
Source: Authors' calculations.

ever, the marginal gains from HIV testing are considerably larger,
ranging from $US 3.4 million to approximately $US 30.7 million.

If we allow for the possibility of downstream infections, the
marginal benefits from HIV testing are significantly larger. For
example, under the COI approach, the monetary estimates of the
benefits from testing range from $US 1.7 million to $US 15.4
million under the low and the high scenarios respectively.[59] When
using the WTP approach, the estimates range from $US 25.1 mil-
lion to $US 228.6 million.

Our calculations do not take account of the fact that testing
blood for HIV could also reduce the risk of hepatitis B infection
(as well as the risk of other STDs) to the extent that the chance
of being infected with HIV and with other STDs are correlated
(see for example, Over and Piot 1993). Unfortunately, little
evidence is available on the contribution of HIV testing of blood
to the reduced risk of hepatitis B and other STDs, although one
can conjecture a reduction in such risk. Thus, our monetary estimates should be viewed as lower bounds to the true monetary
benefits from HIV testing.

The costs of HIV testing are the sum of: (a) the costs of personnel and equipment used during testing; (b) the costs of destroying unusable blood; and (c) the costs of replenishing blood lost
through discarding.

59. These calculations are based on a discount rate of 3 per cent. If the discount
rate is 5 per cent, the estimates under the COI approach would range from $US 1.3
million to $US 12.2 million.

The average price for a single ELISA or SERODIA kit is approximately $US 0.70, and for the Western Blot test about $US 12.40 (commmunication with WHO, Sri Lanka). These figures do not include the costs of equipment, personnel, and the like.[60] Under the current NBTS strategy for blood screening, all 100,000 samples of donated blood will be tested for HIV using the ELISA or SERODIA tests. If any blood sample tests positive, it is retested, and if the retest is positive it is subjected to a confirmatory Western Blot test (communication with Nandrani de Zoysa).[61] Testing costs make up the bulk (more than 95 per cent) of the screening costs (see Table 13).

Disposing of blood that cannot be used for transfusion can be costly. In the United States, estimates indicate that the cost of disposing of blood could be as high as $US 69 per unit (Eisenstaedt and Getzen 1988). In Sri Lanka, however these costs are low, some $US 3 per unit of blood destroyed according to our estimates, because of the relatively primitive method (i.e. burying contaminated blood) the NBTS uses to dispose of such blood (personal communication with Nandrani de Zoysa). The full cost of blood disposal is then derived by estimating the total volume of blood to be destroyed.

Currently, Sri Lanka does not face a shortage in the supply of voluntarily donated blood (de Zoysa 1995). Thus, the cost of replacing blood that has to be destroyed is quite low. However, if a shortage were to arise, then an estimate of this cost can be derived from the cost of commercially supplied blood in India— about $US 3 to $US 4 per unit (Bloom and Mahal 1995a)—plus the cost of testing (see Table 13).

---

60. We assume that the full cost of testing a single sample of blood is $US 7.30 using the ELISA/SERODIA kit and $US 30.00 using the Western Blot. The former estimate is based on the price for getting an 'AIDS-free' certificate for overseas workers and the latter estimate is from Bloom and Glied (1993) for India.

61. In addition to true positives, there are false positives as well, which adds to the cost of testing. In our analysis we assumed that only the ELISA and Western Blot tests are used. In individual testing, average sensitivity of the ELISA, SERODIA, and HIVSPOT tests is about 98.5 per cent, with a specificity of 97.7 per cent (Eisenstaedt and Getzen 1988; Spielberg and others 1989).

Table 13 shows that under the COI method, the current practice of blood screening by the NBTS is not cost-beneficial if we do not include downstream infections, primarily because of the low rate of HIV prevalence among the donor population. However, if we include downstream infections, the current NBTS strategy yields a net return of 117 per cent on investment, a very high rate of return indeed. Moreover, HIV testing is cost-benefical if we evaluate benefits in WTP terms, even under the low scenario and without considering downstream infections. Under the high prevalence scenario, HIV testing is clearly beneficial in all cases, with rates of return exceeding 162 per cent in the least favourable case (under the COI method, and excluding downstream infections).

It can be quite plausibly argued that the net gains from HIV testing, although substantial, can be increased further by pooling samples for the purposes of testing, (especially in a situation with low levels of HIV prevalence and high levels of test sensitivity and specificity) in pools of five or less (Cahoon-Young and others 1989; Emmanuel and others 1988; Monzon and others 1992). However, the difference in the net benefits under the two strategies is not large (about $US 600,000 annually), so the viability of the pooling strategy would depend on the ability of Sri Lankan laboratory technicians to master the intricacies of pooled testing.[62]

Using Reusable Instead of Disposable Injecting Equipment

A July 1992 news article in the *Island* (Wijetunge 1992) quoted four leading doctors in Sri Lanka as saying that existing methods of sterilizing medical instruments were inadequate, exposing users and employees of Sri Lanka's medical system to unnecessary risks of HIV and hepatitis B infection. One suggested solution was to make the use of disposable syringes mandatory by law. (In a recent survey of health care workers at Colombo's General Hospital, respondents indicated that disposable injecting equipment was used only 50 per cent of the time. Especially disconcerting was

62. Allowing for downstream infection, the gains from pooled testing (which is likely to reduce HIV testing costs by 80 per cent) are significant as a percentage of total net benefits (about 66 per cent) only in the case of the low scenario under the COI methodology. In all other scenarios, these savings from pooled test procedures account for less than 4 per cent of total net benefits as reported in Table 13.

the observation that staff sometimes *reused* the disposable equipment.) However, policy makers have expressed concern about the costs of disposable injecting equipment (personal communication with Dr George Fernando). In this section, we report the results of a cost-benefit analysis that compares the use of disposable syringes and needles in Colombo General Hospital with two alternative regimes: one that focuses on strict sterilization and continued use of reusable syringes and needles; and one in which existing (and possibly imperfect) practices of sterilization continue, with reuse of needles and syringes.

As in the section on HIV testing of blood, we calculate the benefits by first estimating the number of HIV cases averted under each strategy, and then multiplying this number by the monetary value of a single averted HIV infection. In the absence of proper sterilization of injecting equipment, HIV infections in hospitals will typically result in one of three ways: (a) a patient gets infected as a result of an injection from a previously contaminated needle or syringe; (b) medical personnel get infected as a result of needle stick injuries in the process of recapping needles or washing instruments following an injection (Kuruppuarachchi and Jayasinghe 1992a, 1993); and (c) in the absence of proper disposal facilities, garbage collectors and other handlers of medical waste could get infected.

With proper sterilization of injecting equipment, the risks to patients will probably become zero. However, medical personnel will still face a risk (probably reduced) from post-injection needle stick injuries to the extent that some of those injected are HIV-positive. This would also be true for garbage handlers. If, however, disposable injection sets were being used, the greatest increase in the risk of infection would be to those who handle medical waste, although accidental needle stick injuries among doctors and nurses have also been reported in the case of disposables, primarily in the process of recapping injecting equipment (Stock, Gafni, and Bloch 1990). Nonetheless, the probability of needle stick injuries among doctors and nurses is likely to be lower than in the case of reusables because the equipment does not have to be cleaned or recapped. We do not consider here the possibility that disposable injection sets are reused.

Considering existing practices at the General Hospital, which rely on the reuse of needles and syringes with possibly imperfect sterilization, we estimate that nurses and doctors can expect about 33 needle stick or sharps injuries per person per year.[63] With a staff of about 1,800 doctors and nurses, we estimate that the number of injuries in the General Hospital, Colombo, is about 59,400 annually. To translate the estimates of needle stick injuries into an estimate of the expected number of new HIV infections, we require estimates of (a) the probability that the injecting equipment is contaminated with HIV; and (b) the probability of transmission from a contaminated needle, in case of an injury. On the assumption that all needle stick injuries occur after a parenteral episode, we estimate the probability that a reusable injection set is contaminated with HIV to be 0.115 per cent at the time of a needle stick injury.[64] Assuming an HIV transmission probability of 1/250 in case of injury with an infected needle, we calculate that the expected number of HIV infections among doctors and nurses in General Hospital Colombo will be approximately 0.273.[65]

63. According to our survey at the General Hospital, doctors, nurses and midwives experience about 0.89 sharps injuries per person per week. Earlier studies at the General Hospital indicate the frequency of needle stick injuries to be about 0.39 per person per week (Kuruppuarachchi and Jayasinghe 1992a,b). We use the mid-point of the two estimates for weekly estimates of needle stick injuries per person.

64. This requires an estimate of the cumulative probability of infection over the life cycle of a reusable injection set. This probability P is given by the formula

$$P = \{\theta/[1 - y(1 - \theta)]\}\ \{1 - [y(1 - \theta)]^t\}$$

where t is the average number of times is needle has been used previously, y is the chance that sterilization is ineffective, and θ is the probability that patients are HIV-positive. On the assumption that needles typically last for sixty uses, we assume that the average number of times that a needle has been used previously is about thirty. Moreover, we assume y to be 67 per cent, on the basis of our survey among health care workers calculations. Finally, we have assumed that the HIV infection rate among hospital patients is 0.038 per cent, the same as for the general population.

65. In our calculations we used the formula

Expected infection = risk of transmission
× probability that injecting equipment is contaminated
× number of injuries among health care workers.

To account for potential infections among patients as a result of existing injecting practices in the General Hospital, we note that the risk of infection faced by a patient on any one injection episode is somewhat smaller than that faced by medical personnel. This is because the risk of infection that the patient faces is from poor sterilization of injecting equipment; on the other hand, needle stick injuries to medical personnel must also account for the chance that the patient who is being injected may himself be HIV-positive. We estimate that the chance of the needle that is used to inject the patient being HIV-positive is 0.077 per cent. To estimate the potential HIV infections that might arise among patients in General Hospital, Colombo, we assume that patients experience an average of 1.5 parenteral events per day (based on a survey carried out by one of the study team). With an average daily occupancy of 2,480 beds, the annual number of inpatient days at the General Hospital is approximately 906,000 (Ministry of Health and Women's Affairs 1992). Using these facts, we estimate the number of HIV infections among patients to be approximately 4.185 annually.

Finally, we estimate the chance that handlers of medical waste get infected with HIV through to needle stick injuries. In general, there is little information on needle stick injuries to such individuals. In our survey we found that among labourers and attendants at General Hospital, the sharps injury rate was 0.003 per person per week. Assuming that these individuals are most likely to handle medical waste, we estimated the annual number of needle stick injuries in this group to be 2,230.[66] With an estimated probability of a needle being infected of about 0.115 per cent, and a transmission probability of 1/250, the expected number of HIV infections in this group is 0.010 annually.

Thus, we conclude that under existing practices, 4.47 HIV infections will occur annually among health care workers and patients. If downstream infections are included, continuing with current injecting practices for one more year could lead to 33.3 HIV infections over the next decade. The previous calculations

---

66. Based on our estimate of the total number of attendants and labourers at General Hospital as about 1,300.

were undertaken under a low scenario, with HIV infection rates among patients assumed to be of the order of 0.038 per cent. Under a high scenario with the HIV prevalence in the population as in 2005, we estimate the expected number of infections among hospital patients and medical personnel to be 39.78, excluding downstream infections. If we include downstream infections, the number of new HIV infections that could result from following existing patterns of injecting-equipment use in the General Hospital for one more year would be nearly 296 over the next decade.

To estimate the number of HIV infections averted under a strategy of fully effective sterilization (after each injection) of injecting equipment, we proceed by tracing its impact on the probability of infection faced by each of the groups (patients, doctors and nurses, and medical waste handlers), as well as on the chance of injury. In general, continued use of reusable equipment suggests that the probability of needle stick injury is likely to remain unchanged, both for doctors and nurses as well as for waste handlers. However, with properly sterilized needles and syringes, the risk of infection from injections would fall to zero for hospital patients. Moreover, the chance that a needle is contaminated at the time of a needle stick injury would fall to 0.038 per cent in our analysis, as the only way a needle can now be contaminated is if the injectee was HIV-positive.[67] It immediately follows that under the low scenario, the expected number of new infections among medical personnel would be approximately 0.12 annually (that is, 4.35 averted cases). With downstream infections, the expected number of HIV infections would be 0.89 over the next decade. Under the high scenario, the expected number of HIV infections would be 8.05, including downstream infections. Thus, under the low scenario, a strategy of fully sterilizing needles would result in 32.4 averted HIV infections over the next decade, with 288 averted infections under a high scenario.

When using disposable syringes and needles, the risk to patients is virtually negligible, just as for fully sterilized injecting equipment. Moreover, for medical personnel experiencing needle

---

67. In our calculations, we assume that the patient to needle transmission probability is one.

stick injuries, the chance of injecting equipment being contaminated is 0.038 per cent under the low HIV prevalence scenario, just as in the case of fully sterilized needles. However, the frequency of needle stick injuries is likely to be different. As noted earlier, for doctors and nurses at least, the frequency of injuries should fall given that there is less need for recapping needles or washing injecting equipment.

Unfortunately, little is known about the decline in needle stick injuries among doctors and nurses following the replacement of reusable injecting equipment with disposable sets. We do, however, have estimates of needle stick injuries in a Canadian hospital that uses only disposable injecting equipment (Stock, Gafni, and Bloch 1990). Using that data, we estimate that the number of needle stick injuries among doctors and nurses would decline to 2,810 following the introduction of disposable kits.[68] As a consequence, the expected number of infections in this group would fall to 0.004 annually. However, with increased use of disposables, one would expect an increase in the frequency of needle stick injuries among handlers of medical waste. On the assumption that each unit of reusable equipment can be used about sixty times (personal communication with W. Ransi at the General Hospital), we can expect a sixty-fold increase in the frequency of injuries among waste handlers—to about 134,000 annually. This translates into 0.204 infections annually among waste handlers, excluding downstream infections. In other words, the expected number of HIV infections under the low scenario would be 0.208 annually. This would result in 4.27 averted HIV infections annually (31.8 infections over the next decade, including downstream infections). Under the high scenario, our estimate of averted infections is 37.9 per year (282 averted over the next decade,

68. Stock, Gafni, and Block (1990, p. 941) estimated the number of needle injuries to be 510 per year in a 450-bed teaching hospital in Hamilton, Ontario. Noting that the occupancy rate in the General Hospital is 2,480 per day and assuming full occupancy in the Canadian hospital, we scale the estimate of needle stick injuries to arrive at 2,810 (= 510 × 2,480/450). This estimate may be biased downwards to the extent that one believes that fewer precaution would be taken in Sri Lankan hospitals.

including downstream infections). Note that if disposable bins were also made available, the estimate for averted cases would range from 33 to 296 under the low and high scenarios, respectively (including downstream infections over the next decade), because the risk of needle stick injury among handlers of medical waste would become negligible.

Table 14 indicates the benefits, measured in monetary terms, under alternative strategies. In the low scenario, a strategy that focuses on better sterilization (but continued reliance on reusable injecting equipment), will result in benefits of $US 77,000 under the COI approach, and US$ 1.14 million under the WTP method. These calculations exclude averted downstream infections. If these were included the benefits would range from $US 572,000 under the COI methodology, and $US 8.5 million under the WTP approach.

If disposable injecting equipment were used instead (but without disposable bins), then under the low scenario the benefits in averted HIV cases would range from $US 75,000 (COI approach) to $US 1.12 million (WTP method) excluding downstream infections. If those were included as well, then under the low scenario the benefits would range from $US 561,000 thousand to $US 8.34 million. If disposable bins were used the benefits are somewhat higher (see Table 14).

Our analysis compared the monetary benefits of each strategy to the additional costs imposed by it. Table 14 indicates these costs for the General Hospital for one year. They include the costs of sterilizing equipment (personnel, electricity, and sterilizers), and the costs of purchasing reusable injecting equipment to meet the hospital's needs for one year.[69] The full cost of sterilizing injecting equipment was discounted by 67 per cent (the perceived failure rate of existing sterilization practices suggested by our sur-

---

69. We estimated these requirements as follows. Taking the annual inpatient load as 2,480 times 365 (Ministry of Health and Women's Affairs 1992), we multiplied it by 1.5 (the average number of parenteral events experienced by an impatient per day). This yields the estimated number of parenteral events in one year. Assuming that syringes last for 225 uses, and needles for sixty, we have an estimate of the number of items of each type that are required. Price data was supplied by Lanka Laboratories Ltd.

Table 14: Disposable Injecting Equipment Versus Reusable Injecting Equipment: A cost–benefit analysis

Benefits and costs	Fully sterilized equipment (reusable)	Disposable Equipment	
		with Bins	No bins
Expected infections averted			
Low scenario[a]			
No downstream infections	4.35	4.46	4.27
Downstream infections	32.40	33.23	31.81
High scenario[a]			
No downstream infections	38.70	39.74	37.91
Downstream infections	288.32	296.06	282.42
Marginal Benefits[b] ($US millions)			
COI method			
Low scenario	0.08–0.57	0.08–0.59	0.08–0.56
High scenario	0.68–5.09	0.07–5.22	0.67–4.98
WTP method			
Low scenario	1.14–8.50	1.17–8.72	1.12–8.34
High scenario	10.15–75.64	10.42–77.67	9.94–74.09
Marginal Costs[c] ($US thousands)	17.24	321.09	229.31
Net benefits ($US millions)			
COI method			
Low scenario	0.06–0.55	(–)0.24–0.27	(–)0.15–0.33
High scenario	0.66–5.07	0.38–4.90	0.44–4.75
WTP method			
Low scenario	1.12–8.48	0.85–8.40	0.89–8.11
High scenario	10.13–75.62	10.10–77.35	9.71–73.86

a. Two scenarios were considered, a low scenario, with the 1994 rate of HIV infection among patients, and a high scenario, with the 2005 rate of HIV infection among patients.

b. The range of marginal benefits for each scenario indicates the benefits with and without the inclusion of averted downstream cases of HIV.

c. Cost calculations assume that each inpatient receives, on average, 1.5 injections per day, and that reusable syringes and needles can be used upto a maximum of 225 times and 60 times, respectively. Having obtained the full cost of using sterilized needles for the year (by taking account of personnel and equipment costs involved in needle sterilization), we obtained the marginal cost for the strategy of sterilized needles by discounting the personnel and equipment costs by 67 per cent. We eveluted the additional costs of using disposable equipement based on (a) estimated usage rate of disposables in the General Hospital in any year; and (b) price data from Lanka Laboratories Ltd., and Doebbeling and Wenzel (1990).

Source: Authors' calculations.

vey of medical personnel) to obtain the costs of the current system. The difference between the full costs of sterilization and the costs of the existing system, approximately $US 17,000, is the marginal cost of instituting more careful sterilization practices in Sri Lanka. In similar fashion, we estimated the total cost of disposables using price data supplied by Lanka Laboratories Ltd., and the number of disposables required for meeting the annual needs of General Hospital (see footnote 67). The marginal cost of adopting disposable injecting equipment is the total cost of disposables, less the cost of operating the existing system of sterilization in Sri Lanka. We estimate this to be about $US 229,000.

Table 14 also indicates the net benefits, in monetary terms, of replacing the existing system of needle use and sterilization in General Hospital, Colombo. Under the COI approach, it is clear that in all cases improved sterilization of reusable injecting equipment is the most socially beneficial option. If, however, this option is not feasible, then our analysis suggests that adopting disposables is cost-benefical, unless we choose to ignore downstream infections. If downstream infections are accounted for, our results suggest that the rate of return to investments in disposables strategy would be in excess of 100 per cent. The benefits would be even higher if we accounted for the reduced number of hepatitis B cases that would result from this. There is little to choose between a policy with or without disposable sharps containers (bins), so the simultaneous introduction of disposable injecting equipment and disposable bins appears to be economically well justified.

Instituting Universal Precautions in Health Care Settings

The practice of universal precautions is founded on the assumption that all contact with patients, whether direct or indirect, should be considered as a potential source of infection with HIV and other infectious diseases irrespective of whether the patient is known to be HIV-positive or not. According to the Centers for Disease Control (CDC 1987), the practice of universal precautions means that medical staff should wear gloves whenever they might come into contact with blood or other bodily fluids; wear masks, goggles, and gowns if there is a possibility of being splashed; not recap needles; keep disposable sharp objects in safe containers near the place of use; and wash hands in case of contact. Both anecdotal and research evidence suggests that health care workers in Sri Lanka dot not adhere to this practice (Eswaaratchige 1993). Two explanations are usually offered for this. Firstly, Sri Lankan hospitals suffer from a shortage of adequate facilities and equipment: gloves, disposable bins, incinerators, and so on. As a consequence, the practice of co-disposing of equipment contaminated with bodily fluids with other hospital garbage is still common (Rahulla and Jayasinghe 1993). Secondly, a discrepancy appears to exist between health workers' knowledge of the correct procedure and their actual practice. As a result, the risk of hepatitis B and HIV infection faced by health care workers appears to be several times higher than the risk faced by the general population.

We carried out a cost-benefit analysis of universal precautions in Colombo General Hospital. We evaluated the benefits in terms of the number of averted HIV infections among health workers multiplied by the value of each averted infection. This method obviously undervalues the benefits of adopting universal precautions, as such a practice will protect medical staff from other infections in addition to HIV. It also does not include the concomitant benefits of averted patient-to-patient and health-worker-to-patient transmission of HIV and other infectious diseases. We calculated the costs by examining the expenditures needed to provide gloves and other disposable equipment and to educate health workers about precautionary measures.

We calculated the number of averted HIV infections on the assumption that the primary source of HIV infection among health care workers is their occupational setting, and ignored the risks from sexual transmission. Furthermore, we assumed that the only HIV risk of significance is the one resulting from injuries such as needle sticks. This assumption is justified on the basis of evidence from a large number of studies that suggest little risk of infection from other forms of contact with blood or other fluids (Marcus 1988; McCray 1986; Stock, Gafni, and Bloch 1990 and articles cited therein). We considered two HIV prevalence scenarios: a low prevalence scenario in which we assumed HIV prevalence among hospital patients was 0.038 per cent, and a high prevalence scenario in which we assumed it was 0.342 per cent (these percentages are the estimated and projected population seroprevalence rates for 1994 and 2005 respectively). In the interest of simplicity, we assume that health care workers are uninfected (have a zero prior probability of infection) with HIV at the time they begin working.

In the absence of reliable evidence about the risk reduction among medical personnel that accompanies the adoption of universal precautions, we conducted a hypothetical experiment (as in Stock, Gafni and Bloch 1990) whereby the adoption of universal precautions reduces the risk of sharps injuries by 25 per cent, 50 per cent, and 75 per cent. Moreover, since most discussions of universal precautions presume the use of disposable injecting equipment in health care settings (for example, CDC 1987), we shall evaluate universal precautions in a setting where disposable injecting equipment is already being used. There is, however, some concern as to whether additional precautions are needed in a hospital setting.

Table 15 indicated the benefits and costs over one year under each of these possibilities, with benefits per avoided infection valued at $US 17,600 and $US 262,300 under the COI and the WTP approaches. In the previous section, we estimated that if disposable injecting equipment were used, the number of injuries among doctors and nurses at the General Hospital would be 2,810 per year, but about 134,000 among waste handlers. Assuming a transmission probability of 1/250 and the chance that a needle is contaminated with HIV to be 0.038 per cent we can expect 0.208 HIV infections per year among medical personnel, or 1.55 infections over the next decade, if we allow for downstream infections.

Thus, under a low scenario of HIV prevalence (the current situation in Sri Lanka), we can imagine benefits ranging from 0.052 to 0.156 avoided HIV infections (depending on the degree of risk reduction achieved—25 per cent to 75 per cent). Including downstream infections, expected infections averted would range from 0.39 to 1.16 over the next decade. Thus, in COI terms, the benefits from universal precautions could range from $US 6,900 to $US 20,500, if we include downstream infections. With WTP

Table 15: A Cost–Benefit Analysis of Universal Precautions in General Hospital, Colombo

	Magnitude of risk reduction					
	25 per cent		50 per cent		75 per cent	
	low scenario	high scenario	low scenario	high scenario	low scenario	high scenario
Expected number of infections averted						
No downstream cases	0.052	0.463	0.104	0.926	0.156	1.389
Downstream cases included	0.387	3.449	0.774	6.898	1.162	10.348
Benefits ($US thousands)						
COI method						
No downstream cases	0.917	8.167	1.835	16.335	2.752	24.502
Downstream cases included	6.827	60.840	13.653	121.681	20.498	182.539
WTP method						
No downstream cases	13.641	121.459	27.282	242.918	40.923	364.376
Downstream cases included	101.522	904.776	203.043	1,809.552	304.827	2,714.591
Costs ($US thousands)						
Low estimate	277	277	277	277	277	277
High estimate	2,140	2,140	2,140	2,140	2,140	2,140

Source: Authors' calculations.

valuations, the benefits would range from $US 102,300 to $US 304,300.

Under the high scenario, the number of cases likely to be averted by instituting universal precautions will be greater—ranging from 3.49 to 10.32 HIV cases over the next decade (that is, inclusive of downstream infections). In COI terms, the monetary benefits, from such a reduction range from $US 61,600 to $US 182,000. Expressed in WTP terms, the benefits range from $US 915,500 to $US 2.7 million.

We calculated the costs of adopting a strategy of universal precautions in two ways. First, we estimated the costs using information on the expenses on disposables for two private hospitals in Colombo. On average, these hospitals spent about $US 3.40 on disposables per patient. Deducting the cost of disposable injecting equipment from this estimate (as our estimate presupposes that such injecting equipment is already being used), we estimate that the amount spent on other disposables is about $US 1.77 per patient. This is probably a lower bound to the true cost of adopting universal precautions since hospitals in Sri Lanka are unlikely to have adopted the full range of practices and equipment under this strategy.[70] Thus, we also estimated the cost of these materials using Doebbeling and Wenzel's (1990) estimate (for the United States) of the cost of isolation materials per inpatient, which was about $US 13.70. This is the lower bound of the Doebbeling and Wenzel estimates, as the cost of materials is probably somewhat lower in Sri Lanka than in the United States.

Assuming a cost per inpatient of $US 1.77, we estimate the annual costs of universal precautions to be $US 265,000. To this we add the costs of educating health care workers and lost productivity on account of such educational programmes. Assuming that these costs as a proportion of total equipment costs are the same as in Stock, Gafni, and Bloch (about 4.3 per cent), we get an estimate of the costs of instituting universal precautions of about $US 277,000. If, however, the costs are assumed to be $US 13.70 per patient, we have an estimated total cost of adopting universal

70. Typically these would include examination gloves, surgical gloves, disposable gowns, sharps containers, disposable masks, protective eye wear, training of health care workers in precautionary measures, etc.

precautions of about $US 2.14 million. This constitutes the upper bound of our total cost estimates. To the extent that some of the equipment needed for universal precautions may already be in use at the General Hospital, these bounds continue upwardly biased measures of the lower and upper bounds of the marginal cost of adopting universal precautions.

Under the COI methodology, there is little economic justification for supporting the introduction of universal precautions in a health care setting where disposable injecting equipment is being used. This is so even if we use the lower bound of our cost estimates in the calculation of social net benefits. Moreover, under the low HIV prevalence scenario, universal precautions are cost-beneficial only when they achieve a 75 per cent reduction in risk even with calculations based on WTP estimates of the cost of an HIV infection. The only cases where the net social benefits are unambiguously large is where we use the WTP method to evaluate the net benefits under the high HIV prevalence scenario.

It would seem, therefore, that the introduction of universal precautions in Sri Lanka's hospitals may not be cost-beneficial at the present time. To the extent that these measures would bring about a reduction in risk of contracting other infections such as hepatitis B, our analysis understates the gains from adopting universal precautions in General Hospital. However, we believe that the bulk of the gains from reducing the risk of hepatitis B can be captured through the use of disposable instead of reusable injecting equipment.

Conclusion

The first case of HIV infection in Sri Lanka was detected in 1987. By early 1996, Sri Lanka had reported 172 cases of HIV, including 58 cases of AIDS. Reported cases of HIV infection and AIDS, however, are only the tip of the iceberg and reflect little more than the limited amount of costly HIV testing that has been conducted. They are grossly misleading with respect to the full extent of the epidemic, which needs to be estimated using statistical tools to infer the level of infection among the population, from sample data. One such set of estimates recently prepared for Sri Lanka indicated that there are 6,800 cases of HIV infection, a figure that will grow to 80,000 by the year 2005 if it remains on its current trajectory.

These figures suggest that Sri Lanka is not immune to the rapid spread of HIV. It will not be spared because of its culture or through some non-traditional medical cure. On the contrary, Sri Lanka is extremely vulnerable to the epidemic. Many factors contribute to this vulnerability: the country's proximity to India (which is already the HIV capital of the world); high rates of internal and international mobility associated with overseas contract work, tourism, military activity, refugees, and domestic labour migration; unsafe medical practices, particularly with regard to the use of disposable injection equipment; an active commercial sex industry; and the population's age distribution, which has a large proportion of the population in the sexually active years.

Because of the disease's complexity in both biomedical and socio-economic terms, no single discipline has a monopoly on the information and expertise needed to address the AIDS epidemic. Rather, effective responses will have to draw upon skills and experiences from a wide range of fields, working in co-operation.

It is in this spirit that we have undertaken the foregoing comprehensive analysis of social and economic aspects of the AIDS epidemic in Sri Lanka. By utilizing tools from economics, statistics, anthropology, sociology, and medicine; building upon existing knowledge and research in other countries; paying close attention to regional and international experience; and analyzing both existing and new data, we have reached a great many conclusions which we hope will not only advance understanding of the epidemic, but also inform policy making, both within and outside Sri Lanka. Indeed, we hope this study catalyzes further research and discussion on the HIV and AIDS epidemics and contributes momentum to efforts to promote deeper understanding of the epidemic as a basis for the development of prevention and care strategies that are rooted in local realities.

References

Abednego, Hadi. 1993. 'Indonesian AIDS Update'. UNDP/ADB Inception Workshop on the Economic Implications of AIDS in Selected DMCs, Manila, Philippines, September 8–10.

Abeynayake, Rajpal. 1993. 'Lankans Prepare for the AIDS Epidemic'. *Sunday Observer,* June 6.

Ainsworth, M. and A.M. Over. 1994. 'The Economic Impact of AIDS on Africa.' In M. Essex and others eds., *AIDS in Africa.* New York: Raven Press.

Aloysius, Carol. 1993. 'Sri Lanka—Where the White Man Finds his Child-Lovers'. *The Sunday Observer,* June 27.

Attanayake, Nimal, and U.H.S. de Silva. 1987. 'Economic Analysis of Health Sector Resource Flows in Gampaha District of Sri Lanka'. Colombo, Sri Lanka: Ministry of Health. Draft.

Barnett, Tony. 1995. 'The Potential Social and Economic Impact of HIV/AIDS in Rajasthan, India: Some Observations from Experience in Uganda, Tanzania, Kenya, and Zambia'. New Delhi, India: United Nations Development Programme. Draft Report.

Barnett, Tony, and Piers Blaikie. 1992. *AIDS in Africa: Its Present and Future Impact.* London: The Guilford Press.

Basu, Alaka, 1995. 'Poverty and AIDS: The Vicious Circle'. Ithaca, NY: Cornell University, Division of Nutritional Sciences. Draft.

Basu, Alaka, Devendra Gupta, and Geetanjali Krishna. 1995. 'The Household Impact of Adult Morbidity and Mortality: Some Implications of Potential Epidemic of AIDS in India'. New Delhi, India: Institute of Economic Growth. Draft.

Berenger, Leon. 1992. 'Health Officials Remain Mum on Condition of AIDS Patient'. *The Island,* October 14.

Bloom, David, and Geoffrey Carliner. 1988. 'The Economic Impacts of AIDS in the United States'. *Science* 239 (4840): 604–10.

Bloom, David, and Sherry Glied, 1991. 'Benefits and Costs of HIV Testing'. *Science* 252 (June 28): 1798–804.

——1992. 'Projecting the Number of New AIDS Cases in the United States'. *International Journal of Forecasting* 8(3): 339–66.

——1993. 'Who is Bearing the Cost of the AIDS Epidemic in Asia?' In David Bloom and Joyce Lyons, eds. *Economic Implications of AIDS in Asia.* New Delhi, India: United Nations Development Programme.

Bloom, David, and Joyce Lyons. 1993. *Economic Implications of AIDS in Asia.* New Delhi, India: United Nations Development Programme.

Bloom, David, and Ajay Mahal. 1993. 'The Cost of Illness'. New York: Columbia University, Department of Economics. Draft.

——1995a. 'The Economic Implications of AIDS in Asia'. New York: Columbia University, Department of Economics. Draft.

——1995b. 'The AIDS Epidemic and Economic Policy Analysis'. *Current Science* 25(10): 865–9.

———1996. 'Does the AIDS Epidemic Threaten Economic Growth?' *Journal of Econometrics*. Forthcoming.

Bloom, David, Neil Bennett, Ajay Mahal, and Waseem Noor. 1996. 'The Impact of AIDS on Human Development'. New York: Columbia University, Department of Economics. Draft.

Bloom, David, Ajay Mahal, and Brendan O'Flaherty. 1995. 'The Economics of Needle Use and Reuse'. New York: Columbia University, Department of Economics. Draft.

Brooke, Blair, Chalintorn Burian, and Doris Mugrdtchian. 1994. 'Trip Report'. Washington, D.C.: Family Health International.

Broome, John. 1978. 'Trying to Value a Life'. *Journal of Public Economics* 9: 91–100.

Brown, Tim, Chirapun Gullaprawit, Werasit Sittitrai, Sombat Thanprasertsuk, and Apichat Chamratrithirong. 1994. 'Projections for HIV in Thailand 1987–2005: An Application of EPIMODEL'. Bangkok, Thailand: National Economic and Social Development Board Working Group. Draft.

Brown, Tim, and Werasit Sittitrai. 1993. *Estimates of Recent HIV Infection in Thailand*. Research Report No. 9. Bangkok. Thailand: Thai Red Cross Society, Program on AIDS.

Brown, Tim, and Werasit Sittitrai, Suphak Vanichseni, and Usa Thisyakorn. 1994. 'The Recent Epidemiology of HIV and AIDS in Thailand'. *AIDS* 8 (suppl 2): S131–41.

Cahoon-Young, Barbara, Ann Chandler, Timothy Livermore, James Gaudino, and Robert Benjamin. 1989. 'Sensitivity and Specificity of Pooled versus Individual Sera in a Human Immunodeficiency Virus Antibody Prevalence Study'. *Journal of Clinical Microbiology* 27(8): 1893–5.

Carvell, A., and G. Hart. 1990. 'Risk Behaviours for HIV Infection among Drug Users in Prison'. *British Medical Journal* 300: 1383–4.

CDC (Centers for Disease Control). 1987. 'Recommendations for Prevention of Transmission of HIV in Health Care Settings'. *Morbidity and Mortality Weekly Report* 36 (suppl 2): 1S–18S.

Central Bank of Ceylon. 1984. *Report on Consumer Finances and Socio Economic Survey 1981/82, Sri Lanka (Part II)*. Colombo, Sri Lanka: Statistics Department.

Central Bank of Sri Lanka. 1990. *Report on Consumer Finances and Socio Economic Survey 1986/87, Sri Lanka (Part II)*. Colombo, Sri Lanka: Statistics Department.

———1994. *1993 Annual Report*. Colombo, Sri Lanka.

Ceylinco Insurance Company, Ltd. 1992. *Annual Report 1992*. Colombo, Sri Lanka.

Ceylon Tourist Board. 1993. *Annual Statistical Report.* Colombo, Sri Lanka.

Chan, Robert. 1992. 'AIDS in Singapore: Some Aspects of Epidemiology and Management'. Singapore: Singapore National University. Draft.

Chin, James. 1992. 'Estimation/Projection of HIV/AIDS in Southeast Asia'. WHO Assignment Report. New Delhi, India: WHO, Southeast Asia Regional Office.

——1994. 'Estimation and Projection of HIV Infection and AIDS Cases in Hong Kong'. Berkeley, California: University of California, School of Public Health. Draft.

——1995. 'Estimation and Projection of HIV Infections and AIDS Cases'. *Current Science* 25(10): 828–32.

Chin, James, David Dunlop, and Hnin Hnin Pyne. 1994a. 'The HIV/AIDS Situation in Nepal'. Washington, D.C.: World Bank, Asia Technical Department. Draft.

——1994b. 'The HIV/AIDS Situation in Bangladesh'. Washington, D.C.: The World Bank, Asia Technical Department. Draft.

Chin, James, and S.K. Lwanga. 1991. 'Estimation and Projection of Adult AIDS Cases: A Simple Epidemiological Model'. *Bulletin of the World Health Organization* 69(2): 399–406.

Cohen, Desmond. 1993. 'The Economic Impact of the HIV Epidemic'. New York: United Nations Development Programme. Issues Paper.

Cuddington, John. 1993a. 'Modeling the Macroeconomic Effects of AIDS, with an Application to Tanzania'. *The World Bank Economic Review* 7(2): 173–89

——1993b. 'Further Results on the Macroeconomic Effects of AIDS: The Dualistic, Labor-Surplus Economy.' *Journal of Development Economics* 4(3): 363–8.

Daily News. 1994. 'AIDS: The Red Light is Flashing in Sri Lanka'. August 1.

de Zoysa, Nandrani. 1985. 'Survey of Blood Donors in Sri Lanka, 1985'. *Ceylon Medical Journal* 37: 129–30.

——1995. 'Making the Blood Supply Safe From HIV: The Sri Lankan Experience'. Colombo, Sri Lanka: National Blood Taransfusion Service. Draft.

Department of Census and Statistics. 1991. *Sri Lanka National and District Life Tables: 1980–2.* Colombo, Sri Lanka: Government of Sri Lanka, Ministry of Policy Planning and Implementation.

——1992a. *Quarterly Report of the Sri Lanka Labour Force Survey: Third Quarter 1991.* Colombo, Sri Lanka: Government of Sri Lanka, Ministry of Policy Planning and Implementation.

—1992b. *Survey of Demographic and Social Aspects—1986/87, Sri Lanka: Health and Housing.* Final Report. Colombo, Sri Lanka: Government of Sri Lanka, Ministry of Policy Planning and Implementation.

——1993a. *Statistical Abstract of the Democratic Socialist Republic of Sri Lanka 1992.* Colombo, Sri Lanka: Government of Sri Lanka, Ministry of Policy Planning and Implementation.

——1993b. *Quarterly Report of the Sri Lanka Labour Force Survey: Third Quarter 1992.* Colombo, Sri Lanka: Government of Sri Lanka, Ministry of Policy Planning and Implementation.

Dharmasene, M.D., and L.W. Karunaratne. 1992. *Report of the Study on Knowledge and Attitudes on HIV/AIDS.* Colombo, Sri Lanka: Ministry of Health and Women's Affairs, Health Education Bureau.

Doebbeling, B.N., and Wenzel, R.P. 1990. ' The Direct Costs of Universal Precautions in a Teaching Hospital'. *Journal of the American Medical Association* 264(16): 2083–7.

Economic and Social Commission for Asia and the Pacific. 1991. *Tourism Development in the Asian Region.* Bangkok: United Nations.

Economist. 1989. 'AIDS Homes In'. February 4.

Eisenstaedt, Richard, and Thomas Getzen. 1988. 'Screening Blood Donors for Human Immunodeficiency Virus Antibody: Cost-Benefit Analysis'. *American Journal of Public Health* 78(4): 450–4.

Emmanuel, J., M. Bassett, H. Smith, and J. Jacobs. 1988. 'Pooling of Sera for Human Immunodeficiency Virus (HIV) Testing: An Economical Method for Use in Developing Countries'. *Journal of Clinical Pathology* 41: 582–5.

Ernst and Young Company. 1994. 'Current Financing of Health Care and its Implications'. Colombo, Sri Lanka. Draft.

Eswaraaratchige, Padmasiri. 1993. 'A Study on the Prevalence of Hepatitis B Surface Antigen Carrier Status in a District in Sri Lanka and Prevalence and Risk Factors of Hepatitis B Infection among Nursing Personnel in the Same District'. Colombo, Sri Lanka: University of Colombo, Faculty of Medicine. MD Thesis.

Fernando, C.R.S., K. de Abrew, K.S.A. Jayasinghe, L. Mendis, K. Jayawardena, and H. Nanayakkara. 1992. 'The Prevalence of Hepatitis B Infection in Insulin Dependent Diabetics Attending General Hospital, Colombo'. Abstract No. 5, 105th Anniversary Academic Sessions. Colombo, Sri Lanka: Sri Lanka Medical Association.

Gallwey, John, and Frank Judson. 1991. *Report of Visit to Sri Lanka.* Colombo, Sri Lanka: WHO.

256 *The Economics of HIV and AIDS*

Gelles, Gregory. 1993. 'Costs and Benefits of HIV-1 Antibody Testing of Donated Blood'. *Journal of Policy Analysis and Management* 12(3): 512–31.

Giraud, Patrick. 1993. 'The Economic Impact of AIDS at the Sectoral Level: Developing an Assessment Methodology and Applying It to Thailand's Transport Sector'. In David Bloom and Joyce Lyons, eds., *Economic Implications of AIDS in Asia*. New Delhi, India: United Nations Development Programme.

Griffin, Charles. 1990. *Health Financing in Asia*. Washington, D.C: The World Bank, Asia Technical Department. Report No. 8553–ASI.

Griffin, Charles, Ruth Levine, and B. Kelly Eakin. 1994. 'Government and Private Health Care Facilities in Sri Lanka'. Washington D.C.: The Urban Institute. Draft.

Gurubacharya, V., and B. Suvedi. 1992. 'HIV Infection/AIDS in Nepal'. Paper Presented at the Second International Conference on AIDS in Asia and the Pacific, New Delhi, India, November 8–12. Abstract no. B215.

Hanemann, W. Michael. 1991. 'Willingness To Pay and Willigness To Accept: How Much Can They Differ?' *American Economic Review* 81(3): 635–7.

Health Insurance Association of America. 1995. *Source Book of Health Insurance Data 1994*. Washington, D.C.

Hellinger, Fred. 1993. 'The Lifetime Cost of Treating a Person with HIV'. *Journal of the American Medical Association* 270(4): 474–8.

Hettiarachchi, T. 1994. 'Female Labour Force at Katunayake Export Processing Zone: Social Impact of the Coping Behavior Patterns'. *Economic Review* (July): 33–5.

Holtgrave, David, Ronald Valdiserri, and Gary West. Forthcoming. 'Quantitative Economic Evaluations of HIV-Related Prevention and Treatment Services: A Review'. *Risk*.

Htoon, Myo, Hla Lwin, Khin San, Edward Zan, and Min Thwe. 1994. HIV/AIDS in Myanmar'. *AIDS* 8 (suppl 2): S105–9.

The Island. 1992. 'Number of HIV Patients may Escalate Alarmingly'. 23 May.

———1993. 'AIDS Can be Transmitted by Dental Equipment'. July 21.

———1994. 'Lesbians Safe From AIDS Transmission—Report'. July 25.

Jain, Manoj, T. Jacob John, and Gerald Keusch. 1994a. 'A Review of Human Inmmunodeficiency Virus Infection in India'. Boston, Massachusetts: New England Medical Center, Division of Geographic Medicine and Infectious Diseases. Draft.

———1994b.'Epidemiology of HIV and AIDS in India'. *AIDS* 8 (suppl 2): S61–75.

Jalal, Fasli, Hadi Abednego, Tonny Sadjimin, and Michael Linnan. 1994. 'HIV and AIDS in Indonesia'. *AIDS* 8 (suppl 2): S91–4.

Jayakuru, Gamini. 1992. 'Country Situation and Status of the National AIDS Programme'. Colombo, Sri Lanka: STD/AIDS Control Programme. Draft.

Jayasinghe, Wasu. 1994a. 'Injecting Infections: The Nightmare Scenario of Disposable Syringes in the Country'. *The Sunday Times,* September 25.

——1994b. 'Helping the Helpless: AIDS Patients Get Comfort at IDH'. *The Sunday Times,* December 4.

Jianhua, Y., and C. Yanlin. 1993. 'Epidemic Situation and Research on HIV/AIDS in China'. Paper presented at the Inception Workshop on the United Nations Development Programme/Asian Development Bank Study on the Economic Implications of HIV/AIDS Epidemic in Asia, Manila, Philippines, September 8–10.

Jones-Lee, Michael W. 1974. 'The Value of Changes in the Probability of Death or Injury'. *Journal of Political Economy* 82: 835–49.

Kahnemann, Daniel, and Amos Tversky. 1979. 'Prospect Theory: An Analysis of Decision Under Risk'. *Econometrics* 47: 263–91.

Kaldor, John, Paul Effler, Rabin Sarda, Georg Petersen, Dorota Gertig, and Jai Narain. 1994. 'HIV and AIDS in Asia and the Pacific: An Epidemiological Overview'. *AIDS* 8 (suppl 1): S165–72.

Kallings, Lars. 1992. 'The AIDS Pandemic'. *CARC Calling* 5(1): 7–11.

Kambou, Gerard, Shantayanan Devarajan, and Mead Over. 1992. 'The Economic Impact of AIDS in an African Country: Simulations with a Computable General Equilibrium Model of Cameroon'. *Journal of African Economies* 1(1): 109–30.

Kaplan, Edward, and Elaine O'Keefe. 1993. 'Let the Needles Do the Talking—Evaluating the New Haven Needle Exchange'. *Interfaces* 23(1): 7–26.

Kitamura, Takashi. 1994. 'Summary of the Epidemiology of HIV/AIDS in Japan'. *AIDS* 8 (suppl 2): S95–7.

Kleiber, D., and M. Wille. 1993. 'Sexual Behavior of German (Sex) Tourists'. Abstract no. WS-D10-2. IX International Conference on AIDS, Berlin, Germany, June 7–11.

Kremer, Michael. 1995. 'Integrating Behavioral Choice into Epidemiological Models of AIDS'. Cambridge, Massachusetts: Massachusetts Institute of Technology, Department of Economics. Draft.

Kuruppuarachchi, L., and S.S.A. Jayasinghe. 1992a. 'Injuries Due to Sharps in Health Care Workers: A Preliminary Report'. Abstract no. 7. Paper presented at the Sri Lanka Medical Association's 10th Anniversary Academic Sessions, March 25–8.

——1992b. 'Injuries Due to Sharps During Surgery: A Preliminary Report'. Abstract no. 8. Paper presented at the Sri Lanka Medical Association's 105th Anniversary Academic Session, March 25–8.

——1993. 'When Do Injuries Due to Sharps Occur in Health Care Workers'. Colombo, Sri Lanka: University of Colombo, Faculty of Medicine. Draft.

Lichtenstein, S., P. Slovic, B. Fischoff, M. Layman, and B. Combs. 1978. 'Judged Frequency of Lethal Events'. *Journal of Experimental Psychology: Human Learning and Memory* 4:551–78.

Mahawewa, W., and A. Soma. 1993. 'The Process of International Female Migration: The Case Study of Sri Lanka'. Adelaide, Australia: Flinders University of South Australia. Masters Thesis.

Mann, Jonathan, Daniel Tarantola, and Thomas Netter. 1992. *AIDS in the World.* Cambridge, Massachusetts: Harvard University Press.

Marcus, R. 1988. 'Surveillance of Health Care Workers Exposed to Blood from Patients Infected with the Human Immunodeficiency Virus'. *New England Journal of Medicine* 319:1118–23.

McCray, E. 1986. 'Occupational Risk of the Acquired Immunodeficiency Syndrome among Health Care Workers'. *New England Journal of Medicine* 314:1127–32.

Merson, Michael. 1992. 'AIDS in Asia and the Pacific: The Reality, the Opportunity, and the Challenge'. Keynote address at the Second International Conference on AIDS in Asia and the Pacific, New Delhi, India, November 8–12.

Milhuisen, Ivor. 1992. 'Interested Parties Blow Up AIDS Scare'. *Daily News,* May 18.

Ministry of Health and Women's Affairs. 1992. *Annual Health Bulletin 1991.* Colombo, Sri Lanka: Government of Sri Lanka.

Mishan, E.J. 1971. 'Evaluation of Life and Limb: A Theoretical Approach'. *Journal of Political Economy* 79: 687–705.

Monzon, Ofelia, Fem Paladin, Efren Dimaandal, Angelita Balis, Celso Samson, and Sheila Mitchell. 1992. 'Relevance of Antibody Content and Test Format in HIV Testing of Pooled Sera'. *AIDS* 6(1): 43–8.

Moore, Michael, and Kip Viscusi. 1988a. 'The Quantity-Adjusted Value of Life'. *Economic Enquiry* 26(3): 369–88.

——1988b. 'Doubling the Estimated Value of Life: Results Using New Occupational Fatality Data'. *Journal of Policy Analysis and Management* 7(3): 476–90.

Moreau, Ron. 1992. 'Fighting a Killer'. *Newsweek,* June 29: 10–16.

Murray, Christopher, Karel Styblo, and Annik Rouillon. 1993. 'Tuberculosis'. In Dean Jamison, W. Henry Mosley, Anthony

Measham, and Jose Bobadilla, eds., *Disease Control Priorities in Developing Countries.* Washington, D.C.: Oxford University Press.

NAP (National AIDS Programme). 1994. *HIV/AIDS Estimates for Sri Lanka.* Colombo, Sri Lanka.

National AIDS Prevention and Control Programme. 1994. *Report of the External Programme Review.* Colombo, Sri Lanka: Ministry of Health and Women's Affairs. Draft.

Orubuloye, I., Pat Caldwell, and John Caldwell. 1993. 'The Role of High-Risk Occupations in the Spread of AIDS: Truck Drivers and Itinerant Market Women in Nigeria'. *International Family Planning Perspectives* 19(2): 43–8.

Over, Mead, 1992. 'The Macroeconomic Impact Of AIDS in Sub-Saharan Africa'. Washington, D.C.: World Bank, Africa Technical Department, Population, Health, and Nutrition Division. Technical Working Paper no. 3.

——1993. 'The Economic Impact of AIDS'. Washington, D.C.: World Bank, Africa Technical Department. Draft.

Over, Mead, and Peter Piot. 1993. 'HIV Infection and Sexually Transmitted Diseases'. In Dean Jamison, W. Henry Mosley, Anthony Measham, and Jose Bobadilla, eds., *Disease Control Priorities in Developing Countries.* Washington, D.C.: Oxford University Press.

Panos Institute, The. 1992. *The Hidden Cost of AIDS: The Challenge of HIV to Development.* London: Panos Publications.

Panyarachun, Anand. 1995. 'AIDS and Social and Economic Progress in the Asian and Pacific Countries'. Speech at the Third International Conference on AIDS in Asia and the Pacific, Chiang Mai, Thailand, September 17–21.

Peterson, Georg, and Rabin Sarda. 1995. 'The HIV and AIDS Epidemic in the Western Pacific'. *Current Science* 25(10): 835–9.

Philipson, Tomas, and Richard Posner. 1993. *Private Choices and Public Health: The AIDS Epidemic in an Economic Perspective.* Cambridge, Massachusetts: Harvard University Press.

Rahman, M. 1995. 'Wages of Success'. *India Today,* May 31.

Rahulla, S., and K.S.A. Jayasinghe. 1993. 'Disposal of Sharps by Private Institutions in Colombo'. Colombo, Sri Lanka; University of Colombo, Faculty of Medicine. Draft.

Ratnapala, Nandasena. 1994. *Report on the Sexually High-Risk Groups in Sri Lanka.* Colombo, Sri Lanka: WHO.

Rice, Dorothy. 1966. *Estimating the Cost of Illness.* Washington, D.C.: Government Printing Office. Health Economics Series #6, U.S. Public Health Service Publication no. 947–6.

Richardson, Clive, Rosemary Ancell-Park, and George Papaevangelou. 1993. 'Factors Associated with HIV Seropositivity in European Injecting Drug Users'. *AIDS* 7(11): 1485–91.

Richardson, Michael. 1992. 'In Unprepared Asia, AIDS. Hits Hard'. *International Herald Tribune,* July 20.

Sandler, S., and J. AuBuchon. 1987. 'Qualification and Management of Blood Donors'. In L. Petz and S. Swisher, eds., *Clinical Practice of Transfusion Medicine,* 2nd edition. New York: Churchill Livingstone.

Schelling, Thomas. 1987. 'Value of Life'. In John Eatwell, Murray Milgate, and Peter Newman, eds., *The New Palgrave: A Dictionary of Economics.* London: Macmillan Press.

Seneviratne, Maureen, and Shirley Peiris. 1991. 'Tourism and Child Prostitution in Sri Lanka'. In Koson Srisang, Sudarat Srisang, Sarah Sexton, Baw Tananone, June Rogers, Chris Wiebe, and Alison O'Grady, eds., *Caught in Modern Slavery: Tourism and Child Prostitution in Asia.* Bangkok, Thailand: The Ecumenical Coalition on Third World Tourism.

Shenon, Philip. 1992a. 'After years of denial, Asia Faces Scourge of AIDS'. *The New York Times,* November 8.

——1992b. 'Brash and Unabashed, Mr. Condom takes on Sex and Death in Thailand'. *The New York Times.* December 20.

Shogren, Jason, Seung Shin, Dermot Hayes, and James Kliebenstein. 1994. 'Resolving Differences in Willingness to Pay and Willingness to Accept'. *American Economic Review* 84(1): 255–70.

Simons, Marlise. 1992. 'In French Court, Tales of HIV Transfusions'. *The Island,* August 11.

Sisk, Jane. 1995. 'Economic Evaluation of HIV/AIDS Education and Primary Prevention'. New York: Columbia University, School of Public Health. Draft.

Sittitrai, Werasit, Praphan Phanuphak, Jean Barry, and Tim Brown. 1992. *Thai Sexual Behavior and Risk of HIV Infection.* Bangkok, Thailand: Thai Red Cross Society and Chulalongkron University, Institute of Population Studies.

Sivaratnam, Dinesh. 1992. 'Prevention of HIV Transmission among Clients of Commercial Sex Workers and Among Commercial Sex Workers Themselves in Sri Lanka'. Thesis, Monash University, Faculty of Medicine, Melbourne, Australia.

Solon, Orville, and Angelica Barrozo. 1993. 'Overseas Contract Workers and the Economic Consequences of the HIV and AIDS Epidemic in the Philippines'. David Bloom and Joyce Lyons, eds., *Economic Implications of AIDS in Asia.* New Delhi, India: United Nations Development Programme.

Spielberg, Freya, Claire Kabeya, Robert Ryder, N. Kifuani, Jeffrey Harris, Thomas Bender, William Heyward, and Thomas Quinn. 1989. 'Field Testing and Comparative Evaluation of Rapid, Visually Read Screening Assays for Antibody to Human Immunodeficiency Virus'. *The Lancet,* March 18: 580–4.

Srisang, Koson, Sudarat Srisang, Sarah Sexton, Baw Tananone, June Rogers, Chris Wiebe, and Alison O'Grady, eds. 1991. *Caught in Modern Slavery: Tourism and Child Prostitution in Asia.* Bangkok, Thailand: The Ecumenical Coalition on Third World Tourism.

Stalker, Peter. 1994. *The Work of Strangers: A Survey of International Labour Migration.* Geneva: International Labour Office.

Stewart, Hamish. 1992. 'Rationality and the Market for Human Blood'. *Journal of Economic Behavior and Organization* 19: 125–43.

Stock, Susan, Amiram Gafni, and Ralph Bloch. 1990. 'Universal Precautions to Prevent HIV Transmission to Health Care Workers: An Economic Analysis'. *Journal of the Canadian Medical Association* 142(9): 937–46.

Tan, Michael, and Manuel Dayrit. 1994. 'HIV/AIDS in the Philippines'. *AIDS* 8 (suppl 2): S125–30.

Tantrigama, Gunatillake. 1994. 'Tourism and the Economy of Sri Lanka'. *Economic Review* August: 3–12, 31.

Tantrigama, Gunatillake, and Alan White. 1994. 'Coastal Environment and Tourism: Can Hikkaduwa, Sri Lanka, Afford to Clean Up?' Paper presented at the Third Meeting of the International Society of Ecological Economics, San Jose, Costa Rica, October 24–9.

Thant, Myo. 1993. 'The Economic Implications of AIDS in Southeast Asia: Equity Considerations'. In David Bloom and Joyce Lyons, eds., *Economic Implications of AIDS in Asia.* New Delhi, India: United Nations Development Programme.

Titmuss, Richard. 1971. *The Gift Relationship: From Human Blood to Social Policy.* London: George Allen and Unwin.

UNDP. 1992. 'Hong Kong: Country Report'. Presented at the Subregional Seminar on the Social and Economic Implication of AIDS, Kunming, China, September 22–6.

———1994. *Human Development Report 1994.* New York: Oxford University Press.

UNDP and WTO. 1993. *Tourism Master Plan: Sri Lanka,* Vols. I–III. Madrid: World Tourism Organization.

UNICEF. 1991. *Children and Women in Sri Lanka: A Situation Analysis.* Colombo, Sri Lanka.

U.S. Bureau of the Census. 1993. *HIV/AIDS Surveillance Database.* Washington, D.C.: Center for International Research.

U.S. News and World Report. 1992. 'Selling Sex Does Not Pay'. July 27.

Viravaidya, Mechai, Stasia Obremskey, and Charles Myers. 1993. 'The Economic Impact of AIDS in Thailand'. In David Bloom and Joyce Lyons, eds., *Economic Implications of AIDS in Asia.* New Delhi, India: United Nations Development Programme.

Viscusi, Kip, and Wesley Magat. 1987. *Learning About Risk: Consumer and Worker Responses to Hazard Information.* Cambridge, Massachusetts: Harvard University Press.

Viscusi, Kip, Wesley Magat, and Joel Huber. 1987. 'An Investigation of the Rationality of Consumer Valuations of Multiple Health Risks'. *Rand Journal of Economics* 18(4): 465–79.

Viscusi, Kip, and Michael Moore. 1989. 'Rates of Time Preference and Valuations of the Duration of Life'. *Journal of Public Economics* 38:297–317.

Vorakitphokatorn, S., and R. Cash. 1992. 'Factors that Determine Condom Use among Traditionally High Users: Japanese Men and Commercial Sex Workers (CSW) in Bangkok, Thailand'. Abstract no. PoD5237. VIIIth International Conference on AIDS, Amsterdam, July 19–23.

Waningasundara, Mallika. 1991. 'Risky Trade-Off for Beach Boys'. *WorldAIDS,* May. London: Panos Publications.

Wijesinghe, Sisira. 1993. 'War Against Child Sex Abuse Hots Up'. *The Island,* June 22.

Wijetunge, Shan. 1992. 'Patients Face Threat of AIDS Infection'. *The Island,* June 17.

World Bank. 1992. *Tanzania: AIDS Assessment and Planning Study.* Washington, D.C.: Oxford University Press.

——1993. *World Development Report 1993.* Washington, D.C.: Oxford University Press.

——1994a. *World Tables 1993.* Baltimore, Maryland: Johns Hopkins University Press.

——1994b. *World Development Report 1994.* Washington, D.C.: Oxford University Press.

1995. *World Development Report 1995.* Washington, D.C.: Oxford University Press.

WHO (World Health Organization). 1991. *Guidelines for the Clinical Management of HIV Infection in Adults.* Geneva: WHO, Global Programme on AIDS.

——1993. *The HIV/AIDS Pandemic: 1993 Overview.* Geneva: WHO, Global Programme on AIDS.

——1994. *AIDS: Images of the Epidemic.* Geneva: WHO, Global Programme on AIDS.

——1995. *In Point of Fact.* Geneva: WHO, Press Office.

WTO. 1992. *Yearbook of Tourism Statistics,* 44th ed., Vol.II. Madrid, Spain.

Xinhua, Sun, Nan Junhua, and Guo Qili. 1994. 'AIDS and HIV Infection in India'. *AIDS* 8 (suppl 2):S55–9.

Yang, Bong-Min. 1993. 'Case of the Republic of Korea'. Paper presented at the Inception Workshop of the United Nations Development Programme/Asian Development Bank on the Economic Implication of the HIV/AIDS Epidemic in Asia, Manila, Philippines, September 8–10.